"This groundbreaking book introduces readers to the practice of *muraqabah*, an important mindfulness technique in Islamic spirituality. The book incorporates a wealth of research, covering the practice of *muraqabah* in contemporary Sufi orders, *muraqabah* in classical Islamic texts, insights from psychotherapy and Islamic spiritual care, and Buddhist, Christian, and Jewish mindfulness techniques. The book can easily be utilized as a textbook for courses on *muraqabah*, Islamic spiritual care, or mindfulness techniques more generally. It also comes with an appendix with seven sample sessions, which are very helpful for clinicians, teachers, or practitioners. This book is a milestone in the emerging discipline of Islamic spiritual care and psychospiritual therapy and its innovative approach, comprehensiveness, and easy-to-read style make it a delight to read. A noteworthy accomplishment!"

Nevin Reda, associate professor of Muslim studies, Emmanuel College, Victoria University, the University of Toronto, Canada

"This book presents the Islamic beliefs and traditions of *muraqabah* and applies its numerous insights to Islamic spiritual care and psychotherapy. Dr Isgandarova also connects *muraqabah* to Christian, Buddhist and Jewish practices. The book is well done and is a great resource for scholars as well as practitioners. I highly recommend it."

Thomas St. James O'Connor, PhD, professor emeritus, Martin Luther University, Ontario, Canada

"This book is a masterpiece authored by a leading expert in the field. With precision and depth, Dr Isgandarova merges Islamic mindfulness practices with modern psychotherapy by connecting past holistic therapeutic knowledge with the present. The book is enriched by the author's experience in spiritual care and offers a profound exploration of healing and self-discovery."

Salih Yucel, associate professor and accredited clinical pastoral supervisor, Centre for Islamic Studies and Civilisation, Charles Sturt University, Australia

Mindfulness Techniques and Practices in Islamic Psychotherapy

Mindfulness Techniques and Practices in Islamic Psychotherapy is a guide for Muslim spiritual care providers, psychologists, psychiatrists, psychotherapists, and others who use spiritual and religious concepts, values, and rituals as novel interventions to offer culturally appropriate mental health services. Chapters lay out the practice of *muraqabah* as a strategy for addressing mental and emotional disturbances such as depression, anxiety, personality disorders, attention-deficit disorders, and more. Using hermeneutical data, *Mindfulness Techniques and Practices in Islamic Psychotherapy* presents the processes and ethics of the *muraqabah* technique in Islamic spiritual care and psychotherapy.

Nazila Isgandarova, PhD, DMin, RSW, RP, is a director of the supervised psycho-spiritual education programme and assistant professor at Emmanuel College of Victoria University in the University of Toronto. She is recipient of the Ontario government's 2023 Champion of Diversity Award and the 2022 Order of Vaughan.

Mindfulness Techniques and Practices in Islamic Psychotherapy
The Power of *Muraqabah*

Nazila Isgandarova

Taylor & Francis Group
NEW YORK AND LONDON

Designed cover image: ©Getty Images

First published 2025
by Routledge
605 Third Avenue, New York, NY 10158

and by Routledge
4 Park Square, Milton Park, Abingdon, Oxon, OX14 4RN

Routledge is an imprint of the Taylor & Francis Group, an informa business

© 2025 Nazila Isgandarova

The right of Nazila Isgandarova to be identified as author of this work has been asserted in accordance with sections 77 and 78 of the Copyright, Designs and Patents Act 1988.

All rights reserved. No part of this book may be reprinted or reproduced or utilised in any form or by any electronic, mechanical, or other means, now known or hereafter invented, including photocopying and recording, or in any information storage or retrieval system, without permission in writing from the publishers.

Trademark notice: Product or corporate names may be trademarks or registered trademarks, and are used only for identification and explanation without intent to infringe.

ISBN: 9781032623566 (hbk)
ISBN: 9781032623498 (pbk)
ISBN: 9781032631387 (ebk)

DOI: 10.4324/9781032631387

Typeset in Optima
by codeMantra

Contents

List of Figures and Tables ix
Acknowledgements x
About the Author xi
Invitation xii

Introduction 1
Description of the Chapters 9

1 **Introduction to Mindfulness** 12
Mindfulness in Contemporary Western Psychotherapy 13
Questions for Discussion 29

2 **An Overview of *Muraqabah* as a Spiritual Practice** 30
Muraqabah *and Sufism or Islamic Spirituality* 31
Muraqabah *as a Spiritual Practice* 32
Purpose of Muraqabah *in Sufi Tradition* 35
The Practice of Traditional Muraqabah 39
Sufi Orders and Muraqabah 41
Muraqabah *in Naqshibandi Order* 42
Muraqabah *in Ni'matullahi Order* 47
Other Details in Muraqabah: *Space, Music, and Dance* 50
Questions for Discussion 52

3 ***Muraqabah* and the Human Nature** 54
Overview of Human Nature 56
'Aql *(Mind; Reason; Intellect)* 57
Qalb *(Heart)* 59
Ruh *(Spirit)* 62

Nafs *(Soul)* 64
Stages of the Nafs 66
The Development of the Soul 66
Questions for Discussion 71

4 The Relevance of *Muraqabah* in Islamic Psychotherapy   73
Questions for Discussion 86

5 The Techniques of *Muraqabah* in Islamic Psychotherapy   87
Mushahadah 87
Tasawwur 88
Muhasabah 95
Stages of the Human Condition during Muraqabah 96
Questions for Discussion 98

6 Incorporating Dhikr, Music, and Physical Movement in *Muraqabah*   99
Contemplating on Asma al-Husna—99 Names of Allah 105
Physical Movements in Muraqabah 110
Questions for Discussion 113

Conclusion   116

Glossary of Key Terms   *119*
Appendix: Overview of Sample Muraqabah *Practices before Individual, Couple, or Group Sessions*   *122*
References   *141*
Index   *153*

Figures and tables

Figures

2.1	The power of *Muraqabah*	34
4.1	Summary of definitions of *Muraqabah*	85
4.2	Levels of *Muraqabah*	86
5.1	*Muraqabah* techniques	96
6.1	Asma ul-Husna	100

Tables

1.1	A working definition of mindfulness	14
1.2	Mindfulness and contemplative practices suggested by Young (2016)	17

Acknowledgements

Many colleagues, friends, family members, and other individuals supported me in completing this book and for whom I have a deep gratitude. One of them is my husband, Akbar Majidov, who has always believed in me and supported me since our marriage. My readers also encouraged me to continue reflecting and elaborating more on *muraqabah* after my first article on Islamic mindfulness practices. My colleagues, Professor Nevin Reda, Professor Pam McCarroll, Professor Thomas O'Connor, and Malak El-Tahry, and my editor Anna Moore provided valuable insights, constructive ideas, and comments. I also deeply thank my students at Emmanuel College of Victoria University in the University of Toronto, who engaged in our discussions of spirituality, mental health, disability, and spiritual resources in mental health.

I am grateful to Emmanuel College of Victoria University in the University of Toronto, who supported and facilitated this book's completion. My colleagues at Emmanuel College encouraged me and helped me with their opinions and concepts that expanded my fusion of horizons on Islamic mindfulness techniques in spiritually integrated psychotherapy.

About the Author

Nazila Isgandarova has a PhD from the University of Toronto, a doctor of ministry degree in pastoral counselling, marriage, and family studies from Wilfred Laurier University, and a master of social work from the University of Windsor. She is a registered psychotherapist at the College for Registered Psychotherapists of Ontario and a registered social worker at Ontario Social Workers and Social Service Workers. Nazila is the recipient of the Order of Vaughan, the Forum for Theological Exploration Research Award for her study on domestic violence against Muslim women, the Canadian Association for Spiritual Care Senior Research Award, and the Society for Pastoral Counselling Research Award. Nazila is an assistant professor at Emmanuel College of Victoria University in the University of Toronto. Her book *Muslim Women, Domestic Violence, and Psychotherapy: Theological and Clinical Issues* was published by Routledge in 2018, and *Islamic Spiritual Care: Theory and Practice(s)* was published by Pandora Press in 2019.

Invitation

This book explores the practice of *muraqabah* from the perspectives of theory and practice. The discussion investigates historical, comparative, and theoretical perspectives on the topic and includes practical suggestions for using *muraqabah* techniques within the context of individual, couple, or group treatment processes.

In this book, I invite you to consider Islamic mindfulness traditions as well as the more recent impacts of mindfulness-based approaches within the field of psychotherapy. From my work as a Muslim psychotherapist and social worker, I have witnessed among the Muslim healthcare professionals in the field and also the clients a profound desire to become more attentive, empathetic, tolerant, and understanding. In this regard, mindfulness practices can act as helpful guides when dealing with intrapersonal issues, such as self-regulation and stress reduction, and when nurturing interpersonal relationships, such as the cultivation of trust, compassion, positive regard, kindness, and generosity.

Beyond such practical applications, however, I hope this book will inspire more scholarship. I also hope that Muslim psychotherapists, spiritual care providers, psychologists, and social workers will continue sharing our collective wisdom regarding how Islamic mindfulness practices can be implemented. I hope that *muraqabah* might also be one of the techniques to help our Muslim clients achieve a state of happiness, satisfaction, self-care, self-awareness, well-being, and clarity of mind.

By reflecting on traditional and contemporary mindfulness practices, I also hope this book might encourage more research in the field, and I invite the reader to think about future directions for research and evidence-based practices. For example, how new methods and analytical approaches, such as paradox research, can be employed in the service of randomized controlled trials, blinded studies, or case studies. These studies could focus on the roles played by different ethnographies, epistemologies, and ontologies.

In whatever direction this book takes you, I offer a simple invitation: as you read, explore, and be mindful of our existence on this beautiful earth!

Introduction

Along other evidence-based treatment modalities, spiritually integrated psychotherapy techniques play an essential role in treating mental health problems. As such practices gain popularity, Islamic mindfulness techniques are also quickly achieving prominence among Muslim mental health professionals. Muslim spiritual care providers, psychologists, psychiatrists, and psychotherapists employ religious rituals inspired by the Islamic tradition and contemporary mindfulness-based therapies in their clinical practices as novel interventions to address a need for culturally appropriate mental health services.

Many references in the Qur'an and the Hadith, the canonical collection of the sayings, approvals, and disapprovals of the Prophet Muhammad, point to the reality that people live their lives in a state of *ghafla*, which can be translated as "forgetfulness of divine reality" or "dissociation from the present moment." *Ghafla* also refers to being disconnected "from the love and contentment that comes from an acute awareness of God's reality" (Rothman, 2018, p. 37). In brief, *ghafla* is a state of disconnection or detachment and may manifest as animalistic impulses usually attributed to lower urges. External factors, such as trauma or adverse childhood experiences, can also cause detachment from the reality.

The Prophet Muhammad used to say that a cure awaits all diseases except old age and death. In cases of *ghafla*, where the distress relates to a detachment from reality, becoming mindful of present emotional and psychological states has become an effective clinical intervention. Within the Islamic traditions, this can be achieved through the mindfulness practice—*muraqabah*—a tool used in the treatment of detachment, disconnection, and dissociation caused by various illnesses, including mental health issues. Throughout the book, I prefer to use the original word, *muraqabah*, over existing translations. As Scott Kugle (2021) notes, "meditation" might not be the right word to describe *muraqabah* or similar spiritual practices in Islamic traditions. Similarly, in Arabic, Turkish, Urdu, or Persian, even the word "prayer" cannot fully capture the meaning of these mindfulness practices.

Drawing upon its Arabic roots, the word *muraqabah* derives from the verb *raqeeb*, which means "to watch over," "to take care of," or "to keep an eye on." In the Qur'an, the word *raqeeb* appears in 24 different forms, including *raqeebun* (an observer) and *fartaqib* (so watch). *Ar-raqeeb*—a name or attribute of the Creator—refers to God's role as a protector or caretaker. The Qur'an says, "Verily, God watches over you…" (Q. 4:1). From a broader perspective, the word can also be translated as meditation, vigilance, contemplative vigilance, self-examination, watchfulness, or spiritual surveillance. For example, Sufi practices translate *muraqabah* as meditation (Amini, 1999; Ernst, 2007; Husain & Hasan, 2021; Mirdal, 2012; Rothman, 2018), contemplation (Azeemi, 2005) or vigilance and contemplative watchfulness (Amini, 1999), and heightened awareness (Lobel, 2007). Bearman et al. (2012) use the term "spiritual surveillance" to describe the self-evaluation process or examine the purpose of any action by asking questions, why? how? for whom? According to Husain and Hasan (2021):

> *Muraqabah* is an intentional practice of the *qalb* (heart). During the practice of *muraqabah*, saints and the learned and common people keep vigil of the holy essence of Allah, or His attributes, or some other aspect in the mind with devotion.
>
> (p. 132)

Rothman (2018) defines *muraqabah* as tuning into our inner self holistically—*qalb* (spiritual heart), *aql* (intellect, mind), *nafs* (soul, ego), and *ruh* (spirit)—and connecting with God spiritually through the *ruh*. Sometimes, Rothman uses the word *tafakkur* (contemplation) (p. 49) to describe a similar phenomenon. It can be achieved simply by sitting in any comfortable position, with eyes closed or open, while maintaining awareness of the entire body, focusing attention inwardly, and paying special attention to the physical location of the heart.

Regardless of its English translation, *muraqabah* also refers to a certain type of spiritual and/or religious practice. In this type of meditation, the disciple watches over or takes care of the *nafs* (soul). This includes watching over thoughts, actions, and spiritual states. Through this process of meditation, the disciple acquires knowledge about the soul and its relationship with the creator. By becoming mindful of one's inner feelings and outer surroundings, the disciple achieves spiritual growth and makes progress towards becoming an *insan-i kamil* (a "perfect" or "universal" human being, depending on the translation). In Sufi traditions, the *salik* (the disciple who follows the spiritual path) understands and learns to feel how God watches over us at every moment. Therefore, the disciple must protect the heart from all earthly distractions and evil thoughts. For this purpose, the disciple learns to meditate with *muraqabah* and/or *dhikr* (chanting, prayers, and self-examination), both of which aid the disciple in contemplating God. In this respect, *muraqabah* is "a mutual 'keeping watch' between the Creator and the wayfarer on the Sufi path" (Amini, 1999, p. 105).

A disciple can engage in the traditional *muraqabah* with or without the physical presence of a Sufi master. During *muraqabah*, the disciple needs to observe *batin* (inner), *zahir* (outward), and *ghayb* (hidden) states of being. In addition, disciples of *muraqabah* achieve ascending levels of competency with practice (low-level, medium-level, and high-level *muraqabah*).

Unfortunately, important psychological theorists and practitioners have ignored or regarded spiritual and religious beliefs with suspicion. For example, Sigmund Freud (1955), the father of modern psychology, dismissed the concept of the Divine and viewed it as an illusion. Simply put, he categorized religious beliefs as delusional ideas occurring within the psyche. For him, the psyche consists of three elements: the *superego* (conscience), the *id* (pleasurable instincts that demand release), and the *ego* (conscious mind). From a Freudian perspective, the *superego* develops amidst the influences of family and culture, forming the rules by which a person "should" abide; when the pleasurable instincts within the *id* arise, they are confronted by the *superego*, causing rebellious energies to surface that weaken or confuse the *ego*. A battle then erupts between the *superego* and the *id*. Under the influence of the Freudian school of thought, the field of psychology anchored itself with the secular sciences, relegating natural healing techniques, especially those with roots in religious or spiritual traditions, to the realm of care for the soul.

Not all theorists in the field of psychotherapy agreed with Freud; for example, Carl Jung (2009) and Victor Frankl (2003) viewed the soul as an essential component of the inner life. For Jung, the soul, which often expresses itself by means of human imagination, facilitates the relationship between the conscious mind and the unconscious. Building on Freud's understanding of the psyche (*superego*, *ego*, and *id*), Jung advocated for an integration of these seemingly separate components, a process that requires conscious association with the material that arises from the unconscious. For him, this unconscious material contains a multitude of symbols, including images of God.

In the 1990s, later generations of mental health professionals were drawn to the concept of spirituality, preferring this notion over and against the idea of religion. Various reasons for this shift have been highlighted by researchers, including Pargament (2007) and Koenig et al. (2012). Researchers at that time focused on discerning the role of religion in the domain of mental illness. Positions varied from seeing religion as providing solutions for a variety of situational and emotional conflicts, to it being described as mental illness itself. Koenig (2018) begins by defining religion according to the relatively simple definition, such as acknowledgement of a higher controlling power, often a personal God, deserving obedience. Although he found that church attendance, an extrinsic expression of a religious system, may have little to do with mental health. Koenig also stated that religious beliefs and practices may protect against stress from hospitalization and medical issues. Those who cope through faith show lower prevalence of depressive symptoms and disorders, experiencing less depression over time (p. 185).

In their research, Koenig and Larson (2001) discovered that the vast majority of psychiatrists felt neither comfortable nor competent when addressing religious issues or spiritual needs in depth. This finding may reflect a general lack of training, even though clinical best practices recommend that a religious or spiritual history be taken for all patients and clients. To increase professional competency in this area, Koenig and Pritchett (1998) provided practical information and guidelines to facilitate the integration of spirituality and religion into mental health professions such as psychotherapy. Since then, multiple studies have demonstrated the benefits of spiritually integrated interventions, including mindfulness practices. That being said, these guidelines come with precautions. First, therapists must never function beyond their scope of practice; competent practitioners need to identify when referral to a religious authority may be warranted. Second, the interests of the patient or client may be best served by holistic approaches that include various strategies, such as the use of pharmaceutical treatments.

Mindfulness practices have been discussed and employed in psychology and psychotherapy since the 1960s. Kabat-Zinn (1994) describes mindfulness as "paying attention in a particular way: on purpose, in the present moment, and non-judgmentally" (Kabat-Zinn, 1994, p. 4). He adds that mindfulness practices help us to:

> commit fully in each moment... to be present ... inviting ourselves to interface with this moment in full awareness, with the intention to embody as best we can an orientation of calmness, mindfulness, and equanimity right here and right now.
>
> (p. 22)

This moment of awareness is only possible through being attentive "to the unfolding of experience moment by moment" (Kabat-Zinn, 2003, p. 145).

Although mindfulness practices have been woven into psychology and psychotherapy for decades, these practices have not always been accepted within religious, political, or academic systems without prejudice and bias. For example, in Soviet Azerbaijan, where I was born and grew up, religion and spirituality were not officially outlawed, but the Soviets discouraged such practices. Within the Communist Party and in academic circles, spirituality and religion were labelled as superstitious; consequently, those who felt drawn to explore existential meaning in their lives did so with judicious discretion, not wanting to reveal anything that might be conceived as weakness, lest they be accused of cult worship. By contrast, such political persecution against religious and spiritual beliefs did not occur to the same extent in the West.

Nevertheless, "the Soviet men" discovered powerful expressions of their spirituality through art, literature, music, film, and nature. One compelling example emerged in 1973 with the release of the Azerbaijani film *Nasimi*, portraying the life of the 14th-century Azerbaijani Hurufi poet, Imadaddin Nasimi (d. 1417). The screenplay was written by Isa Huseynov and directed by Hasan Seyidbayli. A well-known actor, Rasim Balayev, was cast as Nasimi, and Ismayil Osmanli as Naimi, the leader of the sect of Hurufism. The film also featured powerful female roles, such as Fatma, the daughter of Naimi. Critics who regarded religion and spirituality as mere superstitions identified the images of dervishes or desert wanderers in the movie as cogent evidence of what they believed. For others, the film awakened untoward images of the Muslim Sufi as one who wears cheap sackcloth and whose hair and beard are kept long and unkempt. At the same time, the film also offered viewers a powerfully spiritual reference of the divine. In general, the film demonstrated how the belief can overcome suffering manifested on a personal level. Rather than portraying Islam as a "dry, legalistic, and formulaic" and "Semitic" religion (Ernst, 2011; Kugle, 2021), the film put forwards powerful spiritual images and visions of social justice that revealed how the self could be transformed into a spiritual being. For example, Nasimi and his followers called upon the divine to witness their suffering souls, thereby developing spiritual strength, courage, dignity, and cultivating a deep and profound trust in God. For them, entry into the spiritual world diminished earthly or worldly suffering. Through this film, one can begin to discern the difference between religious systems and personal spirituality. Spiritual poetry of Nasimi, the chanting of the Sufi dervishes, and creative expressions of spirituality in the film transcend "dry" and "rigid" religious system and encourage making connections between spirituality, resilience, and power. These connections are supported by studies that have established strong correlations between resilience, mental health, and spirituality, and that demonstrate positive evidence in clinical work such as mindfulness-based spiritual practices.

Although strong links have been confirmed between mindfulness practices, psychology, and psychotherapy, establishing similar connections between the Islamic practice of *muraqabah* and mindfulness has not been easy. To begin with, many Muslims believe that mindfulness techniques are rooted in Buddhist traditions; however, through Sufism, Muslim psychiatrists, psychologists, spiritual care practitioners, and psychotherapists have come to appreciate how mindfulness practices are also embedded within the Islamic tradition. Furthermore, the benefits of using this spiritual practice have been documented in clinical studies. In the light of its benefits in Sufi practices, *muraqabah* is also becoming a crucial Islamically based mindfulness technique for Islamic practitioners.

Even though strong correlation exists between mindfulness practices and Sufism, incorporating these practices and other spirituality-based tools within an Islamic practice of psychotherapy can be challenging. What arises is the lack of and need for comprehensive guidelines demonstrating how to integrate *muraqabah* practices into Islamic psychotherapeutic clinical settings. Therefore, this book addresses that need and demonstrates how *muraqabah* has been used as a spiritual assessment and treatment tool in classical Islamic spirituality and psychotherapy since the emergence of Sufism. Even though not many resources establish the clinical and spiritual validity of these earliest practices, important contemporary research studies confirm their application and subsequent benefits.

When I gathered relevant texts using search engines and databases such as the ATLA Religion Database with ATLASerials (EBSCOhost databases), PubMed, and PsycINFO, using key word searches yielded very few results. In my search for terms such as "muraqabah," "muraqaba," "murakaba," and "murakebe," I had to widen the search to include qualitative, peer-reviewed, and hermeneutical studies. More specifically, the search for the term "muraqabah" yielded 12 results, including instances where the word was used in the direct title of the books and articles. Authors included Nūrbakhsh (1979), Karimpour (2020), and Kamada (1977). Some of these sources were written in Arabic, Turkish, Japanese, and/or other languages.[1] The word "muraqaba" yielded 17 results in primary and secondary sources (for example, al-Ghazali, 2015; Ibn 'Ajībah et al., 2011; Isgandarova, 2019a; Kugle, 2021; Lobel, 2007; Mulyati, 2003; Netton, 2000; Omar et al., 2017). The term "murakaba" generated only three results, and only one addresses the subject of this study directly (Bearman et al., 2012). As previously stated, for the sake of consistency, I will use the word *muraqabah*, as many studies in the field have chosen it over other representations.

In his classic work, *Ḳut al-Qulub*, Abu Talib al-Makki (d. 996) explores *muraqabah* through the lens of *murabaṭa*, which is derived from the word *ribaṭ* and literally means "to mount guard" or "connectedness." According to Bearman et al. (2012), *muraqabah* is one of the six degrees of *murabaṭa*, or "measures of vigilance and these six degrees are":

1 *Musharaṭa*: the anticipatory accounting of the soul in the morning every day.
2 *Muraqabah*: spiritual surveillance to examine the motives of actions and intentions.

3 *Muḥasabat al-nafs ba'd al-'amal*: inward accounting after the action.
4 *Mu'akabat al-nafs 'ala takṣiriha:* examination of the conscience to check for negligence in the pursuit of virtues or in the accomplishment of acts of devotion.
5 *Tawbah al-nafs wa-mu'atabatuha:* reprimanding and admonishing the soul constantly.

Abunasr Sarraj (d. 988) identifies *muraqabah* as the first phase or stage of ten mystical graces in his *Kitab ul Luma.'* The other phases or stages include *qurb* (realization of the nearness of God), *mahabba* (love), *wara'* (fear), *raja'* (hope), *shauq* (longing, yearning), *uns* (a state of loving familiarity with God), *itminan* (a sense of security and serene dependence), *mushahada* (contemplation), and *yaqin* (certainty) (Rice, 2017, p. 56).

One of the fundamental spiritual treatises on *muraqabah* was written by Muhammad bin Muhammad Abu Hamid al-Ghazali (d. 1111), a famous Muslim theologian whose works are still used in Islamic psychotherapy. The 38th chapter of the *Revival of the Religious Sciences* is named *Kitab al-muraqabah wa'l muhasaba* (*The Book of Vigilance and Self Examination*). The main purpose of the chapter is to provide guidance "on how to observe the soul and how to maintain its faithfulness to its Lord" (al-Ghazali, 2015, p. xvii).

Javad Nurbakhsh (d. 2008), a psychiatrist and influential Sufi leader of the Nimatulllah order, made a considerable contribution by authoring very comprehensive books about *muraqabah,* Sufi psychology, and Sufism and psychiatry. Nurbakhsh lived and preached in different parts of the world, including the United States. His book *Muraqabah* was first published in 1978 by Khaniqahi Nimatullahi.

It is also important to mention Farzaneh Amini's (1999) doctoral dissertation, *Sufi Psychology and Jungian Analytic Psychology: Treatment of Narcissistic Personality Disorder*, submitted to the Wright Institute Graduate School of Psychology. In this dissertation, Amini discusses how to integrate Jungian analytic psychology with the spiritual insights and practices of Sufism and provides a detailed account of *muraqabah* and other Sufi techniques relevant to psychotherapy. Amini demonstrates how Sufi psychology and Jungian analytic psychology encourage emotional and mental processes of differentiation, integration, and individuation as part of a journey towards psychological wholeness.

This book weaves together studies on *muraqabah* and its clinical implications, reviewing spiritual studies conducted in traditional Sufi settings and relative investigations from clinical contexts. This body of research clearly supports the importance of Islamic mindfulness techniques and practices in helping empower the mind and enrich one's soul. Without a doubt, *muraqabah* is getting more attention recently, especially as it relates to its benefits within mindfulness-based psychotherapeutic modalities. Today, *muraqabah* is recommended not only as a spiritual discipline, but also as an evidence-based practice for addressing mental and emotional disturbances such as depression, anxiety, bipolar disorder, personality disorders, attention-deficit disorders, and so forth. The practice of *muraqabah* has also been used as an effective strategy for managing blood pressure, increasing life expectancy, improving vision, enriching cardiovascular health, supporting immunity, and treating insomnia.

In this book, I explore *muraqabah* practices through the lenses of social sciences (psychotherapy, psychology) and Islamic psychotherapy, and I illustrate how *muraqabah* techniques can be incorporated effectively and ethically within Islamic spiritual care and psychotherapy. Throughout the book, I consistently use the Arabic word *muraqabah* instead of referring to the practice as Islamic mindfulness. I agree with Shah (1980), who believed in drawing upon the added benefit that comes when certain Islamic words are vocalized in their original Arabic. This practice is comparable to other mindfulness customs where sacred Sanskrit mantras such as *Om Mani Padme Hum* are recited or chanted. Shah argues that sounds produce resonance in the body, through which certain words produce a positive, uplifting, and peaceful state of mind, which is also a long-standing belief in Islamic tradition. For example, Muslims who do not understand or speak Arabic learn to recite the Qur'an and prayers in their original language. Similarly, we do not translate certain terms such as yoga, karma, tai chi, qigong, and so forth when used within a practice of psychotherapy.

With these points as background, this book will focus on accomplishing the following:

- To explore how *muraqabah* can be used as a mindfulness practice in Islamic psychotherapy. More specifically, I aim to develop a bio-psycho-social-spiritual mental health framework for providing mental health services to Muslims, one which incorporates spirituality and the practice of *muraqabah*.
- To review the history and context of existing mindfulness practices (MBSR and MBCT) as important spiritual exercises. I will also honour the rich spiritual practices that are found in other religious traditions by including an exploration of Christian traditions (spiritual exercises of Ignatius of Loyola, Lectio Divina, Orthodox Christian Contemplative Practices, the silence in Quaker tradition, and so forth), along with Buddhist contemplative practices.
- To explore how *muraqabah* is used in contemporary clinical settings to manage stress and anxiety. I will specifically highlight how the

techniques used in *muraqabah* can become effective interventions in a clinical context.
- To address how *muraqabah* can be used ethically in clinical settings. It is my belief that Muslim clinicians must receive adequate training in classical religious and theological traditions—particularly Sufi practices—before using *muraqabah* techniques in their clinical practice.
- To provide sample outlines for incorporating *muraqabah* practices.

My research foundations will include primary and secondary sources, highlighting recent studies in the field of Islamic psychotherapy that directly examine the role of *muraqabah* in psychotherapy. I am grateful for these scholarly accomplishments that have contributed greatly to our practice today. Even so, I acknowledge that the application of *muraqabah* in Islamic psychotherapy finds itself in the early stages of exploration.

Description of the Chapters

This book combines various research methods and methodologies, including the direct observation of *muraqabah* practices in traditional settings and the hermeneutical study of original sources.

In Chapter 1, I introduce the general concept of mindfulness and the unique role it plays in various modalities such as Mindfulness-Based Stress Reduction (MBSR), Mindfulness-Based Cognitive Therapy (MBCT), Dialectical Behavior Therapy (DBT), Acceptance and Commitment Therapy (ACT), and Mindfulness-Based Relapse Prevention (MBRP). From a religious perspective, I provide historical narratives from Buddhism, Judaism, and Christianity that illustrate how these foundations provide a framework for contemporary approaches to mindfulness that incorporate psychotherapy and religious traditions. Drawing on Islamic sources, I show how emerging mindfulness practices have been used as a tool to enhance spiritual and psychological well-being. This chapter also demonstrates the theoretical underpinnings that support the use of mindfulness to enhance spiritual, emotional, and mental health in these traditions.

In Chapter 2, I provide an overview of *muraqabah* as a spiritual practice. This includes a reflection on the path of spiritual tradition, or Sufism, that provided a system for *muraqabah* for Sufi disciples and for those in the psychotherapy field who wish to incorporate this practice. As exemplified by the Prophet Muhammad, the Qur'an provides the primary foundation for the main schools of the Sufi tradition and their key teachings and techniques of *muraqabah*. Different examples from the Sufi masters and their followers are provided, as these lay the foundation for mindfulness practices and illustrate how to apply this model in clinical settings.

In Chapter 3, I discuss *muraqabah* as it relates to human nature, describing the theological, spiritual, and psychological underpinnings of Islamic psychotherapy. This includes an examination of how human nature is understood from an Islamic psychotherapeutic perspective and how this foundation provides a platform for integrating the practice of *muraqabah* within Islamic psychotherapy. This perspective plays an important role, as the practice of *muraqabah* in Islamic psychotherapy and Islamic spirituality focuses on improving human nature on the path to perfection.

In Chapter 4, I underscore the relevance of *muraqabah* in Islamic psychotherapy. I show how this unique spiritual practice can be effective in assessing and treating clients with mental health problems such as clinical stress, adjustment problems, depression, anxiety, and so forth. I also bring to light some of the challenges that might be encountered when using *muraqabah* in a clinical setting; however, obtaining proper training and education can help the practitioner apply this therapeutic technique in the effective treatment of clients.

In Chapter 5, I offer techniques for using *muraqabah*, and I discuss how these can be used in Islamic psychotherapy. More specifically, I focus on topics such as *tafakkur* (contemplation), *tasawwur* (imagination), *muhasabah* (self-assessment), and *mushahadah* (observation), offering perspectives on their meanings and applications. This chapter will clarify terms and key concepts associated with the practice of *muraqabah*, especially as these definitions and elements relate to the unique role *muraqabah* can play in psychotherapy.

In Chapter 6, I look more closely at topics including *dhikr*, music, and physical movements, as well as their relevance in *muraqabah*. For example, I offer a unique way of practicing *dhikr* with deep breathing, which is often an important stage of preparation in *muraqabah*. I describe how these spiritual practices are applied and link these discussions to the Qur'an, the Prophet Muhammad, and the Sufi traditions. As a practice, *dhikr* trains us to expel "consciousness of everything but God, reinforce the conviction that God is responsible for everything in creation" (Ernst, 2011, p. 97). Furthermore, the Sufi traditions encourage us to "engage the heart, the soul, the spirit, the intellect and the innermost conscience called the secret" (Ernst, 2011, p. 93).

Towards the end of the book, I provide sample *muraqabah* sessions. The content of these sessions focuses specifically on the mental, emotional, physical, and spiritual needs of the client or user. I hope that this material will aid in the preparation of the client for therapeutic work and provide grounding for the person who "is in a state of struggle against sources of uncertainty, instability and insecurity and reinforces the view that believers gain a sense of meaning, coherence and purpose from spirituality" (Hussein, 2018, p. 35). Finally, the reader will notice that I delicately interweave the practice of *muraqabah* with spiritual, mental, and emotional layers. In the final analysis, proper knowledge of Islam and its principles is not enough to guide the therapist who wishes to incorporate *muraqabah* within a clinical practice; indeed, to follow the *adab* (correct conduct; ethics) requires proper training in classical Sufi psychology. Training in mindfulness-based therapies also provides a strong foundation. Embracing a holistic approach that combines spiritual, theological, and psychotherapeutic foundations will equip Islamic therapists with the necessary knowledge and skills to help their clients develop self-awareness, loving-kindness, compassion, and empathy in their healing journey.

Note

1 The majority of these books were written in Arabic, Turkish, and Persian. A sample of Arabic studies on *muraqabah* include: al-Intikhābāt al-niyābīyah wa-'amalāt al-murāqabah. (al-Ṭab'ah 1.). (1999). al-Markaz al-Lubnānī lil-Dirāsāt al-Qānūnīyah wa-al-Iqtiṣādīyah. Mujtama'at al-muraqabah. (1993). Alif (Cairo, Egypt), 13, 74–; Bin-Yahyá, M. (2002). Mīzānīyat al-dawlah: al-i'dād, al-tanfīdh, al-murāqabah (al-Ṭab'ah 1.). al-Majallah al-Maghribīyah lil-Idārah al-Maḥallīyah wa-al-Tanmiyah; Fayḍ al-Kāshī, M. ibn M. (2005). al-Rujū' ilá Allāh: al-murāqabah, al-muḥāsabah, al-tawbah, al-mawt (al-Ṭab'ah 1.). Dār al-Maḥajjah al-Bayḍā'; Ḥannāshī, 'Abd al-Laṭīf. (2003). al-Murāqabah wa-al-mu'āqabah bi-al-bilād al-Tūnisīyah: al-ib'ād al-siyāsī anmūdhajan, 1881–1955: fī jadalīyat al-idṭihād wa-al-muqāwamah (al-Ṭab'ah 1.). Kullīyat al-Ādāb wa-al-'Ulūm al-Insānīyah.

1 Introduction to Mindfulness

Mindfulness in the Pali language, which is the canonical language of Theravada Buddhism, is translated as *sati*. The word "mindfulness" might not exactly reflect the original meaning of the Asian term, as:

> although the Asian terms are closely related, they are not quite synonyms. Moreover, Southeast Asian, East Asian, and Tibetan traditions do not necessarily agree among themselves as to how to define those terms. Indeed, even within a given cultural area, there can be disagreement among different scholars and lineages as to what a given term specifically designates.
>
> (Young, 2016, p. 30)

Nevertheless, the word mindfulness in English refers "to any one or combination of three things: (1) a form of awareness, (2) the practices that elevate that form of awareness, and (3) guidelines for applying that awareness to specific perceptual, behavioural, or psycho-spiritual goals" (Young, 2016, p. 30). Such an approach to the translation of the original Asian term into English invites us to differentiate between state mindfulness (how mindful a person happens to be at a given time) and trait mindfulness (how mindful a person is in general) (Young, 2016, p. 30).

Mindfulness practices can help their practitioners achieve a state of happiness and improve attention-related skills such as concentration, sensory clarity, and equanimity. As a result, the associated Buddhist practice became a subject of interest among Westerners who travelled to Asia in the 19th century. Later, in the 1960s and 1970s, many practitioners in the Western world visited temples in Southeast Asia to learn the secrets and techniques of mindfulness practices. The passion and love for Buddhist mindfulness practices motivated practitioners to bring them back to the West, where the practices could be taught either as part of Buddhist teachings or outside the doctrinal framework of Buddhism. Young (2016) notes that, in the 1980s and 1990s, mindfulness practices were used in

DOI: 10.4324/9781032631387-2

various secular contexts to remedy various issues and problems in sports, education, and business.

Mindfulness in Contemporary Western Psychotherapy

Contemporary Western psychotherapy has been using concepts of Buddhist meditation as stress-reduction techniques since the 1990s. For example, Mindfulness-Based Stress Reduction (MBSR) was developed by Kabat-Zinn (2003) in the 1990s; he conducted his first systemic application of mindfulness in a clinical context, focusing on the benefits of mindfulness in stress reduction through sitting meditations, body scanning, and hatha yoga. Being inspired by the Buddhist teachings, Kabat-Zinn defined mindfulness as "the awareness that emerges through paying attention on purpose, in the present moment, and non-judgmentally to the unfolding of experience moment by moment" (Kabat-Zinn, 2003, p. 145).

Table 1.1 highlights the most accepted definitions of mindfulness in a psychotherapeutic context based on the summary of Skinner and Beers (2016, p. 107), who present their summary of the most used definitions and conceptual applications of mindfulness by referring to the works of Brown et al. (2007), Kabat-Zinn (2003), and Chambers et al. (2009).

Later, Mindfulness-Based Cognitive Therapy (MBCT) was specifically designed by Segal (2002) to help prevent relapse when treating clinical depression for people with recurrent depression, and it proved to be effective in reducing the risk of depression relapse by approximately half. MBCT was also an effective tool for treating people dealing with anxiety, stress, irritability, and exhaustion (Frostadottir & Dorjee, 2019).

According to Bruno Cayoun (2011), in mindfulness-integrated CBT (MiCBT), the concept of equanimity is used. This concept teaches a Buddhist awareness of the impermanence of all things. During the MiCBT, participants are trained to focus on their bodies, observing the sensations with acceptance and detachment. Of course, the clients are responsible for their own reactions. It is expected that the client will disown taking responsibility for the reactions of others. During the MiCBT, the focus is also on empathy and compassion, forgiveness towards the self and others, and a sense of connection or attachment to all living things.

Linehan (1993) developed dialectical behaviour therapy (DBT) for treating patients with borderline personality disorder and as a tool for behavioural control. Hayes (2004) developed Acceptance and Commitment Therapy (ACT) for a range of mental and emotional issues, encouraging commitment and behaviour change to increase psychological flexibility, and then MBRP to address substance use (Simkin & Black, 2014). All these practices use Buddhist meditation techniques such as Sahaha meditation, Sahaja Sadadhi meditation, Sahaja yoga meditation, tai chi, qigong, yoga,

Table 1.1 A working definition of mindfulness

Present-oriented	"Focus of awareness and attention to the direct and immediate experience of present events as they arise and unfold from moment to moment, without distraction by past or future concerns" (Skinner & Beers, 2016, p. 107).
Receptivity	"Openhearted, friendly, affectionate, compassionate, and accepting awareness and acknowledgement of experience, that is nonjudgmental and nonevaluative, without the chatter of self-centered thoughts ('quiet ego')" (Skinner & Beers, 2016, p. 107).
Clarity	"Dispassionate clear seeing of internal and external phenomena (including thoughts, emotions, sensations, actions, or surroundings) as they are, and not as distorted by conceptual filters or habitual ways of seeing" (Skinner & Beers, 2016, p. 107).
Empirical stance	"Explorative, interested, and curious observation of the full objective facts of life, without preferring self-enhancing or shying away from distressing or threatening information and experiences" (Skinner & Beers, 2016, p. 107).
Flexibility	"Voluntary fluid regulation of states of attention and awareness from narrow focus to broad vista, without confusion or loss of contact to present moment experience" (Skinner & Beers, 2016, p. 107).
Steadiness	"Composed intentional continuity of sustained awareness and attention, without distraction or fixation" (Skinner & Beers, 2016, p. 107).
Presence	"'Integrative awareness' as the agent of action. The integrated 'I' is actively engaged with, has direct contact with, and ownership of experience while also being immersed in it" (Skinner & Beers, 2016, p. 107).

etc., that encourage self-management, self-control, and self-improvement (Simkin & Black, 2014).

Although self-compassion was also important in MBSR and MiCBT, Paul Gilbert and his colleagues (2009) developed Compassion Focused Therapy (CFT), which was meant for clients who suffered from long-term emotional problems associated with high levels of shame and self-criticism. In the beginning, CFT was provided as an individual therapy to help clients develop compassion for themselves and others (Gilbert, 2017). Gilbert defined compassion as being aware of suffering in ourselves and others, with a strong drive to alleviate or prevent it. The client must first identify the "threat mind," which is the mind motivated by survival. The goal is to then develop a "compassionate mind," which is a mind open to feeling compassion for others and oneself (Frostadottir & Dorjee, 2019). In the sessions, the client becomes aware of the brain's three emotion-regulation systems: threat, drive, and soothing. After the client is taught about these systems, the client then learns the role of self-compassion in deactivating the threat system and activating the self-soothing system (Frostadottir & Dorjee, 2019).

Acceptance and commitment therapy (ACT) is another third-wave psychotherapy modality, one with six core concepts that refer to the Buddhist worldview of self: (1) cognitive diffusion, (2) acceptance, (3) contact with the present moment, (4) self-as-context, (5) values, and (6) committed action. These concepts are based on the Four Noble Truths, a key teaching of Buddhism that significantly impacted the theoretical foundation of ACT (Fung & Zhu, 2018). These Four Noble Truths are: (1) there is suffering; (2) the origin of suffering can be known, and it is caused by ignorance, desire or attachment, and aversion; (3) the cessation of suffering is possible; and (4) the cessation of suffering is through the Eightfold Path.

The Eightfold Path can be grouped into three categories: (1) wisdom, within which are right view and right intention; (2) ethical conduct, within which are right speech, right action, and right livelihood; and (3) concentration of the mind, within which are right effort, right mindfulness, and right concentration (Fung & Zhu, 2018). In this respect, Buddhist healing encourages practicing ethical conduct, maintaining focused attention, and gaining wisdom, in order ignorance can be eliminated. This paves the way for enlightenment and liberation from suffering in this life and, eventually, from the cycle of rebirth and death (Fung & Zhu, 2018).

Later on, yoga, tai chi, qigong, ayurveda, herbalism, and other ancient Eastern practices were included in Western clinical work (Moodley et al., 2018; Okamoto, 2017). Their popularity was largely due to their focus on mindfulness and physical exercise. Furthermore, the application of mindfulness meditation techniques in clinical work demonstrated the compatibility of Asian spiritual, religious, philosophical, and healing traditions with psychotherapy; clients experienced positive emotional, mental, and even spiritual transformations. These applications also revealed shortcomings in contemporary Western psychotherapeutic approaches with respect to spirituality and religion.

In addition to the aforementioned summary of the Buddhist view of suffering and healing, it is also important to mention three Dharma Seals briefly. These seals are used to test and evaluate one's adherence to the core Buddhist belief system. These Dharma Seals are: (1) impermanence—all phenomena changes, arising and disintegrating; (2) emptiness/nonself—there is no entity or self that is truly permanent and independent; and (3) nirvana—the extinction of ignorance can ultimately lead to peace and liberation from the cycle of *saṃsar*.

Although the Buddhist beliefs of nirvana and karma are not discussed or presented in any mindfulness-based psychotherapy modalities, including

ACT, the following Buddhist transcendent perfections (paramitas) inspired the following core ACT processes:

- Present moment with *dhyāna pāramitā* (concentration, contemplation)
- Acceptance with kṣānti (kshanti) pāramitā (forbearance, acceptance)
- Defusion with s'īla *pāramitā* (discipline, proper conduct)
- Values with *dāna pāramitā* (generosity, giving of self)
- Committed action with *vīrya pāramitā* (diligence, energy, effort)
- Self-as-context with *prajñā pāramitā* (wisdom, insight) (Fung & Zhu, 2018).

Fung and Zhu (2018) also demonstrate the integration of ACT experiential exercises and metaphors from Dharma talks, poetry, and traditional stories. They reported that Buddhist concepts of rebirth, karma, and past lives facilitated change such as loving-kindness towards the self and others, becoming compassionate, and acceptance from a spiritual perspective.

However, in China, Japan, and other Asian countries, there were attempts to convert traditional spiritual knowledge and practice into psychotherapy. For example, a branch of traditional Chinese medicine psychotherapy (TCMP) emerged as a form of psychotherapy in China. The TCMP practitioners explained mental and emotional health problems as:

> the imbalance of the seven modes of emotion (joy, anger, shock, anxiety, thinking, fear and sorrow), personality factors (classified according to the five elements; yin and yang), organic functional factors (e.g. the interactions between the seven modes of emotion and their respective metaphorical organs, the imbalance of *qi*), and environmental factors (e.g., wind, air).
>
> (Lee, 2018, p. 23)

In order to treat these problems, their recommended treatment methods include talk therapy, psychoeducation, emotional rebalance and control, work and rest, change of personality types through moral education and herbal treatments, qigong (QG), tai chi, herbs, and acupuncture.

There are many overlapping features between mindfulness-based therapies and techniques, such as cultivating mindfulness, body awareness, grounding mentalization training, and the use of psychoeducation; however, each of them has its own focus. For example, the main aim of MBCT is to cultivate mindfulness, whereas CFT mainly focuses on self-compassion (Gilbert, 2009).

In general, many research studies provide empirical support for mindfulness in treating many mental health problems. For example, some studies found a positive correlation between mindfulness, an increased sense of

Table 1.2 Mindfulness and contemplative practices suggested by Young (2016)

Mindfulness exercises are of various types, such as mindfulness of the breath, mindful walking, mindful reading, mindful listening, and mindful viewing and have in common the application of moment-to-moment, non-judgemental awareness
MBSR (Mindfulness-based Stress Reduction) exercises (Kabat-Zinn, 1990)
Concentration exercises
Exercises for cultivating emotional balance (CEB)
Beholding a work of art
Visualization
Silence
Alternation between "focused attention" and "open monitoring" (Lutz et al., 2008)
Meditative movement: yoga, tai chi, qigong, authentic movement, eurythmy, contemplative dance, etc. (Helberg et al., 2009)
Empathy, compassion, and loving-kindness practices (e.g., Center for Compassion and Altruism Research and Education)
Analytical and settled meditation

---

well-being, reduced psychological symptoms and emotional reactivity, and improved behavioural regulation. Mindfulness, distraction, self-awareness skills, and cognitive coping skills are among the best treatment approaches for complex trauma (Cohen et al., 2012, p. 535). Furthermore, mindfulness techniques benefit some clients who may not have the language to articulate their thoughts in psychotherapy sessions.

Overview of Mindfulness and Mindfulness-Based Practices in Jewish and Christian Traditions

Many Jewish and Christian scholars also conducted research highlighting the historical legacy of mindfulness on topics such as self-seclusion, contemplation, compassion, and loving-kindness in the Abrahamic traditions. These studies also reflected on the compatibility of a contemporary application of mindfulness in Christian and Jewish contexts (Choe et al., 2021; Hess, 2020; Hoover, 2018; Jones et al., 2023; Symington & Symington, 2012). For example, *merkabah*, also known as *merkavah* mysticism or Chariot mysticism, is considered an early Jewish mystical tradition that dates from around 100 BCE to 1000 CE and focuses on the nature of the human being; self-purification; visionary experiences, as described in the book of Ezekiel or in *hekhalot* literature; ascending to heavenly palaces; and encountering the Throne of God. The main body of *merkabah* literature, which was written between 200 and 700 CE, is also known as the Maaseh Merkabah, which translates to "Work of the Chariot," and circulated among the Ashkenazi Hasidim during the Middle Ages (Neusner, 2020). However, the *Merkabah* was not recommended to people without the necessary preparation, and, even then, it was limited to only those who were considered worthy sages (Drob, 2000; Verman, 1992).

The other Judaic spiritual practice is *hitbodedut* (self-seclusion), a practice popular within Judaism wherein practitioners seclude themselves and attempt to connect with the Divine (Persico, 2014). This practice is used prominently, especially among the Bratslav Hasidic Jews who follow the teachings of Rebbe Nachman (b. 1772). The Bratslav Hasidic Jewish community is a "primary site for welcoming secular Jews 'back into the fold' of observant Judaism" (Persico, 2014, p. 99). These converts come from a postmodern Western culture and desire experiential religion, and *hitbodedut* offers them "new age" Jewish spirituality. Persico (2014) notes that according to its founder, R. Nachman, the practice entailed seclusion and a candid talk with God, with the objective of annulling one's earthly existence. This mystical path includes the individual's effort to root the self in God's path. This is accomplished first through the stilling of the mind, then through divine conversation, and finally by experiencing emotional arousal almost to the point of death. In contemporary practice, the danger involved in *hitbodedut* is absent, and it is aimed instead at "the spiritual light [that] will shine on the complicated net of our feelings, and expose the sources of wrong patterns of thought and behaviour, which we were not aware that existed" (Persico, 2014, p. 105). In contemporary practice, rather than an emotional or physical experience, one seeks a cognitive experience. A "right vision" is cultivated with a detachment from the senses, or a "temporary disconnection of consciousness from the senses, thus creating a relaxation of consciousness" (Persico, 2014, p. 108). Contemporary practices of *hitbodedut* focus more on patterns of thought and behaviour than on annulment of the self and emotional experiences, perhaps influenced by contemporary spirituality. The inward, subjective mind is emphasized rather than the outward, external concentration, as influenced by New Age "Eastern" religious trends. Persico (2014) suggests that inward-directed spiritual practices might threaten *halakhah* and one's relationship with the divine, so practitioners emphasize that any thought that contradicts the Torah must be disregarded.

In his article, Alan Lew (2000) talks about how his friend's Buddhist practices helped him practise his faith as a Jew: "Zen meditation had opened me to the great richness of ordinary Jewish prayer, a richness that was no longer apparent to most Jews" (Lew, 2000, p. 93). Reflecting on the lack of spirituality felt by Jews in contemporary worship, especially in the United States, he recognizes both the need to educate (both in the Hebrew language and in the structure and history of Jewish practices) and also "the rhythm of the service… the flow of gesture and sound, and in the silences of between and behind the language. Spirituality is non-verbal and a-rational" (Lew, 2000, p. 94). Lew compares the mindfulness of being Jewish in Israel, where one's identity is taken for granted almost as a part of their everyday life, and being Jewish in the United States, where an identity must be actively cultivated through worship practices. A focus on the verbal and nonverbal in Jewish prayer practices, such as the historical use of the Amidah, the communal "we" voice, and gestures (kissing, stepping, bowing, and covering the eyes), makes Jewish worshippers aware of their physical presence in a sacred time and space and as part of the historic Jewish consciousness. As Moshe Greenberg (d. 2010) has shown by identifying what appeared to be spontaneous prose prayer in the Hebrew scriptures, Jewish ritualistic milieus shaped the way they "pour out the contents of their hearts... not unlike jazz musicians improvising on a standard" (Lew, 2000, p. 100).

Highlighting the mindfulness practices in the Christian tradition, Miu (2018) states that *hesychasm* ("silence," "quiet," "calm," or "peace") was originally a monastic practice originating among the 4th-century Desert Fathers in the Egyptian Desert, who isolated themselves, prayed continually, and practised asceticism. Although *hesychasm* was condemned in the 4th and 14th centuries since it led to begging and the rejection of the Mysteries and Sacraments, it remains a marginal practice and is currently practised among laity in the Eastern Orthodox Church. *Hesychasm* is the private, silent repetition of the Jesus Prayer: "Lord Jesus Christ, Son of God, have mercy on me, a sinner." This repetition either facilitates another prayer or is to be repeated throughout the day to keep one's mind away from negative distractions. This practice is based on the Apostle Paul's imperative to pray continually (1 Thess 6:17), Jesus' imperative to pray in secret (Matt 6:6), and the belief that, through the recitation of Jesus' name, humans can accommodate the divine (Exod 23:20–21). "The constant repetition of Jesus' name maintains the soul focused and keeps it safe from sinful deviations" (Miu, 2018, p. 47). Repetition of the Jesus Prayer chases away intrusive thoughts when meditating or praying. The power of the Jesus Prayer rests on the belief that, as the apostles invoke Jesus' name to heal, revive, and exorcize, the repetition of Jesus' name also absolves the supplicant's mind of intrusive thoughts. It has been reported by individuals who practise *hesychasm* that they experienced the "uncreated light" or the Holy Spirit, undergoing theosis (deification), or a unity with or closeness to God.

Lippard's (1988) example of the Society of Friends (Quakers) also helps us understand worship and mindfulness in the Christian tradition. The Society of Friends originated in the 17th century and today numbers only 200,000 members in the United States. They practise "unprogrammed" worship, or worship devoid of leadership, liturgy, teachings, sacraments, symbolism, or structure. A typical meeting starts when the first person enters the worship space and ends when the last person leaves. This meeting is completely silent. Friends believe that the Inner Light, the communication that God has with every human, is experienced through waiting to receive the

Divine in silence. Those taking part in this worship come to understand that "the individual human is the living temple of God" (Lippard, 1988, p. 148). "If God reveals Himself, then worship can be nothing less than reverent waiting in His Presence. If He speaks to man, then it is man's highest privilege to listen" (Lippard, 1988, p. 148). Unlike other Christian worship practices, the Inner Light is placed in the individual rather than in leaders and the pulpit. Friends do not consider silence to be passive, but focus on and attune the human will to the will of God. Group identification is premised on releasing intransigent forms of life and focusing instead on the Divine perspective. This silence is sometimes, but not always, met with a vocal ministry by any member who feels like they have a divine message or prophecy. The member often breaks the silence by saying, "I have a concern" or "I have a leading." The message they share is not coercive but seeks cooperation that is achieved after months or years of contemplation. Only when there is consensus and acceptance of the message is it believed to be a true prophecy.

Quakers have historically used this method to come to a consensus on issues such as abolition and emancipation. This practice is also used in Quaker meetings, retreats, schools, and in their homes. Quakers practise a "commitment to a 'continuing insight'" with "their unity upon a constantly unfolding, living Truth, a process of knowing rather than a known reality" (Lippard, 1988, p. 154).

Pickell (2019) states that Apophatic (negative) prayer is the Christian practice of decentring and deconstructing the self to avoid of the burning preoccupation with self (p. 69). This decentring mimics Biblical figures like Samuel's response to Yahweh (1 Sam 3:10), Mary's words to Gabriel (Luke 1:38), Jesus' prayer at Gethsemane (Matt 26:42), and the Church's response in the recitation of the Lord's Prayer (e.g., "Your kingdom come, Your will be done…"). It is best exemplified in *The Cloud of Unknowing*, a book written by an anonymous 14th-century monk who contended that the only path to knowing God is through unknowing. Such a position claimed that God is not understood through intellectual labour, but through love and a reorientation of one's mind and will, which is accomplished through negating the self and intrusive thoughts.

Apophatic prayer is the displacement of negative or harmful thoughts and can be facilitated with the repetition of a single short word, such as "God" or "love," which is used in the "renunciation of the notion of control, a patient waiting, and a de-centering of the self and its desires in the hope" (Pickell, 2019, p. 71). This is similar to Quaker prayer meetings and *glossolalia*, or the Jesus Prayer.

The semantic value of the word is not meditated on; instead, its repetition is used mechanically to drown out intrusive thoughts and empty the mind. This emptying (*kenosis*) is similar to the way Jesus emptied himself of his divine nature to be incarnated, filled (*plerosis*) with the Holy Spirit, and later do the will of God. This emptying and filling create a dependency on the divine and move the individual beyond regular patterns of thought or a preoccupation with the self, which can be especially helpful in managing fear or stress.

According to Barnes (1989), Ignatius of Loyola, a 16th-century Spanish Jesuit priest, composed a manual for an aesthetic, mindful practice called Spiritual Exercises. These exercises were also known as Loyola's Exercises and were distributed as a little handbook to those he encountered. They detailed a loose set of exercises that helped Ignatius with his own spiritual life.

The goal of Exercises was "control of desire" and to "build up a contemplative mood from which purified desires naturally arise" (Barnes, 1989, p. 264). The text indicates that they are practical guidelines for how to continue praying after the exercitant returns to everyday life. These spiritual exercises last up to four weeks, with each week devoted to a different theme, such as sin and mercy, the life of Jesus, the Passion, the resurrection, etc.

Loyola's spiritual exercises and instructions are still read and preached today; however, some modern practitioners have expressed their regret that these exercises are often theologized and developed beyond Ignatius' intent. For example, they are being used as "a Christian equivalent, perhaps, of the Zen return to the marketplace" (Barnes, 1989, p. 271). Nevertheless, the text still consists of various prayers, meditations, and instructions for praying, with each section making frequent references to the body and the senses. In the prayer section (each prayer is appended with a meditation), only one mention of the body is made, wherein the person praying is instructed to feel the power of sin around them with all their senses, not just think about it. Later in the text, in the notes and rules section, the body and the senses play an important role. Since the themes change based on the week, Ignatius instructs those praying to adopt a posture suitable for the content being contemplated (e.g., upright posture for contemplating the resurrection, lowly posture for contemplating sin). Believing self-discipline is important to the act of contemplation, Ignatius includes instructions for everyday life while taking part in Exercises. He includes instructions such as planning ahead to avoid eating impulsively, focusing on where one is walking and why, focusing on the meaning of each word in prayer and on the rhythm of the breath while praying, and saying the Lord's Prayer one word and one breath at a time while doing chores.

> It is no part of Ignatius's intention to remove the exercitant from the world but to return him or her to that world strengthened by an experience of prayer which is now to be maintained in the midst of ordinary occupations.
>
> (Barnes, 1989, p. 267)

Howard (2012) uses the concept of *Lectio Divina* (divine readings) to explain mindfulness in the Christian tradition. He states that *Lectio Divina* is a term that originated in *The Rule of St. Benedict* (6th century) as part of an instruction for monks to regulate their time between work and reading, but today it refers to a diverse devotional practice among both Catholics and Protestants. It has four common components—reading, meditation, prayer, and contemplation—and often includes one additional component: action. Though these components of *Lectio Divina* may not be identified as such in many Protestant denominations, they are nevertheless present in their prayer practices. This scripture reading is not an academic reading, but a repetitive reading that "aims to bear fruit in the spiritual growth of the reader" (Howard, 2012, p. 58). The procedure and elements of *Lectio Divina* are not of primary importance, but instead what is sought is an attitude that assumes the Holy Spirit is the primary exegete. While most Christians support the perspicuity of Scripture, it is still believed that its interpretation is only accomplished through the Holy Spirit. The reading component is usually a short section, from a few verses to a chapter, while meditation often includes a repetition of certain words or phrases and a slow re-reading of passages. Prayer often includes either an oral reading of the passage or extemporaneous prayer that uses language from the passage, and contemplation involves sitting in silence and using either the words or individual words of the passage to block intrusive thoughts and focus on the Divine message.

Brian Butcher (2017), who is a rising prominent contemporary voice in liturgical theology, also points out that Eastern Orthodox spirituality has its central characteristic liturgically rich worship practices and deification (*theosis*), including mindfulness. Butcher (2017) uses taekwondo as a contemplative practice, noting many affinities between Eastern Orthodox practices and the *dojang* (taekwondo's instructional space). He notes that liturgy has often been compared to games, being meaningful without serving another purpose or having a *theosis*. For example, the *dojang* is a sacred space, like a church, that requires a certain etiquette, like bowing to the Korean flag once anyone enters the space. There is a hierarchy of various instructors and various students, like the hierarchical order in the Orthodox church, and there are rituals to begin and end each taekwondo class (e.g., formulaic phrases, silent meditation, choreographed movement, etc.), just like how there are rituals to the process of *theosis*. Both taekwondo and Orthodox worship have a patterned structure and cosmology, and both require a bodily dedication; the former involves kicking and punching, while the latter involves bowing, singing, making the sign of the cross, and kissing icons. Finally, both taekwondo and Orthodox worship require the participant to regulate breathing and keep rhythm. Like Paul Ricoeur's "surplus of meaning" and "reorientation through disorientation," the meaning of the repetitive practices and values in taekwondo and Orthodox liturgy can be extended into daily life and shape an individual's reactions to events. "The very tedium and predictability of these prayers serve to recall me from any distractions and invite me into a different space where I cultivate certain kinds of capabilities" (Butcher, 2017, 203).

In his article, *The Influence of Swami Satyananda's Meditation on John Main's Christian Meditation*, Jaegil Lee (2020) discusses the influence of Hindu meditation on Christian meditation through an example from the life of John Main (d. 1982). Main, a Benedictine monk, created a form of Christian meditation influenced by both John Cassian's (d. 435) *The Conferences* and the Hindu meditation practices taught to him by Swami Satyananda (d. 1961), creating an interreligious meditation practice. Main met Swami, a Hindu monk, while in the British Colonial Service in Malaysia. Swami founded the Pure Life Society and accepted Main as a student who, until then, had used an Ignatian method of meditation. Main then used his initiation into mantra meditation when he was the headmaster of St. Anselm's School in Washington, D.C., after he read about Cassian's Conferences. Cassian taught a form of unceasing, repetitive, contemplative prayer using only a few words, suggesting Ps 70:1. The prayer is encouraged to recite these words whenever troubling thoughts enter their mind and to cultivate an open spirit. Main's adoption of John's contemplative prayer adds three additional elements characteristic of Hindu mantra meditation.

Main suggests prayers speak the repetitive phrase rhythmically, paying attention to syllables, the inhaling and exhaling of one's breath, and to the sound of the words being prayed, not their meaning. Main's mixture of contemplative prayer and Hindu mantra meditation satisfied the needs of Christians in the 1970s who were turning to Eastern spirituality because Christianity did not satisfy their spiritual hunger.

I would say that one of the essential books on Christian meditation and mindfulness in clinical settings is Knabb's *Christian Meditation in Clinical Practice: A Four-Step Model and Workbook for Therapists and Clients*. In this book, Knabb (2021) presents a model that helps Christian therapists integrate mindfulness-based therapy with Christian meditation in counselling. He notes that, in recent decades, many clinicians have embraced mindfulness meditation originating from the Buddhist tradition and mindfulness-based therapy as a means of addressing a long list of symptoms. He suggests that mindfulness and meditation have always been integral to a Christian life. Therefore, he provides a foundation for a Christian-sensitive approach to meditation in clinical practice and differentiates Christian-based mindfulness from secular and Buddhist forms of mindfulness meditation.

Knabb (2021) tried to harmonize the features of the Christian approach with psychology and research-based evidence for the benefits of Christian meditation. For example, he provides examples from the practices of early desert fathers of Christian tradition, Ignatius of Loyola, Celtic Christians, the Puritans, and contemporary writers, then suggests guidance for targeting transdiagnostic processes (a new approach to understanding mental disorders): cognition (repetitive negative thinking), affect (impaired emotional clarity and distress intolerance), behaviour (behavioural avoidance), the self (Perfectionism), and relationships (impaired mentalization) that may lead to psychological suffering (Knabb, 2021, p. 21). In this respect, the unique psychospiritual benefits of Christian mindfulness techniques in counselling can be to engage clients in meditative exercises and help them develop healthier responses to difficult experiences. This becomes possible by developing a deeper awareness of and contentment with God. Using the Christian tradition of mindfulness, Knabb explores topics such as the increase in mindfulness and differences between secular and Christian literature, and comparing and contrasting meditation in the Christian, Buddhist, and secular schools of thought. Of course, Knabb also discusses the differences between secular and Christian meditations, for which he presents historical narratives of Christian practices for embracing the presence of God. This kind of approach is closely related to Acceptance and Commitment Therapy (ACT), which also uses concepts of noticing internal processes, present-moment awareness (including spiritual awareness), acceptance, and committed action. In brief, the exercises begin with learning to "notice," then practicing "shifting" from earthly to heavenly mindedness, and finally "accepting" God's active loving presence and providential care; these steps are thoughtfully explained and practically laid out.

Ford and Garzon (2017) also introduced a three-week Christian accommodative mindfulness (CAM) programme to a traditional mindfulness programme in a university setting. They demonstrated how to integrate mindfulness and Christian-derived meditative practices in counselling. They also reported that such integration resulted in significantly positive outcomes.

Wilhoit (2014) notes that centring prayer, a prayer practice that has much in common with *hesychasm* and apophatic prayer, stands alone as an organized and responsive development to the focus on contemplative mindfulness practices of "Eastern" religions in the middle of the 20th century. In the 1960s, Fr. Thomas Keating turned to *The Cloud of Unknowing* to introduce Christian youth to a Christian form of mindfulness, which he called "centering prayer." Keating utilized training, retreats, and numerous publications (e.g., *Foundations for Centering Prayer and the Christian Contemplative Life*, 2002) to promote centering prayer. Unlike the aforementioned prayer practices, centering prayer is done in groups, either in youth groups, religious retreats, or in other settings that help the individual make and keep an "appointment with God" (Wilhoit, 2014, p. 109).

Centering prayer is a practice that prepares individuals for contemplative prayer. Keating outlines four stages: (1) individuals sit for 20 minutes or more in silence to be in the presence of God; (2) they are to pick a sacred word with the help of the Holy Spirit; (3) they are to introduce that word slowly into God's presence with eyes closed and with a receptive posture, using it in extemporaneous prayer or to ward off distracting thoughts to help them return to the intent of the prayer, which is to be in the presence of God; and (4) the prayer is ended with a few minutes of sitting with eyes closed and praying the Lord's Prayer. It is emphasized throughout Keating's writings that this practice is not one of attention, but rather of intention. "Centering prayer is not so much an exercise of attention as intention... you intend to go to your innermost being, where... God dwells. You are opening to Him by pure faith" (Wilhoit, 2014, pp. 116–17). The intent to be in the presence of God is not accomplished through human will, but through the aid of the Holy Spirit.

In 2003, Avants and Margolin (2003) produced a manualized treatment plan for an eight-week group, non-sectarian intervention for addiction and HIV risk behaviours by applying meditation, prayers, affirmation, and training in spiritual virtues. The goal of the group is to replace the "addict self-schema" with a "spiritual self-schema." Ano (2005) presented a four-session Christian-based therapy using spiritual visualization, purification, prayer, and Scripture. McCorkle, Bohn, Hughes, and Kim (2005) developed a treatment manual that presented sanctification, meditation, ritual, and spiritual support to treat social anxiety from a spiritual perspective. We can also add to this list the manuals for spiritually integrated psychotherapy by Rye and Pargament (2002), Worthington (2004), and McCarthy-Jones et al. (2013).

Islam and Mindfulness

A detailed account of mindfulness in Islamic psychotherapy practice will be made in the following chapters of this book; however, I would like to indicate briefly that, similar to the implementation of Buddhist practices in contemporary Western psychotherapy, the application of a classical Sufi understanding of human nature and mental and spiritual health issues has stimulated a new and dynamic discourse about the use of *muraqabah*, or the Sufi practice of mindfulness, in contemporary Islamic psychotherapy (Chishti, 1985; Dwidiyanti et al., 2021; Hussein, 2018; Isgandarova, 2019; Saniotis, 2018).

In this respect, in his work *Sufi Varieties of Transformative Practice: Transformation of the Ego-Self,* Arthur F. Buehler (2016) notes that, in most contemplative practices, the initial step usually involves calming the mind. To access the inner realms and unveil hidden truths, one must transcend the senses and rational thinking. For this, Buehler (2016) recommends to take a watch with a second hand and observe how it rotates without any thoughts. Note how quickly a thought arises. Many individuals struggle to focus for even a minute without thoughts intruding. He also recommends to contemplate on the following question: where do these thoughts originate? It becomes evident that our most potent tool, the mind, often operates uncontrollably. While we have mastered control over our bodies and emotions over time, many have not learned to tame their minds. If the Sufi path of transformation is a journey, the traveller cannot embark until the mind is liberated from thoughts.

In this respect, the Sufi masters developed a whole set of contemplative practices, including *muraqabah* and *dhikr,* which can be compared to mantras in the Buddhist tradition. Unlike the Buddhist tradition, however, contemplation happens not only in the mind of the person, but also in the heart. The second important difference is with respect to the goal of classical *muraqabah,* which is highlighted by Lobel (2007) as "the human being's heightened awareness of God's loving perception of him" (p. 225). God possesses deep insight into the human heart and remains ever-watchful and aware. It is essential for individuals to maintain a continuous awareness of God's presence. The Quran's depiction of God as all-knowing serves as a motivation to align behaviour and inner intentions. The notion of *muraqabah* highlights the significance of human reactions to God's all-knowing nature. Sufis also emphasize the idea that the human consciousness of God can be nurtured and enhanced to be more persistent.

Similarly, some elements of *muraqabah* might remind certain elements of practices in yoga. The desired outcomes, such as action, love, sacred knowledge, and freeing the self from temporary material bondages, might be the same; however, Nasr (2007) points out one fundamental difference between the Islamic tradition, which is the theological foundation of *muraqabah,* and Hinduism, for example, which is the theological and spiritual foundation of yoga. In Islam, one does not regress from the heavenly state upon entering Paradise, even if it is achieved through virtuous deeds grounded in faith rather than knowledge and love of God. This differs from Hinduism, where following only the path of action or *karma yoga* may lead to falling back into the lower realms of *maya* associated with cycles of birth and death once good karma is depleted in the next world (Nasr, 2007).

Although Muslim therapists need to engage in a deeper and more meaningful discourse about the implications of Sufi practices, the practice of *muraqabah* can be used as mindfulness-based Islamic psychotherapy. I personally prefer to integrate this technique with the social sciences, such as family therapy, psychology, etc. For example, its integration with psychotherapeutic modalities and techniques such as MBSR, MBCT, DBT, ACT, and MBRP can help the client understand and manage the problem in a more effective way. The benefit of such integration is that it provides a direct, whole body-spirit-mind awareness of the present moment with a focus on spirituality.

When it comes to Islam and its impact on our attitude towards illness and healing practices, we can argue with confidence that there is no distinction between religion and spirituality for many Muslims. Muslims put the Divine at the centre of their attempts to seek meaning and purpose in this life and the hereafter. Therefore, healing practices are a direct product of Islamic beliefs and cultural practices. Illness is an opportunity to serve, clean, purify, and balance the physical, emotional, mental, and spiritual domains (Isgandarova, 2019b; Rassool, 2016). Muslims generally view physical doctors as healthcare providers who care for the body and spiritual "doctors" as those who heal the soul. A pure soul is a "sound heart… free of character defects and spiritual blemishes" (Long, p. 49). For this, *tazkiyat al-nafs*, or the purification of the soul, is recommended. *Tazkiyat al-nafs* is defined as "the process of self-purification, conscious intention and religious practice along with the guidance and sincere concern of others" (Long, p. 40).

The main purpose of *tazkiyat al-nafs* is to help the person return to their natural state, called *fitrah* (inner character; nature). A general Islamic belief is that humans are inherently good and free from moral and spiritual diseases; however, too much focus on earthly needs and concerns contaminates *fitrah*. For example, extreme preoccupation with material benefits such as power, money, etc. causes deficiencies in human character and leads to reprehensible morals and deeds, or demoralization. As a result, the person forgets the Divine presence, becoming greedy, jealous, lazy, hypocritical, and delusional with grandiose ideas. With *muraqabah* and other spiritual techniques, one can treat and heal such character deficiencies.

There is a disease in their hearts, to which God has added more: agonizing torment awaits them for their persistent lying. When it is said to them, 'Do not cause corruption in the land,' they say, 'We are only putting things right,' but really, they are causing corruption, though they do not realize it. When it is said to them, 'Believe, as the others believe,' they say, 'Should we believe as the fools do?' but they are the fools, though they do not know it. When they meet the believers, they say, 'We believe,' but when they are alone with their evil ones, they say, 'We're really with you; we were only mocking.'

(Q. 2:10–14)

Some researchers have also discussed certain mental health problems from both the perspectives of Islamic spirituality and the *Diagnostic and Statistical Manual (DSM)-5-TR* (APA, 2013). For example, Subandi et al. (2023) discussed the relationship between the concept of diseases of the spiritual heart (DOTSH) from the Islamic-Sufi perspective, particularly al-Ghazali's interpretation of the spiritual, and mental health issues from the DSM-5. As a result of their study, they presented six DOTSH categories comprised of 40 DOTSH and their correspondence to the DSM-5-TR.

In the case of spiritual health issues, depression, anxiety, and other mental health problems, many Muslims believe that suffering has a purpose. In some cases, it serves as a means of wisdom or reward. The Qur'an reminds us that God does not cause suffering; humans inflict it on themselves and others. I have discussed the position of Islamic schools concerning human suffering in my book, *Muslim Woman, Domestic Violence and Psychotherapy* (Isgandarova, 2019).

Islamic spirituality is deeply rooted in resilience, kindness, mercy, compassion, and hope. Similarly, like all aspects of life, health was also supposed to be, and should be, viewed in the context of justice. Being human means being composed of material, emotional, rational, and spiritual/soul dimensions. Spirit or soul is a heavenly dimension of being human, one which is not always acknowledged in our daily life.

> Man was truly created anxious: he is fretful when misfortune touches him, but tight-fisted when good fortune comes his way.
> (Q. 70:19–21)
>
> [Prophet], have you considered the person who denies the Judgement? It is he who pushes aside the orphan and does not urge others to feed the needy. So woe to those who pray but are heedless of their prayer; those who are all show and forbid common kindnesses.
> (Q. 107:1–7)

In the context of *muraqabah* and its application in Islamic psychotherapy, the question is, then, what is spirit and spiritual? Or what makes us spiritual? It is a challenge to answer this question. Despite multiple suggestions, there is still no all-comprehensive and agreed-upon definition of spirit and spirituality. Healthcare professionals, including psychotherapists and spiritual care providers, still struggle to define spirit, soul, and spirituality clearly. Despite challenges, some have proposed the idea that religion is more about social institutions with their own rules, rituals, practices, and formal procedures. Spirituality, however, is presented as a more personal experience one goes through when they try to seek the sacred in life and look for ways to connect with God (Higher Being), either with religious rituals, practices, and rules, or by reflecting on nature, music, art, etc. For some religion and spirituality are not separate; they are just two sides of the same coin. At the heart of this question of spirituality is one's desire to search for meaning and have purpose in life.

When we think of spirituality and religion in the Muslim context, the task might seem simple at first, but it becomes complex because of the diversity and richness of Muslim traditions. Nevertheless, it can be said that, for many Muslims, both concepts are deeply rooted in their belief in Allah.

Questions for Discussion

1 Discuss the concept of mindfulness in the Christian, Jewish, and other traditions. Discuss the challenges, risks, and benefits of using mindfulness-based practices in various spiritual and religious traditions.
2 Discuss how they might differ from contemporary mindfulness practices in psychotherapy. How can we create opportunities to integrate some of these practices into therapeutic work?
3 In what ways does the increasing tendency to use spirituality-based mindfulness practices suggest a need for more training and education in religion, theology, and spirituality? What else do you want to learn in Christian, Jewish, or other religious and spiritual traditions?

2 An Overview of *Muraqabah* as a Spiritual Practice

Muslims are familiar with *muraqabah* and other mindfulness-based spiritual practices from the Prophetic tradition. It is well known that the Prophet Muhammad engaged in *muraqabah* in the Cave Hira (sometimes it is written and pronounced as Ḥara'). This cave is located in *Jabal al-Nur*, the Mountain of Light, and is three Arabian miles north-east of Mecca, near the *shi 'b*, or quarter of the family of al-Akhnas, on the left of the pilgrim road to 'Irak . Many historical documents show how the Prophet Muḥammad used to spend a month each year in this cave in seclusion. This seclusion, known as *tahannuth*, helped him engage in *muraqabah* consisting of long vigils and prayers. After completing his *muraqabah*, the Prophet would circumambulate the Kaaba seven times (al-Tabari, 1988; Hamidullah, 1981; Kister, 1968). According to historians such as Abu Muḥammad 'Abd al-Malik ibn Hisham ibn Ayyub al-Ḥimyari al-Mu'afiri al-Baṣri, or Ibn Hisham (d. 833), and Abu Ja'far Muḥammad ibn Jarir ibn Yazid al-Ṭabari, known as al-Tabari (d. 923), in one of Prophet Muhammad's seclusions, he was visited by an angel. He was 40 years old at the time. Many spiritual texts consider such angelic visits to be signs of the beginning of revelation. After he received the first revelation through the archangel Gabriel during the last third of Ramadan, Prophet Muhammad continued his practice of *muraqabah*.

> People, be mindful of your Lord, who created you from a single soul, and from it created its mate, and from the pair of them spread countless men and women far and wide; be mindful of God, in whose name you make requests of one another. Beware of severing the ties of kinship: God is always watching over you...
>
> (Q. 4:1)

> I was a witness over them during my time among them. Ever since You took my soul, You alone have been the watcher over them: You are witness to all things.
>
> (Q. 5:117)
>
> God is watchful over all.
>
> (Q. 33:52)

This prophetic experience inspired many Muslim spiritual leaders, specifically Sufi leaders, to develop the concept of *muraqabah* to help their disciples improve their concentration, attention, and contemplation during concentration and breath meditation. Today, we can say with assurance that Sufism directly influences how we see and practise *muraqabah* as a Prophetic tradition.

Muraqabah and Sufism or Islamic Spirituality

As mentioned before, Sufism plays an essential role in how we perceive and practise *muraqabah* today. There is no consensus on what the name "Sufism" refers to, and it is beyond the scope of this study to present the diverse theories of Sufism's nature and origins; however, it would be helpful to summarize some suggestions for when we discuss the role and influence of *muraqabah* on contemporary Islamic psychotherapeutic practices. In brief, there are various explanations for the etymology of the term *tasawwuf* (Sufism). Some believe it is derived from *suf*, the word describing the rough woolen garments or cloaks worn by many Sufis; however, it was also a symbolic name referring to *as-suf libas al-inam* (the garment of faith). Kugle (2021) notes that this cloak symbolized "detachment from outward perception and social engagement—and engaged in meditation to turn the gaze inward to combat the ego" (p. 3). Others, an ascetic group of the Prophet's companions known as the People of the Bench, drew a connection between the term and the *suffa*. Due to the influence of Greek philosophy, the term is often associated with *sophos* (wisdom). It is also possible that the term is connected to the Syrian Sufi, Abu Hashim al-Sufi (d. 767). There may also be a connection with the *safwa* (chosen ones) who practised *tasfiyat al-qulub* (the purification of the heart) (Ernst, 2007). Interestingly, according to Shah (1980), the word "Sufi" may also come from the Hebrew cabbalistic term "Ain Sof," meaning "the absolutely infinite" (p. 15). Shah notes that earlier Sufis also used names such as "The Kindred," "The Recluses," "The Virtuous," and "The Near Ones" (p. 36).

Javad Nurbakhsh (d. 2008) describes the focus of Sufism as follows:

> The science of Sufism deals with the One essence and with Its Names and Attributes in as much as they link the loci of their outward manifestation, together with all related phenomenon, to the Divine Essence. Thus, the subject of this science is the One Essence and its beginningless and eternal Attributes. The questions it investigates include: 1. The emanation of multiplicity from the One Essence and its return thence, 2. The loci of manifestation as reflection of Divine Names and Attributes.
> (Nurbaksh, 1981, p. 31)

It is also important to mention here that there are some controversies about the legitimacy of Sufism as an Islamic tradition. Regardless of these controversial opinions, abundant examples show how prominent Muslim scholars such as Imam al-Shafi 'i, Imam Hanbal, and ibn Qayyim al-Jawziyah followed the Sufi path. Many shaykhs (Sufi leaders) were also prominent Hanbali jurists; for example, 'Abd al-Qadir al-Jilani (d. 1166) founded the Qadiri Sufi order, one of the largest Sufi orders in the Muslim and Western worlds. Therefore, since its emergence, Muslim psychotherapists, psychologists, psychiatrists, and spiritual masters have used Sufi practices as a legitimate tool in their clinical practice to help their clients improve their relationship with God and address their mental and emotional health problems through devotional rituals and practices.

Sufi concepts have also provided a strong foundation for Islamic psychotherapy in the past and continue to do so now. For example, the emphasis on training the *nafs* in Sufi psychology and its approaches to emotional and spiritual diseases have proven helpful in reducing stress and treating depression and anxiety. In Sufi tradition, *nafs* is described as the spiritual reality of all living beings. It is also interpreted as the human potential to actualize self-awareness through the aid of *'aql* (the intellect to control impulses of the lower self) (Esposito, 2016). These examples show how Sufism is still relevant and has been recognized as a life-giving core since the emergence of Islam (Chittick, 2001; Ernst, 2011; Murata & Chittick, 1994; Nasr, 2007; Rahman, 1979; Schimmel, 2011; Sells, 1996: Iqbal & Farid, 2017; Isgandarova, 2019). Therefore, many Muslim psychologists, psychiatrists, spiritual caregivers, and psychotherapists recommend certain spiritual practices, such as *dhikr* (the rhythmic repetition of God's names), prescribed by the Sufi masters. Later, we will discuss the role of *dhikr* in *muraqabah* as a ritual activity, performed either in a group or individually, in the Qur'an (i.e., Q. 33:41–42).

Muraqabah as a Spiritual Practice

Many Sufi masters, such as Ibrahim Adham, al-Harith, al-Qushayri, al-Makki, and al-Ghazali, practised *muraqabah*. A famous 13th-century Sufi leader,

Muhyiddin Ibn 'Arabi (d. 1240), prescribed four levels of understanding to be reflected in Sufi practices, including *muraqabah*: *Shari 'ah* (exoteric religious law; literally means road), *Tariqah* (spiritual or mystical path, a term that was used to refer to the Sufi orders), *Haqiqah* (truth), and *Ma 'rifah* (gnosis) (Frager, 1999). Shari 'ah is the foundation for the practice because it offers genuine guidance for living ethically and morally in this world. Without it, one cannot move to the higher levels. In this respect, Nasr (2007) notes:

> [*Shari 'ah*] is a road that all Muslims are obliged to travel... For most, however, the journey on this road is limited to the place of action, the performance of good acts, and faith in the reality of God. A few wishes to take a step further to discover the ultimate nature of who they are and carry self-knowledge to its end.
>
> (p. 5)

Nasr also states that, as the inner or esoteric dimension of Islam and *Tariqah*, Sufism begins with the Shari 'ah but then proceeds towards *Haqiqah*, which "is the Source of both the Law and Way as well as the Center for one who begins on the circumference, journeys along one of the radii, and finally reaches the Center, which is also his or her own center" (Nasr, 2007, p. 5). In general, Sufism, as a unique branch of the Islamic tradition, embraces "the earlier exemplary life of the Prophet Muhammad" (Green, 2012, p. 4). As Nasr outlines, "Not only certain verses of the Qur'an but also many of the sayings of the Prophet constitute the revealed and canonical basis for the *Tariqah*" (p. 105). Integrating *Shari 'ah* and *Tariqah* supports the disciple or *salik/murid* to discover esoteric knowledge, experience God directly, and follow the practice of *awliya Allah* (God's prophets and friends) in their private and public lives.

Muraqabah has always been an important spiritual practice in other Sufi orders. Al-Ghazali (2015) quotes the followers of the Prophet and later generations, emphasizing it as such:

- Ibn al-Mubarak: "Watch ye God! Exalted is He!" The man asked him to explain his view, he responded, "Act always as if you saw God Almighty and Majestic."
- 'Abd al-Wahid b. Zayd: "When my master watches me, I take notice of nothing else."
- Abu 'Uthman al-Maghribi: "The best thing which man demands of himself is self-examination and vigilance, and to manage his actions through knowledge."
- Ibn 'Ata: "The best act of piety is continual vigilance very moment over the truth."
- Jurayri: "Our affairs are built on two principles: that you keep your soul vigilant for the sake of God and that you manifestly uphold knowledge."

- Junayd: "With your knowledge that the sight of the One who sees you precedes your view of whatever you see... He will verily obtain confirmation through vigilance who fears losing his share from his Lord Almighty and Majestic."
- Muhasibi: "Vigilance being with the heart's knowledge of the proximity of the Lord."
- Murta'ish: "Vigilance is attending to one's secret (interior) in order to be wary of what lies hidden at every moment and with every utterance."
- Muhammad b. 'Ali al-Tirmidhi:

    Examine yourself before the One who ever sees you. Offer gratitude to the One whose blessings to you never cease. Be obedient to the One you cannot but need. Show humility to the One whose dominion and power you cannot escape.

- Sahl [al-Tustari]: "The head is adorned with nothing better or nobler than the servant's knowledge that God sees him as he is" (pp. 13–15).
- Qushayri comments:

    The saying of the Prophet, 'For if you do not see Him, yet he sees you,' is an indication of the state of heightened awareness [muraqaba], because heightened awareness is the servant's knowledge of the Lord's constant awareness [ittila] of him, and his constancy in this knowledge is *muraqaba* of his Lord, and this is the source of all good for him.

    (Lobel, 2007, p. 225)

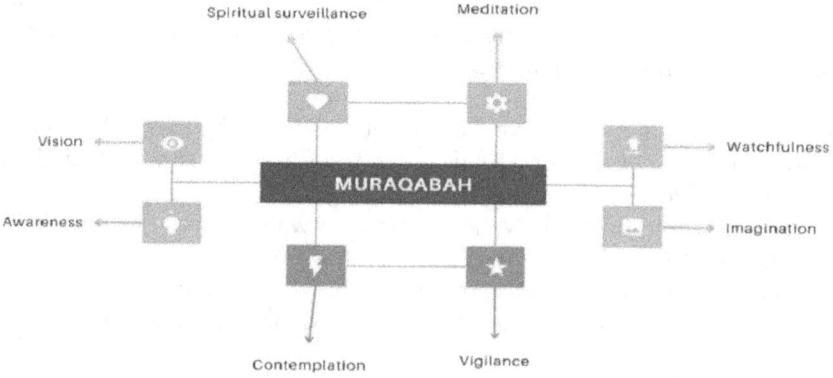

Figure 2.1 The power of *Muraqabah*.

Purpose of *Muraqabah* in Sufi Tradition

As mentioned before, in Sufi practice, *muraqabah* refers to a certain type of meditation in Islamic tradition. In this type of meditation, the disciple watches over or takes care of his/her *nafs* (soul); controls thoughts, intentions, and feelings that prevent the remembrance of the divine; and acquires knowledge about the soul and its relationship with the creator by being mindful of his/her feelings and surroundings. The ultimate goal of *muraqabah* practice in the Sufi tradition is to help the disciple develop and mature emotionally and spiritually, and to gradually achieve the status of *insan-i kamil* through a heightened awareness of and respect for the divine.

Deeply rooted in the Qur'an, Sunnah (the sayings, actions, and approvals/disapprovals of the Prophet Muhammad), and the Sufi tradition of Islam, the concept of *insan-i kamil* emphasizes Islamic ideals such as tolerance, personal and social accountability, peaceful coexistence, and religious broadmindedness. The literary meaning of *insan-i kamil*, in Persian and Turkish, or *al-insan al-kamil*, in Arabic, is interpreted as "the complete human," "a universal person," or "the person who has reached complete perfection"; in other words, a person who has lost himself/herself in God (*fana fillah*) (Leaman, 2006). In Islamic thought, the concept of *insan-i kamil* was initially connected to the beginning of the *nur Muhammad* (the Muhammadan light), which was a movement started in the 8th century.[1] Even in contemporary *muraqabah* practices, contemplation on Muhammad's name, image, or symbol is still an important stage in Sufi practices. Before we discuss how *muraqabah*, as a spiritual tool, was used to become a spiritually and emotionally mature, universal human being, I will provide a brief overview of the concept of *insan-i kamil*.

First, many prominent Sufis, including Muqatil ibn Sulayman al-Balkhi (d. 767), Abu-Said-al-Kharraz (d. 899), Husain ibn Mansur al-Hallaj (d. 922), Hakim Abul-Majd Majdud ibn Adam Sana'i Ghaznavi (d. 1131 or 1141), Fakhraddin Razi (d. 1209), Abu Hamid bin Abu Bakr Ibrahim (d. 1221), Muhyiddin Ibn 'Arabi (d. 1240), Muhammad Bahauddin al-Baytar (d. 1248), Sadraddin al-Konevi (d. 1274), Abdurrazzaq Kamaladdin b. Abi'l-Ganaim al-Kashani (d. 1329), Abd al-Karim al-Jili (d. after 1408), 'Ali ibn Muhammad ibn 'Ali al-Husayni al-Jurjani (al-Sayyid al-Sharif) (d. 1413), and 'Abd al-Ghani ibn Isma'il al-Nablusi (an-Nabalusi) (d. 1731), explored the main principles and practical aspects to being *insan-i kamil*. Their work emphasized that, in order to mature spiritually, one needs to be consistent in practicing mindfulness techniques and lead a proper spiritual lifestyle.

Historically, there were oppositions to the supporters and members of this mystic movement in mainstream Islamic sects; however, the love of the Prophet Muhammad was so deep and profound that many Sufis argued that the honorary title of *insan-i kamil*, as a perfect man or a prototype human being, belonged only to the Prophet Muhammad. This is very explicit in Sahl al-Tustari's (d. 896) explanation of the concept of *insan-i kamil* that contributed to the idea of *nur Muhammad*.

As a concept, *Nur Muhammad* refers to the first of the three lights of God, the foundation for the creation of the first human being and Prophet, Adam. This understanding also influenced the *muraqabah* practice, wherein one contemplates the prophetic image or light. Tustari referred to the Prophet Muhammad's mystical saying, "I am He and He is I, save that I am I, and He is He," and interpreted this as "a mystery of union and realization at the center of the Saint's personality, called the sirr ('the secret'), or the heart, where existence joins Being" (Glasse, 2008, p. 393). Later, Qadi 'Iyad b. Musa (d. 1149) linked Tustari's concept of *nur Muhammad* to the notion of *qalb Muhammad* (the heart of Muhammad), referring to the living reality of Muhammad, or the treasure mine of spiritual knowledge, divine love, and the jewel in the chest that would benefit all believers.

A big portion of Husain ibn Mansur al-Hallaj's (who was Tustari's student) (d. 922) *Kitab al-tawasin* also deals with the idea of the primordial love of God for the Prophet Muhammad and *nur Muhammad*. Al-Hallaj introduced the Prophet Muhammad as the first created being whose "life precedes everything and is part of God's light," by quoting a hadith qudsi: *laulaka ma khalaqtu'l-aflaka*—"if thou hadst not been (but for thee), I would not have created the heavens" (Shimmel, 2011, p. 215). He was also known for saying, "God has not created anything he loves more than he loves Muhammad and his family" (Shimmel, 2011, p. 70). Hallaj has influenced many Sufi practices and also many Sufi mystics and poets such as Shams Tabrizi (d. 1248) and his student Jalal ad-Din Muhammad Rumi (d. 1273), a Persian poet and Sufi leader who lived in Anatolia; the medieval Azerbaijani poet Nasimi (executed in 1417); and Bektashi orders in Anatolia.

Second, in the Sufi tradition, living a life with virtues was important for spiritual perfection and emotional maturity. Abu Naṣr Muḥammad ibn Muḥammad al-Farabi, also known as Alpharabius (d. 950), noted that the characteristics of *insan-i kamil* are one's achievement of a theoretical virtue through the combination of intellectual knowledge and practical moral virtues. Both of these virtues endow the person with effective power; they then assume the responsibility of leadership and become a role model for others (Madkur, 1983, p. 61).

Ibn 'Arabi and al-Jili later expanded the application of the concept to other areas of life, but in the context of *nur Muhammad*. Ibn 'Arabi, for example, explained *haqiqa muhammadiyya*, or the "reality of Muhammad" that Sufis often engage in *muraqabah*, as the manifestation of divine names and particular characteristics of other prophets and messengers. He introduced the Prophet Muhammad as a prototype for humanity and the universe, and likened him to a mirror in which each sees the other.

For instance, he writes that the light of all the Prophets originated from his brilliance, preceding everything, with his name being the first in the book of Fate. He was recognized before all existence, enduring beyond the end of everything. Through his guidance, all eyes have gained insight. All knowledge is but a drop, all wisdom a mere handful from his source, and all time just an hour in his presence (Schimmel, 2011, p. 70).

In his book entitled *Al-insan al-kamil fi ma'rifat al awakhir w-al-awa'il*, which is based on Ibn 'Arabi's discourse on the Perfect Man, al-Jili discussed three stages of spiritual maturity and perfection through meditation, contemplation, and other spiritual practices: (1) *bada'ah*, or the beginning of acquiring divine attributes; (2) *tawassut*, or man as the perfect being (becoming both human and divine) and the beginning of comprehending both realities and knowledge unseen; and (3) attaining power to influence the natural world and beyond (Ritter, 2003).

Nur ad-Din 'Abd ar-Rahman Jami, also known as Mawlana Nur al-Din 'Abd al-Rahman or Abd-Al-Rahman Nur-Al-Din Muhammad Dashti (d. 1492) also suggested three similar major aspects of *insan-i kamil*: "First, the Perfect Man as the locus of manifestation for the name of Allah; second, as the goal of creation; third, God's vicegerent" (Schimmel, 2011, p. 144). Al-Jili also systematized the thoughts of Ibn 'Arabi with a thorough examination of divine manifestations and revelations (*tajalli*). For him, only *insan-i kamil* can attain the divine illumination and attributions of the essence.

When we meditate on spiritual perfection and maturity in *muraqabah*, however, we need to note that the classical Sufi understanding of *insan-i kamil* was a limited concept in the sense that it did not allow the ordinary human to own this title. Some classical Sufi writers even saw ordinary humans as being "like animals" (*ka'l-an'am*), because only the Prophet Muhammad was entitled to be considered a perfect man. With time, however, some prominent members within the Sufi tradition gradually extended this title to other people. This process started by giving this title to mystical people, or a true "man," one who can experience the vision of God through and behind His creation.

The biggest influence on this new trend in the classical Sufi tradition is the *tawhid* perspective of *hamaust*, "everything is He." This new understanding, based on the interpretation of the concept of *hamaust*, implied that if the divine essence can be found in everything and everyone, or "there is nothing but God," then what prevents a common person from reaching the status of *insan-i kamil*?

These new interpretations allowed for the expansion of the circle of *insan-i kamil*, making it applicable to people other than Sufi poets and leaders. Next, we need to mention the role of Ibn 'Arabi's new approach to the concept of *insan-i kamil* and Jami's elaboration of the concept.

These two Sufi masters played a significant role in the extension of the concept to ordinary people. Ibn 'Arabi, who was a great Sufi master and a *qutb* (one who has the knowledge of the unseen world and future) based on the Qur'an, Sunnah, and divine inspiration, used his central concept *wahdat al-wujud* ("Oneness of Being"), the absolute, all-inclusive principle, in his interpretation of *insan-i kamil*.

Ibn 'Arabi's concept of *wujud* in Arabic means to "experience" or "find," and refers to the idea that "being" is not only an idea, but also an experience that must be found and realized. Ibn 'Arabi's belief in *wahdat al-wujud* is located at the heart of the nature of things. In this regard, Ibn 'Arabi recognized "belief" not as an intellectual appreciation or a blind conviction, but as something that is felt only in the heart. Furthermore, for Ibn 'Arabi, spiralling ascent, or *mi'raj*, is the realized spiritual perfection of a true *muhaqqiq* (explorer of the truth). This ascent can be achieved through ongoing interaction between the three essential elements of *tahqiq* (exploring the truth): (1) our actions, experiences, inspirations, and insights; (2) their observed consequences; and (3) the inseparable spiritual processes of reflection and deliberation (*tafakkur, tadabbur, dhikr*, etc.) (Chitttick, 2007, 1983).

Using these principles, Ibn 'Arabi extended the circle of *insan-i kamil* and pointed out that common people can also become *insan-i kamil*, because the world, or a "cosmic orchestra," is intertwined and coherent—the universe, the macrocosm, or *al-insan al-kabir* (the big human), and the human being, the microcosm, or *al-'alam al-saghir* (the small universe) (Shaikh, 2012). For Ibn 'Arabi, the Prophet Muhammad is undoubtedly "the perfect man," which "is the spirit in which all things have their origin; the created spirit of Muhammad is, thus, a mode of the uncreated divine spirit, and he is the medium through which God becomes conscious of Himself in creation" (Schimmel, 2011, p. 224).

The purpose of *insan-i kamil* is to fulfil the needs of the universe as the macrocosm, for—as an ethical and ideal self—*insan-i kamil* has knowledge of how to influence the equilibrium of representation of divine attributes in order to give life/spirit to the universe and transform it "into a polished mirror of the divine attributes" (Shaikh, 2012, p. 80). Ibn 'Arabi argues that each person has the potential to become *insan-i kamil*; however, their lack of proper behaviour, spirituality, and morality prevents them from achieving this capacity: only the prophets and the friends of God, or *awliya*, belong to the category of the sublime human archetype.

These concepts are still relevant in the context of *muraqabah* because the Prophet is one of the practice's symbols of attention. In our sample session section, we will present the meditation on the prophetic light and the spoken blessings to the Prophet Muhammad. This practice comes from the concept of *insan-i kamil,* and Muslims still see the Prophet as a perfect human being who should be followed.

The Practice of Traditional *Muraqabah*

In Sufi traditions, the disciples are trained to perform the traditional *muraqabah* without the physical presence of their master or guide; however, in classical Sufism, the role of the master and guide was so great that there was even the saying, "With a Guide you may become a human being; without one, you will remain an animal" (Shah, 1980, p. 37). Therefore, *muraqabah* was practised in the context of *rabitah* (connectedness), which refers to a close relationship between the master and disciple, who practise visualization of the guide in prescribed spiritual practices. During the *muraqabah*, the disciple needs to observe *batin* (inner), *zahir* (outward), and *ghayb* (hidden) states of being. The one who is engaged in *rabitah* is called *murabit*, a disciple who fights against the harmful impulses and inclinations of the self.

According to Omar et al. (2017):

> *rabitah* plays the role of helping a disciple to be proactive and to be fully dedicated in implementing the practice of dhikr because when the disciple is practicing dhikr the shaykh will control the disciple's emotions so that he is able to achieve his aim in discarding 'passing thoughts' other than Allah. This is because only the heart that is successfully controlled. The whole purpose of this important spiritual practice is to focus on thoughts, feelings and sensations with openness, curiosity, gratitude and acceptance.
>
> (p. 352)

Al-Ghazali discusses *muraqabah* in the context of *sabr* (patience), a certain inner quality that humans obtain at birth. In the path of commitment, he outlines six stations: agreeing upon the conditions (*muharata*), vigilance (*muraqaba*), self-examination (*muhasaba*), punishment (*mu'aqaba*), renewed striving (*mujahada*), and self-censure (*mu'ataba*) (Shaker, 2015, p. xvii). Al-Ghazali states that *murabata*, or steadfast commitment, basically means "attachment" or "the struggle against the self" (*jihad al-nafs*). He quotes from the Prophet: "We returned from the lesser *jihad* to the greater *jihad*" (Shaker, 2015, p. xviii).

Abbadi (d. 1152), who is the author of the treatise on Sufi methodology, presented *muraqabah* as watchfulness because it is "the most important tool in differentiating between different kinds of 'thought-impulses' (*khawatir*). Thought-impulses emerging during the practice of meditation or invocation can give an important implication to the spiritual state of the wayfarer" (Amini, 1999, p. 106). Similarly, Azeemi (2005) notes that humans spend their lives in between their thoughts and imagination, and that human life is a collection of both. Human consciousness is constantly developing and evolving, and has unlimited potential in the journey towards advancement through experimentation, observation, and the senses; however, an undeniable aspect of being human is also the spiritual. In this respect, *muraqabah* opens "the potential for spiritual insights beyond the five senses of Vision, Hearing, Speech, Taste, and Touch, and transforms these senses into vibrant and awake mode" (Azeemi, 2005, p. 11).

In Sufism, the purpose of the *muraqabah* is "to be aware of the one watching (*raqib*)[2] and to turn attention to him…" (Al-Ghazali, 1025, p. 17). It is accepted as a kind of knowledge of God's being watchful and aware of the secrets of the hearts, deeds, and overseeing every soul; it "causes the action in the heart and the limbs… When [certain knowledge] subdues the heart, it makes it mindful in deference to the one who watches and it turns its attention to him" (p. 17). Al-Ghazali states that gaining this kind of knowledge is obligatory for all Muslims; as the Prophet said, whoever knows himself/herself knows the Lord. In this respect, this process happens on two levels:

> First level. The first level is the vigilance of the perfectly truthful among those near to God. This is the vigilance of glorification and exaltation. It is when the heart is engrossed in the awareness of this exaltation, crushed by awe; therefore, it has no room truly to consider another…
> (Al-Ghazali, 2015, p. 17)

> Second level. The second level is the vigilance of the pious (*wari 'un*) among the people of the right hand. This group is that of those whose hearts are overcome by the certainty that God sees the hearts' interiors and exteriors. However, the awareness of divine majesty does not dazzle them. On the contrary, their hears keep within the limit of balance and are capable of attending to states and deeds… He who is at this [second] level needs to be vigilant about everything he does and does not do, this thoughts and glances… He is responsible for them in two respects: before the act and during the act. Before the act, he should observe what appears to him and what actually gives rise to his thought. Is it for God, in particular? Or does the passion of the soul or adherence to the devil give rise to it? This should cause him to pause and settle it, until it is revealed to him through the light of God.
> (Al-Ghazali, 2015, p. 21)

In the light of these instructions and insights, many leaders of the Sufi orders established a set of methods to practise *muraqabah* to help the disciple in his/her spiritual path or journey, which is often expressed in terms of *safar*.

The literal meaning is to travel or move from one place to another, or:

> daylight, to clean, to take something away from another, to light up the day, unveil a face, scatter clouds by the wind, or become manifest.

Similarly, *safar* unveils the faces of travellers and their characters, revealing matters that are hidden.

(Rahmani et al., 2018, p. 127)

In Sufism, *safar* means a spiritual wayfaring or journey from one state or station to another. Sufi masters such as Abu Talib al-Makki (d. 996), Abu Sa'id b. Abi l-Khayr (d. 1049), Ibn 'Arabi (d. 1240), and Jalal al-Din Rumi (d. 1273) extensively talked about the etiquette of spiritual journeys. For example, for Abu Talib al-Makki, the meaning of the journey was related to the purification of the soul.

In general, the Sufi path by itself is a spiritual journey, and *muraqabah* is part of this journey. In this respect, Khawaja Shamsuddin Azeemi (2005) also presents *muraqabah* as "an angle of perception through which the person doing the meditation frees himself or herself from outward senses and begins their journey in the inward feelings" (p. 4).

Sufi Orders and *Muraqabah*

In the West, not many Muslims currently follow the traditional Sufi orders and their methods of *muraqabah*. Some of the most popular Sufi orders that still consider *muraqabah* an important spiritual practice are the Qadiriyah, the Rifa'iyah, the Shadhili, the Suhrawardiyah, the Jerrahi Sufi order, the Naqshibandi, the Tijaniyah, the Mawlawiyah in Anatolia, and the Ahmadiyah in the Nile Delta. The Qadiri order was established around the teachings of 'Abd al-Qadir al-Jilani (d. 1166) in Baghdad; the Suhrawardiyah is based on the teachings of Abu al-Najib al-Suhrawardi (d. 1168) and his nephew Shihab al-Din al-Suhrawardi (d. 1234); the Rifa'i order was founded by Ahmad al-Rifa'i (d. 1182); the Shadhili order was founded by Abu al-Hasan al-Shadhili (d. 1258) in Egypt and North Africa; and the Chishti order was founded by Mu'in al-Din Chishti (d. 1142) in Central and South Asia.

The main difference among these Sufi orders is related to their distinctive historical identity in terms of some Sufi concepts such as *fanaa'* (passing away), *baqa'* (abiding or remaining in God), *sukr* (drunkenness or intoxication), and *sahw* (sober). For example, some Sufi orders, such as the Yasawiyah and the Naqshibandi, followed Abu Yazid al-Bistami (d. 874), who was famous for saying ecstatic utterances, whereas others (i.e., the Kubrawiyah and the Mawlawiyah) followed Abu al-Qasim al-Junayd (d. 910), who emphasized sober Sufism and external aspects of the *Shari'ah* such as ritual purity and fasting.

These differences also impacted how Sufi orders interpreted *muraqabah* and practised it. As Shah (1980) notes, while one may observe differences at the external level explained by environmental factors, there are, however, essentially no significant differences in the *muraqabah* practice itself. Generally, these orders presented and trained their disciples at different levels of *muraqabah*: beginning or low-level *muraqabah*, medium-level *muraqabah*, and high-level *muraqabah*.

1. Low-level *muraqabah* (*La ilaaha illa Huwa*/there's no God but Him): With low-level *muraqabah*, one achieves awareness of the supervision of Allah as the Giver of reward or punishment for human actions. They do deeds that are outward in nature while focusing on the consequences received.
2. Medium-level *muraqabah* (*Laa ilaaha illa Anta*/there's no God but You): With medium-level *muraqabah*, one realizes the supervision of Allah as the Giver of divine pleasure/enjoyment. *Muraqabah* at this level encourages a person to live and act with *qalbiyah* (heart) and *aqliyah* (mind). The aim is to gain the pleasure or enjoyment of Allah.
3. High-level *muraqabah* (*Laa ilaaha illa Ana*/there's no God but I): With high-level *muraqabah*, the person leans how to internalize scared values such that one wants to live and act in line with those values. High-level *muraqabah* becomes evident in *ruhiyah* practice. Those who are at high-level *muraqabah* will perform good deeds and avoid disobedience in order achieve the light of Allah. They no longer act and live for personal gain, but contemplate on their usefulness for life. Allah SWT is very close to them because they have internalized His values and incorporated them into their character (Susanty & Hawadi, 2019, p. 445).

During these stages, the disciple observes and watches over certain signs, including *ihsan, nur, haatif-e ghabi* (subtle sounds of the cosmos, manifestations of the attributes of God), reflection on life after death, the spiritual heart, the purpose of life, nothingness, and also the non-material universe. The role of the master is to observe the spiritual states of the disciple. These states are usually three: counterfeit or imagined, genuine, and irrelevant.

Muraqabah in Naqshibandi Order

Here I would like to elaborate on the aforementioned levels in the practice of *muraqabah* in existing Sufi orders in North America. For example, the tradition which started in Central Asia under the leadership of Baha al-Din Naqshibandi (d. 1389), also known as Shah-e Naqshiband, instructed his followers to pay specific attention to *muraqabah* and developed unique spiritual practices. This tradition not only gained immense popularity in Central Asia, but also extended beyond their borders to become popular in India and the Ottoman Empire.

After the death of Baha' al-Din Naqshband (d. 1389), his disciples, including Emir Kulal (d.772/1370) and Muhammad Parsa (d. 1420), also recommended continuous engagement in a state of *muraqabah* by *sabr* (patience), controlling *nafs*, and living according to the divine rules (Orhan, 2021). Before and during Imam-i Rabbani's lifetime (d. 1624), *muraqabah* was interchangeably used with other concepts, such as *tawajjuh* (meaning to be directed, give preference), and was the foundation of 11 principles of Naqshibandi called *kelimat-i qudsiyye*.[3] In the early stages of Naqshibandi, *muraqabah* was used to protect and control the desires and heedlessness in the heart. It was an important religious and spiritual ritual in the process of *suluk* and was understood and practised in the context of the famous hadith of *ihsan*, which implied "to worship as if you see him" is observable, "Even though you do not see Him, He watches you!" This was accepted as the highest level of *muraqabah*. Later generations expanded the concept of *muraqabah* by adding the *dhikr*, especially chanting *La ilaha illallah*, to cleanse the heart from earthly preoccupations, negative feelings like revenge and anger, bad morals, and worldly desires.

The practice of *muraqabah* depends on the relationship between the Sufi master and the disciple. The disciple, who is called *salik* or *murid*, seeks spiritual guidance based on his/her feeling of *faqr* (spiritual poverty). The realization of this feeling of poverty and emptiness encourages the disciple to initiate a spiritual journey on the path of Truth. The Sufi master can take on this responsibility because he/she has experienced and successfully passed the stages of the spiritual path. This master needs a certification of approval by his/her master. In many Sufi orders, approval is demonstrated with the *khirgah* (cloak of initiation), which is a sign that the master has permission from his/her master to train and guide new disciples.

The spiritual journey requires sincerity and honesty from the disciple. The master also needs to show compassion and empathy, and to suspend his/her biases towards the disciple. In Sufi literature, this is called the love and attention of the master towards the disciple; this is the most important factor in developing a spiritual bond between the master and the disciple. Ahmad Naqshibandi explains how the master and disciple should follow certain procedures:

> Both master and disciple should perform the prayer to request God's guidance (*salat al-istikhara*). When this is done, the shaykh asks the *murid* (disciple) to take a bath of repentance (*ghusl al-tawba*); then he should perform the prayer of repentance (*salat al-tawba*) for two *rak'at*, donate (*adaqa*), and then come to the shaykh to have the ceremony…
>
> (Mulyati, 2003, p. 153)

Then the master checks the disciple's *iradah* or willingness, devotion, and readiness. For this, the master first instructs the disciple to discipline the ego. This would require taking care of chores such as washing the dishes and toilets. Al-Ghazali notes that the disciple is supposed to "regard his teacher like a doctor who knows the cure of the patient. He will serve his teacher. Sufis teach in unexpected ways. Yet the outside observer might be quite amazed at what he is saying and doing…" (Shah, 1980, p. 53).

The master and disciple would regularly discuss unconscious psychological conflicts, disturbances, and hesitations; however, the master is also required to observe, which is called *nazar*, and to know of these psychological conflicts even if they are not reported by the disciple. The master's role is to help the disciple with managing and curing these conflicts (Amini, 1999). For this purpose, the master also uses the method of *talqin*, which means to command, to suggest, or to instruct. In his *'Awarif al-Ma'arif*, Shihab al-Din 'Umar Suhrawardi (d. 1234) notes that the master invokes *talqin* or instructs his disciple to repeat *la ilaha illa Allah* a prescribed 101, 151, or 301 times (Trimingham, 1971). Ibn 'Arabi noted that the master "should possess all that the disciple needs," and should adjust spiritual practices if needed (Shah, 1980, p. 47). It is believed that the master has the capacity to transmit *baraka* (blessing, grace, or gift) to the disciple who consistently performs spiritual practices. Nurbakhsh (1990) notes that the spiritual path programme unravels the disciple's psychological knots, complexes, and emotional tendencies to achieve psychic balance and moral well-being over time. The next phase of the *tariqah* (spiritual path) when the disciple focuses and strives to adopt spiritual virtues and embodies divine Qualities and Attributes.

In later periods of Sufism, *muraqabah* practice emerged as a different kind of systematic and detailed spiritual practice, called *muraqabah ahadiyya* (contemplation of the Oneness), *muraqabah ma'iyya* (mindfulness of the divine togetherness), *muraqabah aqrabiyya* (mindfulness of the divine nearness), and *muraqabah muhabbat* (mindfulness of the divine love). In Naqshibandi order, Mir Valiuddin even suggested eighteen types of *muraqabah*: (1) *muraqabah ahadiyyah*; (2) contemplation of the heart; (3) contemplation of the spirit; (4) contemplation of the *sirr*; (5) contemplation of the *khafi*; (6) contemplation of the *akhfa*; (7) contemplation of the compresence, co-existence of God, or *muraqabah ma'iya*; (8) contemplation of *aqrabiya* (closeness of God); (9) contemplation of love or *muraqabah mahabba*; (10) contemplation of the name "the Outward" or *al-Zahir*; (11) contemplation of the name "the Inward" or *al-Batin* (the superior saintship or the saintship of the angels); (12) contemplation of the perfections of prophethood or *muraqabah kamalat-i-nubuwwa*; (13) contemplation of the perfection of the apostles or *muraqabah kamalat-i-risala*; (14) contemplation of the perfections of the *ulu'l 'azrn*; (15) contemplation of the reality of the ka 'ba or *muraqabah haqiqat-i-ka'ba*; (16) contemplation of the reality of the Qur'an or *muraqabah haqiqat-i-Qur'an*; (17) contemplation of the reality of prayers or *muraqabah haqlqat-i-salat*; and (18) contemplation of the "pure worshipability" or *muraqabah ma 'budiyat-i-sirfa* (Valiuddin & Khakee, 1980). In each of these practices, a disciple would choose one short verse from the Qur'an, deeply contemplate, and expect *fayz* (spiritual pleasure).

Some assume that an Indian Sufi master, Mazhar Jan-ı Janan (d. 1781), introduced this system first after being influenced by the Chishti order, the largest sect in India at the time. It is reported that in the Chishti order, there are 36 types of *muraqabah*, including *muraqabah qurba, muraqabah ma'iyya*, and *muraqabah dhati*, which are similar to *muraqabah aqrabiyya, muraqabah maiyyat*, and *muraqabah dhat-i baht* in the Mujaddidi system (Orhan, 2021).

There are three levels of *muraqabah* in most Sufi traditions, and all these levels are initiated only upon the Sufi master's decision: the beginner, intermediate, and advanced levels. The beginner level of *muraqaba* is called the *muraqabah* of light and is used for basic self-awareness and to cure some diseases. At this level, coloured lights such as violet, indigo, blue, turquoise, green, yellow, orange, pink, and red are imagined. Sometimes, reflection and deep listening are also practised by imagining and reflecting on *noor* (invisible light) or *haatif-e-ghabi* (the unhearable sound of the Cosmos). *Asma al-Husna*, or 99 Names of Allah, which we will elaborate on later, is also counted.

The intermediate level of *muraqabah* focuses on *mawt* (death), to get acquainted with life after death; *qalb* (heart), to mature the Spiritual Heart; *wahdat* (unity), to get more intimate with the divine; *la* (Nothingness), to develop an awareness of the non-material universe; *Adam* (pre-existence), the next level of *muraqabah* of Nothingness; and *fana* (annihilation of self), with the purpose of getting acquainted with the *alpha* and *omega* of the universe.

The third level, which is a more advanced level of *muraqabah*, focuses on: *fana fi Shaikh; fana fi Rasul*—Become One and Annihilated with or in Muhammad; *fana fil Quran*—Become One and Annihilated with or in the Qur'an and its commandments; and *fana fillah*—Become One and Annihilated with or in God.

Sufi masters invited outsiders not to label those who practised *fana fi shaikh* against the *tawhid* principle of Islam. As Shah (1980) notes in *The Study of Sufism in the West*, "The Sufi teacher is a conductor, and an instructor- not a god. Personality-worship is forbidden in Sufism" (p. 31).

In Naqshibandi order, the first level of *muraqabah* is *muraqabah ahadiyyet*, wherein the names of Allah, especially *la ilaha illa Allah*, are chanted with a special focus on the inner world (*khatır*) to attain peace of heart, together with imagining oneself in an inner circle. When the devotee becomes illuminated, they begin to rise with divine attraction, or *seyr ilal-lah*. After completing this stage, the second circle, which is called *velayet-i sugra*, begins. This stage is completed when the devotee achieves the absence of worldly desires in the heart during two hours of *muraqabah*. The aim of *muraqabah ahadiyyet* is to cleanse the heart from associating God with anything else, and to purify the heart from selfish desires and ambitions (Orhan, 2021).

After successfully completing this first level, the second level of *muraqabah*, called *muraqabah maiyyat*, can begin. At this level, the devotee is expected to contemplate the images and subtle essence, or *lataif*, of the prophets Muhammad, Moses, and Jesus. According to Naqshibandi, the *lataif* or essence of each creature consists of the shadows of their names. The *lataif* of the Prophet Muhammad is believed to be *ruh*, spirit; for the Prophet Moses it is *sir*, or secret; and for Prophet Jesus, it is *haif*. The devotee makes a humble request or prayer: "O Allah, deliver the actual manifestations from the heart of the Messenger of Allah to the heart of Adam through the hearts of the sheikhs" (Orhan, 2021, p. 410).

The third level, *muraqabah akrabiyyat*, consists of three small circles and a semicircle. The Qur'anic verse chosen for this stage is "We are closer to him than his jugular vein," from the chapter Qaf. The purpose of this stage is to help the devotee feel the divine presence and achieve inner peace.

The next level is called *muraqabah muhabbat*. At this stage, the devotee contemplates divine love based on the Qur'anic verse "God loves them, and they love God" (Q. 5:54). The purpose of this stage is to help the devotee worship God not out of fear of hell, but out of love for God. Finally, the last level is *muraqabah dhat-i baht*, which is the stage of contemplating God's divine names al-Zahir and al-Batin and adds *Muhammadan Rasulullah* to *la ilaha illa Allah*.

We created man—We know what his soul whispers to him: We are closer to him than his jugular vein.

(Q 50:16)

Say, 'If you love God, follow me, and God will love you and forgive you your sins; God is most forgiving, most merciful'.

(Q. 3:31)

The Lord of Mercy will give love to those who believe and do righteous deeds…

(Q. 19:96)

> Everything in the heavens and earth glorifies God—He is the Almighty, the Wise. Control of the heavens and earth belongs to Him; He gives life and death; He has power over all things. He is the First and the Last; a the Outer and the Inner; He has knowledge of all things. It was He who created the heavens and earth in six Days and then established Himself on the throne. He knows what enters the earth and what comes out of it; what descends from the sky and what ascends to it. He is with you wherever you are; He sees all that you do; control of the heavens and earth belongs to Him. Everything is brought back to God. He makes night merge into day and day into night. He knows what is in every heart.
>
> (Q. 57:1–6)

Muraqabah in Ni'matullahi Order

Muraqabah is also an important spiritual practice in the Ni'matullahi order, which originated in the 14th century under Nur ad-Din Ni'matullah Wali, known as Shah Ni'matullah (d. 1431). It is reported that the Qadiri order influenced this Sufi order. Indeed, Shah Ni'matullah himself was a disciple of the Qadiri Sufi 'Abd-Allah Yefa'i. Nevertheless, he grew to disapprove of seclusion and quietism as a spiritual practice, and did not encourage his disciples to engage in these controversial practices. After the death of Shah Ni'matullah, the Ni'matullahi order became popular in Iran and its surroundings. Nurbakhsh, another influential leader of this order, suggested spiritual practices, including *muraqabah*, that helped the disciple develop unity, or *tawhid*. This process requires two phases. Amini (1999) states that:

> In the first phase, the disciple goes through the process of unravelling and solving psychological conflicts, and decreasing the control of the ego until she achieves a state of psychological balance and harmony. In the second phase, the disciple undergoes a process of becoming illuminated by Divine Attributes and Divine Nature.
>
> (p. 6)

In the Azeemia order, *muraqabah* is also an important spiritual practice. Indeed, this order was established in India in the 1950s by Hassan Ukhra Sayyed Muhammad Azeem Barkhiya, commonly known as Qalandar Baba Auliya (d. 1979), to preach and teach the *muraqabah* method. With that goal, this order established centres across the globe. These centres are called *Muraqabah* Halls. After Hassan Ukhra, the spiritual leadership passed to Shaykh Khwaja Shamsuddin Azeemi. In addition to *muraqabah's* spiritual and religious benefits, Khwaja Shamsuddin Azeemi also extensively discussed its emotional, psychological, and mental benefits with his disciples. He also extended the number of *muraqaba* halls, where disciples and teachers offer colour therapy, amulets, and teach occult sciences using modern techniques and methods.

Azeemi sees *muraqabah* as a crucial spiritual exercise, skill, or way of thinking on a spiritual path. He noted that *muraqabah*:

> improves concentration, immunity, memory, prevents psychological complications, and controls our negative thoughts and emotions, thereby giving us a feeling of serenity and tranquility. Overall, we can perform well in our daily tasks, whether work-related or in relationships.... Emphasis on prayer is always placed on higher focus and contemplation.
>
> (Azeemi, 2005, p. 11)

Azeemi also classified different levels of *muraqabah*, stating that "these different meditations work like a class or grade for the spiritual development of the students, so, their progress would evolve gradually" (p. 45). Each level of *muraqabah* has a certain object or symptom of focus during meditation. The students were exposed to lights of diverse colours and were instructed to focus and observe the pure light. Like other Sufi orders, imagining and focusing on the teacher, guide, or master was also practised. Kugle (2021) notes that this kind of focus is:

> a form of giving thanks and acknowledging the origins of the practice. His [master's] form acts as a *barzakh* or "medium," an intermediary space between the ego and God. Holding that form in one's imagination is an effective way to concentrate one's attention and ward off distracting thoughts that interfere with doing dhikr: one relinquishes one's whole humanity in all its weakness and negligence to one's spiritual guide, so that what is left is the soul's dependency on the pure spirit that animates one and connects one to God. Through this strategy, one can and the strength of resolve to focus on doing dhikr with a whole heart. Sus call this process *fana' fi'l-shaikh* or "effacement of the ego in the person of the spiritual guide."
>
> (p. 6)

Each level has its own purpose and specific benefits. For example, the master might instruct the disciple to observe life after death or the inaudible sound of the cosmos. In this kind of meditation, the purpose is to help the disciple activate hidden senses. In the contemporary era, where the teacher might be geographically distant from the disciple, Azeemi (2005) instructs the disciple to "send monthly journal report of their meditative visions and other experiences that they may face, so whenever necessary, they can receive guidance" (p. 46).

In this respect, in Azeemia order, the focus of the special *muraqabah* programme is:

1. To improve the working of the brain and mind.
2. To improve the individual faculties of the mind, that is, memory, creativity, imagination, and speed.
3. To awaken the hidden abilities of telepathy, *kash*.
4. To improve cognitive and intuitive skills.
5. To activate the spiritual sight or the third eye of the student (p. 47).

Azeemi teaches his disciples to be mindful of consistency in *muraqabah*. For this purpose, he wants his disciples to practise meditation and other exercises, such as respiratory or breathing exercises, almost every day at the same time for a duration of 15–20 minutes. In addition, he also describes the posture of the person in this practice:

> When we see someone performing meditation it seems as if that person is simply sitting in one posture with his eyes closed. That refers to the physical side of it as how to sit and how the surrounding should be. The real aspect of meditation is its mental side… To perform meditation, you would first close your eyes and then free your mind of all the incoming thoughts. Then focus on a single idea or imagination in a way that you are no longer attached to or interested in any other thoughts or ideas. The two main parts of meditation are emptiness of the mind and the idea of imagination. The emptiness of the mind means you should not pay any attention to other thoughts or willingly think about anything. This is what thoughtfulness is. You can perform meditation in different ways…
> (pp. 47–48)

Mirdal (2012) notes that the Sufi meditative tradition's breathing practices create greater awareness. It is also used "as an interruption of habitual maladaptive patterns of breathing" (p. 1210).

In terms of physical posture, Azeemi recommends sitting cross-legged while keeping the back and neck straight. Both hands should be placed on the knees or in the lap. If this posture is uncomfortable, the disciple can change to a position similar to how Muslims sit during prayer. Another posture includes sitting on the hips, folding the legs upwards so the knees touch the chest, and holding the legs with the hands. This will allow the disciple to meditate without getting tired. For those who cannot perform *muraqabah* in these positions, Azeemi recommends using a chair, sofa, ottoman, or bed; however, lying down is not recommended as it encourages sleep.

Azeemi recommends four time periods for *muraqabah*: before dawn, during the early afternoon, in the late evening before sunset, and after midnight. During these natural time periods, nature becomes still and enhances one's ability to meditate. The timespan between sunset and sunrise is the best. In this time period, the human senses are more open to unseen realms, and the subconscious senses are more active. Azeemi instructs beginners not to practise meditation for too long or too frequently. He always advises moderation, as excessive meditation might cause apathy and avoidance. For beginners, the ideal duration of *muraqabah* is a maximum of 15–20 minutes.

In her book titled *The Healing Power of Sufi Meditation*, Nurjan Mirahmadi (2005) also describes a proper sitting posture, breathing and focusing on the image of the shaykh, and saying divine names. Mirahmadi states, "Take care to perform even the smallest details of this form of Sufi meditation, because they are the foundation of your meditation…" (p. 51). After a detailed description, she notes:

> Keep repeating *Ya Sayyidi, ya sayidi madad al-haqa, Mawlana Shaykh Nazim* while holding your index finger and thumb together gently and trying to feel your pulse. It is important to feel your own heart beating and make sure it is in tune with your breathing. Hear your heart beating, Allah, Allah, Remember that each of us in surrounded by a field of energy. You are receiving emanations of Divine Energy.
>
> (p. 53)

I will provide some exercises from Mirahmadi's book in the section where I provide a format for some sample *muraqabah* sessions. Along with Mirahmadi and Azeemi, the reader can also refer to Puran Bair's (1998) *Living from the Heart: Heart Rhythm Meditation*.

Other Details in *Muraqabah*: Space, Music, and Dance

Almost all Sufi orders require their disciples to practise *muraqabah* in a place where they cannot be easily distracted. This reminds us of the Prophet's *muraqabah* in the Cave of Hira; it still inspires many Sufis in terms of space for the effective result of mindfulness. In Sufi practice, this is called *khalwat* (seclusion or isolation), which refers to a space in various places such as Muslim shrines, tombs of sacred men and women, caves, buildings, or mosques that are considered holy for Muslims.

Khalwat also includes a certain body praxis, spiritual/religious practices such as chants, prayers, incantations, and fasting, and psychological techniques that allow a negotiation of space between self and other (Saniotis, 2012). In these spaces, Sufis pray, chant, and practise silence with the purpose of going through purification. They believe these practices have *barakat* (blessedness or grace) that transforms one through the purification of the body, controlling the *nafs*, and elevating the *nafs* to the next level. Some Sufis report a kind of transcendental experience during the process of *khalwat*.

Although we do not expect our clients to experience miraculous signs during psychotherapy sessions, we hope for a positive transformation of the clients' mood, cognition, and emotional state. Sitting in seclusion, or *khalwat*, helps one to sit still, which is very important in *muraqabah* and other mindfulness practices. Thus, the client is instructed to find a space where there is minimal distraction, if any. In our era of technology, earbuds can be used so as not to be disturbed or distracted by external noises. Of course, it is helpful to have the mindset that God watches over us; this suggestion prepares us to have peace of mind psychologically and spiritually, so as to have maximum clarity of awareness.

In *muraqabah*, some Sufi orders use poetry, dance, and music, usually known as *sama'* or ecstatic listening, to enrich the disciples' spiritual experiences. For example, Shah (1980) notes that Attar's works, specifically *The Conference of the Birds*, was a poem where Attar describes "specific stages in human development… sketches individual phases in human consciousness… stages of the human soul in search of perfection" (p. 62). The selected works in *muraqabah* help the disciple reflect upon life's ethical and moral standards. They are also used for the setting and preparation of *muraqabah* practice. For example, in *dhikr* practice, it is common to feel the rhyme and rhythm. According to Dewey (1959), rhythm becomes a manifestation of psycho-physiological energies that is "an indispensable coefficient of aesthetic order" (p. 162). He writes that, "Because rhythm is a universal scheme of existence, underlying all realisation of order in change, it pervades all the arts, literary, musical, plastic and architectural, as well as the dance" (p. 150).

Wolf (2006) gives an example of the Madho Lal Husain:

> During this ceremony, the lamps are lit and even it is called the 'festival of lamps' (mela chir ¯agh ¯an), as this 'urs is sometimes called… The broad tree stump that someone had turned into a fire pit (chir ¯ag hd ¯an) that year was still smoking, flaming, and spewing out coals….
>
> (p. 251)

Fire has a special meaning in mystical Islamic tradition; as Wolf (2006) correctly observes, some Sufi mystics during the spiritual practice call it "the ubiquitous Sufi image of a mystic lover as a moth attracted to a candle's flame…" (p. 251).[4]

In terms of the application of music, there was some criticism towards its misuse in some circles. Shah (1980) gives an example from contemporary dervishes of the Chishti order, who, according to Shah, mistakenly performed their founder's instructions and played or listened to music to induce a dissociated or ecstatic state. Moinuddin Chishti even noted, "Know that every learning must have all its requirements fulfilled, not just music, thought, concentration" (p. 43). In general, we can say a lot about the benefits of music; however, in brief, we can certainly say that music has a tremendous capacity to reawaken our souls. Thus, Sufi masters use music to activate parts of the brain, such as the auditory cortex.

Nasr (2007) notes that music is a natural human need as it is based on harmony. Harmony itself "is the result of the manifestation of the One" (p. 145); it is the core of the functioning cosmos and everything that exists in the universe. In the universe, harmony is expressed in various ways, and music is one way to manifest it. Nasr states that "melodies, rhythms, and harmonies in the technical musical sense can reflect the cosmic harmony and lead us back to the Origin..." (p. 145); however, he also outlines a prerequisite. He states that music should remain "faithful to its traditional nature and [that] cacophony is not mistaken for music" (p. 145). Therefore, as outlined above and going back to the statements by Moinuddin Chishti and others, only sacred music with rites and spiritual practices can take the soul to the divine. Nasr beautifully includes not only Sufi music, but also "the chanting of the Vedas to the sacred songs of Native Americans and including, of course, the great Christian tradition of sacred music going back to Gregorian chants" (p. 145) in his category of sacred music.

Some Muslims might argue that dancing is *haram* (forbidden); however, the Sufi practice of some dance movements, especially whirling, was and is still an important ritual in certain schools. Shah (1980) notes that dance movements in Sufism should be treated as local traditions, as they were prescribed for local reasons. For example, the *Mevlevi* dance was prescribed as a spiritual practice by Rumi for the people of Asia Minor. Taking these dances out of context due to misunderstandings or misapplications does not do any justice to the original use of these spiritual movements. They are not performed for pleasure (Harel et al., 2021). The ultimate purpose of spiritual dance movements in Sufism is "to be with an open heart and unite with God during the whirling, are inseparable parts of the experience..." (p. 3). Nevertheless, the benefits of these movements in *muraqabah* have also been recorded. The following chapters will discuss the application of these *muraqabah* techniques in Islamic psychotherapy.

Questions for Discussion

1. What is the greatest source of *muraqabah* in Islamic tradition? Describe it.
2. What are the foundations of *muraqabah*? How do you think the Qur'an and Sunnah contributed to *muraqabah* traditions in various Sufi disciplines?

3 Discuss the Sufi orders' role in systematically developing *muraqabah* practices in the Islamic tradition. What are the potential effects of these mindfulness practices in classical and contemporary Sufi orders? Discuss the role and responsibilities of the master and the disciple in *muraqabah*.
4 Have you ever had an experience of *muraqabah* or any other Islamic meditative practice before?

Notes

1 Sometimes this word is also translated as Muhammadan mysticism; however, the term "Muhammadan mysticism" was an "orientalist" word, and was used as a derogatory term implying that Muslims worship Muhammad.
2 As mentioned, *Raqib* is also one of God's Names. Based on the Qur'anic verse, Qushayri writes: God is over all things *raqib*. Lobel notes that "In Surat al-Ahzab (33:52), we read that God is watchful over all things (wa kana llahu 'ala kulli shay'in raqzban). The verse appears in a legal context discussing marriage. In the previous verse, we hear that God knows what is in our hearts (wa-llahu ya 'lam ma fi qulubikum); that God is ever knowing ('alfm) and forebearing (~alim). In the next verse, we hear that God is raqzb, watchful over all human doings, inner and outer" (p. 224).
3 These principles are: *hûş der dem, sefer der vatan, nazar ber kadem, halvet der encümen, yâd kerd, bâz geşt, nigâh daşt, yâd daşt, vukûf-i zamânî, vukûf-i adedî, vukûf-i kalbi*.
4 Even some Sufi political leaders also used fire as "a common metaphor for Islamic dynastic succession" (Wolf, 2006, p. 262). Lapidus gives an example from the practice of the Safavid ruler Shah Ismail (d. 1524), who claimed to be "descended from the seventh imam ... and the bearer of the divine [pre-eternal] fire ... that preceded the Quran and the creation of the universe (Lapidus, 2002, p. 234)..." (cited by Wolf, 2006, p. 262).

3 *Muraqabah* and the Human Nature

As a spiritual ritual and practice, great Sufi masters and teachers have, in the past, used *muraqabah* to help their disciples become *insan-i kamil*. Today, its direct purpose is more aligned with goals to help the *muraqabah* practitioner attain awareness of human nature and its direct impact on the human soul. In this respect, it would be helpful to introduce human nature in Sufi psychology to better grasp the purpose of *muraqabah* in Islamic psychotherapy.

First, as Farzaheh Amini (1999) states, Sufi psychology "shares the same goal as modern psychology – to attain self-consciousness" (p. 1). One must also be mindful, however, that the term "psychology" might not adequately describe Sufism (Shah, 1980, p. 20). For example, in Sufi psychology, "self-consciousness is a bridge that guides the individual to higher consciousness of her Divine nature" (Shah, 1980, p. 1). Moreover, as noted by many reputable sources, Sufi masters centuries ago presented spiritual and psychological methods of interpreting human conditions and treating them a hundred years before Freud and Jung (Shah, 1980, p. 38).

Nevertheless, despite ontological and epistemological differences, there are many overlaps between contemporary and Sufi psychology. For example, discussing Sufi psychology in the context of psychoanalysis, Amini (1999) notes that the goal of Sufi psychology is the purification of the heart from the turbidity of oppositions. Jung also discussed a similar concept in the context of the transcendent function, or transcending the dualities to achieve psychic equilibrium, as "there is no consciousness without discrimination of opposites" (Amini, 1999, p. 4). However, Abraham Maslow (1970) elaborated on this in the context of the hierarchy of human needs and referred to it as the "self-actualized" personality.

Furthermore, Sufi psychology provides extensive insight into the psyche, its journey of spiritual crisis, and its resolutions. If the Sufi treatment is successful, the psyche is open to new learning. All these Islamic psychological concepts and approaches, including *muraqabah* as a practice, aim to

DOI: 10.4324/9781032631387-4

perfect the human character, thoughts, and behaviours. These are usually discussed in the context of the following three key terms in the Qur'an:

- *iman* (to be at peace; to be safe; not to be exposed to danger) referring to
- the common tenets of faith,
- *islam* (to be safe; to be whole and integral; not to disintegrate) by following
- the instructions in the Qur'an, and
- *taqwa* (in the hadith it is *ihsan*) referring to piety; fear and consciousness of God.

In *muraqabah*, the last concept is particularly important. The root word of *taqwa* means "to protect from getting lost or wasted" and "to guard against peril" (Rahman, 1987, p. 13). Al-Ghazali (2015) quoted Said 'Ali (Ibn Abi Talib), who described *taqwa* as "the most secure bond" and "the firmest relation" (p. 27). There is a famous hadith where the Prophet responded to Gabriel regarding *ihsan*: "Worship God as if you were looking at Him. Though you see Him not, He sees you."

> Is He who stands over every soul marking its action [in need of any partner]? Yet they ascribe partners to God. Say, 'Name them,' or, 'Can you tell Him about something on the earth He does not know to exist, or is this just a display of words?' But the things they devise are made alluring to the disbelievers and they are barred from the [right] path: no one can guide those God leaves to stray.
> (Q. 13:33)

Al-Ghazali (2015) notes that those with insight (*arbab al-absar*) know that:

> God is ever-watchful over them and that they shall be questioned at the Reckoning and that they will be liable for trifling motes of thoughts and glances. They realize that nothing will save them from those perils but perseverance in self-examination and true vigilance and questioning the soul about breaths and movements and examining her thoughts and glances.
> (p. 3)

In Sufi psychology, an individual's relationship with God is expressed through psychic polarity, known as unity and multiplicity. Amini (1999) notes, "On one hand the realm of unity is based on the relationship between the individual and God. On the other hand, the realm of multiplicity is based on the individual's relationship with the external world and people" (p. 45). Since, hereditary and environmental factors also play an important role, below I will present a developmental view of the structure of the psyche after the discussion on human nature in Sufi psychology.

Overview of Human Nature

According to the Qur'an, humans are the noblest of all creatures, as stated in the verse, "wa laqad karramna bani Adam" (Q. 17:70), with the potential to become the lowest of the low (Q. 95:4). The most fundamental weaknesses of humans are their pettiness, narrow-mindedness, and selfishness. The tendency to worship idols, including power, money, and ego, is also a result of weaknesses in the human soul (Rahman, 1987, p. 13). The starting point of becoming a true human is gaining awareness of transcendence or God-consciousness). In this respect, Rahman (1987) identifies three concepts at the heart of justice and egalitarianism: "One God, one humanity because without this, humans are subject to stagnation and disintegration..." (p. 13). In the context of *iman, islam,* and *taqwa,* we will now present the nature of human being in Islam.

The Qur'an and hadith traditions have played, and indeed still play, an important role in Muslim understandings of human nature, along with the influences of distinguished cultural heritages. Early Muslim scholars, such as Al-Ghazali, ar-Razi, ibn Sina, and ibn Qayyim, also extensively discussed the nature of *nafs, ruh, qalb,* and *'aql* in their seminal works. Even today, their discussions help us to understand the nature of the *nafs* and *ruh* and whether they should be understood as two separate entities. Nevertheless, in previous and present works, some of these concepts are used interchangeably, and some are not even clearly distinguished in traditional Islamic literature. For example, lack of clarity regarding the differences between *qalb* and *ruh* is one of the weaknesses of al-Ghazali's theory of the human psyche (Abu-Raiya, 2012).

Nevertheless, as Murata (1992) points out, Muslim scholars, including cosmologists and psychologists, usually discuss relationships in the context of varying levels or differing intensities and hierarchies that reveal certain qualities. For example, the terms "lower" and "higher" describe a progression from the basic signs of life and activity, seen in plants for instance, to the perfection of these qualities in human beings and beyond. Of special importance is the connection between any two levels, often described as active and receptive, with the higher level typically being active and the lower level being receptive. In Sufi writings, the superior and prevailing aspect of the inner human essence is known as *ruh* (spirit), while the lower aspect is related to receptivity.

These concepts are still relevant in contemporary Islamic psychotherapy literature. Therefore, it is important to clarify them through the lenses of contemporary perspectives on mental, emotional, and spiritual health problems and spiritual imbalances.

Ahmad al-Faruqi al-Sirhindi (d. 1624), also known as Imam-i Rabbani, suggested that humans consist of ten *lataif*, or *lataif-i ashara*. Five of them, or *jevahir-i khamsa* (the heart, the soul, the secret, the light, and the *ahfâ*), belong to the realm of the spiritual world, or *alam-i amr*, and five of them belong to the realm of creation, comprised of *anasır-ı erbaa* (water, fire, air, earth) and *nafs* (ego/soul) (Orhan, 2021). Al-Ghazali also presented the structure of the soul as having four levels. For Rothman and Coyle (2020), these levels are: *nafs*, or "lower self"; *'aql*, or "intellect"; *qalb*, or "heart"; and *ruh*, or "spirit." Below, you will find a brief overview of these concepts in the Qur'an and Sufi psychology.

'Aql (Mind; Reason; Intellect)

The Qur'an refers to *'aql* 49 times. Abu-Raiya (2012) translates *'aql* as intellectual faculty. The most common belief is that the location of the *'aql* is the brain; however, some argue that the seat of cognition is within the *qalb* (Rothman & Coyle, 2018). In the Qur'an, three cognitive processes are mentioned (*ya'qil, yatafkar,* and *ya'lam*) directly related to *'aql*. The main function of *'aql* is "organising the environment's stimuli and, far more importantly, thinking about and contemplating God" (Abu-Raiya, 2012, p. 228). The elements of *'aql* include reason, logic, thoughts, beliefs, knowledge, and biases (Keshavarzi & Khan, 2018).

Al-Ghazali (2015) discussed extensively the role of *'aql* in the soul's struggle for purification. He states that purification of the soul is important because the soul's:

> felicity is through this… Now, as the other party can be adversarial, disputing and rivalling him for profit, he needs to agree on the conditions; second, to be vigilant with him; third, to call him to account; and, fourth, to punish or censure him. By the same token, the intellect first needs to set the conditions for the soul (*musharatat al-nafs*); then to assign tasks to it, lay down the conditions, guide it to the paths of felicity and force it to undertake such paths without for a single moment to keep vigilant over it. Whenever, on the other hand, the intellect neglects the soul, it will find nothing but disloyalty in it and the loss of capital – just like the disloyal servant who, left at liberty, mat abscond with the money.
> (pp. xviii–xix)

According to al-Ghazali (2015), *'aql* refers to intelligence and is responsible for higher intellectual function. He said, "If you want the intellect to prevail over passion, then do not act upon the appetite until you look into the consequence. For regrets dwell longer in the heart than the levity of appetite" (p. 11). When the soul follows the intellect, the chances of experiencing regret also decrease. A famous hadith narrates, "Call yourself to account before being called to account. Weigh yourselves before being weighed." This is possible only through *'aql*.

The *'aql* has an angelic quality, which helps to control satanic influences over the *nafs* in order to assist in gaining a state of harmony (Abu-Raiya, 2012; Yasien, 1996). Najm ad-Din Abu Ḥafṣ 'Umar ibn Muḥammad an-Nasafi, who was a Muslim jurist, theologian, mufassir, muhaddith and historian (d. 1142) notes that the *'aql* has the ability to know the qualities of things. The Prophet himself also noted that "The intellect ['aql] is a fetter ['iqal] against ignorance. The soul is like the worst of beasts. If it does not have intellect, it wanders bewildered, since the intellect is a fetter against Ignorance" (cited by Murata, 1992, p. 239). In this respect, the function of the *'aql* resembles Freudian super-ego. In the Qur'an, the primary function of the *'aql* is guidance. As narrated by the Prophet,

> God created the intellect and said to it, "Turn away from Me" so it looked away. Then He said, "Turn toward Me," so it turned toward Him. Then He said, "By My might and majesty, I have created no creature greater than you nor more obedient than you. Through you I shall begin and through you I shall bring back. What is for you shall be rewarded, and what is against you shall be punished."
>
> Then from intellect branched off deliberation [hilm], from deliberation knowledge, from knowledge right guidance [rushd], from right guidance abstention, from abstention guarding, from guarding shame, from shame gravity, from gravity continuity in the good, from continuity in the good aversion to evil, and from aversion to evil obedience to the good counselor.
>
> (Cited by Murata, 1992, p. 239)

In Islamic psychotherapy, the *'aql* is used as a regulating factor. By reflecting on the nature of the *'aql*, thought is given to wise and proper choices and how to be mindful of the destructive inclinations of the *nafs* (Rothman & Coyle, 2020). It is also the foundational principle behind using cognitive approaches in therapy. In their grounded study, Rothman and Coyle (2020) report that, while participants acknowledged that the cognitive approach to psychotherapy has its place within the Islamic framework, many expressed the view that it should be considered as only one aspect of the conceptualization of the person and of any resultant Islamic therapeutic approach. They all reflected a concern that, like most people, their clients overidentify with thoughts. These therapists believed that, while it is necessary to work with those thoughts, they also need to move their clients beyond that focus.

In this respect, "therapeutic interventions at the *'aql* level may engage cognitive aspects of blocks to the fitrah or higher spiritual self" (Rothman & Coyle, 2020, p. 211). The disadvantage of such interventions is that they "largely do not engage the deeper emotional material that is connected to or causes these blockages and that is found at the level of the *qalb*" (p. 211). In this respect, *muraqabah* plays an important role in strengthening the faculties of *'aql*. Ibrahim ibn Adham (d. 778) also stated that vigilance is the hajj of reason (*al-muraqaba hajj al-'aql*).

Qalb (Heart)

As al-Ghazali has stated, in *muraqabah*, it is the heart that gains a special kind of knowledge. The word *qalb* (translated as "heart" but referring to the spiritual heart) is mentioned 132 times in the Qur'an.

Like the physical heart, the spiritual heart is prone to different kinds of heart diseases. The term *qalb* (heart) is used with dual meanings: one refers to the cone-shaped flesh organ situated on the left side of the chest, while the other alludes to a delicate, ethereal spiritual substance, which is also called *latifah rabbaniyyah ruhaniyyah*, intricately linked with the physical heart (Subandi, 2023, p. 7).

In Sufi psychology, the heart has always been praised as the king of the body. Al-Ghazali, for example, stated:

> The heart's reality does not belong to this world. It has come into this world as a stranger and a passerby. The outward piece of flesh is the heart's mount and instrument. All the parts of the body are its soldiers. The heart is the king of the whole body, and its attribute is knowing God and witnessing the beauty of His presence. Religious prescriptions are made for it, and God addresses it. Rebuke and punishment apply to it, and fundamental felicity or wretchedness belong to it. In all of this, the body follows the spirit.
>
> (Cited by Murata, 1992, p. 230)

In this respect, *qalb* is a "spiritual divine entity... which is the essence of a human being and its knowing, thinking and comprehending part..." (Al-Ghazali, 1995, p. 4), by revealing the secrets of the *ruh*.

Nurbakhsh (1992) also praised the heart by providing philosophical reflections on the core of the heart of the Ideal Individual as a mirror reflecting God's secrets and the essence of exploring the meaning of both worlds (p. 86). The Qur'an also presents various verses in reference to *qalb* in the Qur'an: "hard or harden or hardened" (2:74; 3:159; 5:13; 6:43), "sinful" (2:283), "calm or tranquil or reassure or reassured" (2:260; 3:126; 5:113; 8:10; 13:28), "faithless" (16:22), "regret" (3:156), "earned" (2:225), "go astray" (3:7, 8; 9:117), "fear" (3:151; 8:12), "sealed" (2:7; 2:88; 4:155; 6:25; 6:46; 42:24; 45:23), "reject" (9:8), "rancor" (9:15), "doubt" (9:45; 9:110), "hypocrisy" (9:77), "tranquil by faith" (16:106), "pure" (26:89; 37:84), "set in pleasure" (21:3), "piety" (22:32), "sickness" (2:10; 5:52; 8:49; 33:32), "scornful tyrant" (40:35), "repentant" (50:33), "revealed to" (2:97), "misguided" (18:28), "comforted" (3:126), "strengthened" (8:11; 28:10; 18:14), "guided" (64:11), "believe" (5:41), "comprehend" (6:25; 7:179; 18:57; 63:3), "awe" (8:2; 22:35), "blind" (22:46; 23:63), "humble" (22:52), and "reason with or think" (22:46) (Abu-Raiya 2012, p. 229). When the heart acquires certain qualities and abilities, it becomes able to help a person spiritually (Rothman & Coyle, 2018).

As can be seen, *qalb* occupies a central place in any discussion of spiritual/soul development in the practice of *muraqabah*, as it is the core of the soul. *Qalb* is also associated with *ruh* as the organ. The circulation of *ruh* is via the heart and blood (Abu-Raiya, 2012, p. 230). The heart also affects personality traits, and it is suggested that these traits start in the spiritual heart: narcissism, arrogance, jealousy, envy, deceit, self-consciousness, kindness, openness, shyness, and modesty (Keshavarsi & Khan, 2018). The heart's purpose is to purify the soul, like blood is purified. In this respect, Abu-Raiya (2012) compares the relationship between *qalb* and *nafs* to "the relationship between heart and body" (p. 229). Therefore, both are dependent on each other as they are "intimately connected" (Jackson, 1989, p. 186).

Abu-Raiya (2012) states:

> *Qalb* has two main openings, one to '*aql* which is connected to the external world, and another to the *roh* which is The Truth and ultimate source of spirituality. Further, *qalb* receives messages from *al-nafs al-lawammah* as well as from *nafs ammarah besoa'*. All these messages are processed and integrated in *qalb* which eventually determine the psychological-spiritual state of *nafs*. The desired outcome of this process is, of course, al-*nafs al-mutmainnah*, which lives in a state of peace of mind, is satisfying and satisfied, and eventually reaches heaven. On the other hand, when *qalb* is constantly "hard," "sealed," "fearful," "sinful," and "misguided," then the outcome, the highly undesired one, is what I label *al-nafs al-marid'a* (the sick *nafs*). This *nafs* lacks peace of mind, is discontented and displeasing, and eventually reaches hell…
>
> (pp. 229–230)

The *qalb* is not only the spiritual centre of the person, but it is also the home of the '*aql*, the faculty of intellect or reason, and the seat of the human consciousness. As mentioned in the prophetic tradition, *qalb*, depending on the lifestyle and attitude of a person, can be in either the right or left positions. In the Islamic spiritual tradition, turning to the left means inclining towards or following the lower impulses of the *nafs* under the influence of evil, whereas the right position of the *qalb* means being at peace with the original state of *fitra* (a primordial nature) and keeping the state of *munjiyyat* (virtues) through the guidance of virtues such as justice, wisdom, and benevolence (Rothman & Coyle, 2020).

Therefore, in Islamic psychotherapy, therapeutic interventions beyond the cognitive level include deeper emotional work at the level of *qalb* "by accessing the emotions and unlocking the block to the fitrah self" (Rothman & Coyle, 2020, p. 211). In this respect, Nurbaksh (1992) was a contemporary Muslim psychiatrist who provided insight into the role of the spiritual heart, the mid-point between the *nafs* (ego) and *ruh* (the spirit), in the process of the purification of the psyche (Amini, 1999). In other words, "the heart is the arena between the forces of spirit (unity) and the forces of *nafs*/ego (multiplicity), the two energies clashing to reign the arena" (Amini, 1999, p. 49). He further states that the forces of multiplicity, driven by selfishness, status-seeking, desires, and passions, originate from egocentricity. However, the forces of unity or spirit is stemmed from compassion and love, create a different dynamic. When a heart is usually troubled by multiplicity, it becomes impure, whereas when guided by unity, it becomes pure.

A famous Sufi, 'Aziz al Din Nasafi, noted that *qalb* is subject to "increase or decrease and change from state to state…" (Murata, 1992, p. 232). In *Jami' at-Tirmidhi* (3522, Book 48, Hadith 153), the Prophet's wife, Umm Salamah, was asked: "O Mother of the Believers! What was the supplication that the Messenger of Allah said most frequently when he was with you?" She responded: "The supplication he said most frequently was: 'O Changer of the hearts, make my heart firm upon Your religion (Yā Muqallibal-qulūb, thabbit qalbī 'alā dīnik).'" She then said:

> So I asked: 'O Messenger of Allah, why do you supplicate so frequently?' He responded: 'O Umm Salamah! Verily, there is no human being except that his heart is between Two Fingers of the Fingers of Allah, so whomsoever He wills He makes steadfast, and whomever He wills He causes to deviate.'

In addition to *qalb*, in the Qur'an, *fu'aad* and *sadr* are also used to refer to the heart. The word *fu'aad* comes from *fa'ada*, meaning "burning" or "a flame." When the heart is in an emotional state such as happiness, sadness, anger, sorrow, regret, lust, frustration, or agitation, the word *fu'aad* is usually used to reflect that emotional moment. When the heart becomes spiritually strong, it then becomes *qalb* (see Q. 17:36; 28:10). *Sadr*, which is used 44 times in the Qur'an, refers to the chest that hides motives, whispers, and secrets (see Q. 114:5). When not strengthened, it is open to satanic whispers and suggestions from the lower self. It is also, however, the seat of different feelings and emotions, and even the awareness of divine activities and inspirations. James Winston Morris notes[1]:

> The major difference from the *qalb* (the latter usually referring to the inherent locus of our receptive human awareness of God and the creative Spirit) is that the *sadr*, much like the bodily chest in relation to the bodily heart, also refers to that which can either 'cover over,' hide, obscure and close off – or else open up and reveal – the pure receptivity of the *qalb*. As such, it has a key role in both expressing and accounting for all the dimensions of our apparent human opposition to God's will and of our subjective sense of 'separation' from the divine, especially those aspects of experience – often rather negative or oppressive – that we would express in everyday English usage by reference to what goes on in our 'mind,' 'self,' imagination or even more unconscious levels of subjectivity that may only be perceptible through our corresponding actions, tendencies and attitudes.

Ruh (Spirit)

Ruh and *riyah* (wind) come from the same root. Rumi beautifully says, "Have not the earthen clods—the bodies—come to life through the radiance of the spirit? Marvelous shining light! Wonderful life increasing sun!" (Murata, 1992, p. 229). In this light, Amini (1999) also states:

> When the human psyche has gone beyond the spiritual heart, it ascends to a higher realm called spirit or *ruh*. Spirit is the realm of unity, and love is its attribute. At this point the individual is free from the world of multiplicity and has surrendered to love.
>
> (p. 50)

The Qur'an refers to *ruh* 26 times, and it is one of the Qur'an's more mysterious concepts. Abu-Raiya (2012) suggests a few possible meanings for *ruh*: (1) the angel Gabriel (Q. 26:193' 70:4) or (2) energy of life, divine breath, force of creation, inspiration, revelation, or creation (Q. 15:20; 32:9). In this respect, Abu-Raiya (2012) believes that *ruh* refers to the human spirit, as the Qur'an only mentions it in the contexts of birth and death. By applying the Jungian concept, Abu-Raiya prefers to translate *ruh* as "the collective unconscious portion of *nafs*" (p. 227), God's essence, or the Truth, referring to "innate unconscious knowledge of God (i.e., *fitra*)" (p. 227). In English, however, the most fitting translation of *ruh* is "spirit." In Sufi psychology, the *ruh* is located in the heart, and its essence cannot be comprehended by human intellect (al-Ghazali, 1995), which leads one to *qudrat* (spiritual power) and divine illumination (Saniotis, 2012). The *ruh* might also be interpreted as a part of the soul. It is important to remember, however, that because of its divine nature, it does not change and is always pure. One can also think of the *ruh* as a "location" within the body where the eternal memory of God dwells (Rothman & Coyle, 2018, p. 1736).

Al-Ghazali (1995) writes:

> [it is] a pleasant entity rooted in the bodily heart, spread by blood vessels to the other parts of the body, and its flow from the vessels to the organs of sensation, vision, hearing and smelling is likened to the flood of light from a lamp to the corners of the house.
>
> (p. 4)

According to Murata (1992), Jalal al-Din Rumi identified the *ruh* simply as an awareness that only those who have achieved a greater spirit can acquire, stating, "Then the spirit of God's friends, the Possessors of Hearts, is even greater… That is why the angels prostrated themselves to Adam: His spirit was greater than their existence" (p. 305).

The relationship between soul and spirit can also be interpreted as a cosmic marriage. In this line of thought, "If the perfected rational soul is to be actualized, its parents—spirit and soul—must marry, give birth to it, and nurture it" (Murata, 1992, p. 306). Here, Murata sees the heart as the "perfected rational soul." Such a position is against the contemporary Western view, which is that rationality and the heart are at odds with one another. In Western thought, the heart usually represents the emotional side of a human being. In Islamic psychotherapy, however, the heart is also a rational self, and rationality is not merely seen as "calculative." In this sense, the Islamic understanding of the spirit has the capacity for both reasoning and passion. A soul's ability to properly balance both heart and intellect opens the heart's capacity, which we call *inshirah*.

Most Muslims differentiate the spirit from the soul. The spirit is the source of life (*hayat*) and breath (*nafas*), whereas when the soul is taken from the human body (in sleep, as it is stated in Q. 39:43), death does not occur, but *ruh* remains in the body. Death occurs when *ruh* leaves the body permanently. When commenting on Q. 39:42, al-Muhasibi quoted Ibn Juraj (d. 767), saying, "The *ruh* and *nafs*—their separation is like the separation of a ray of sunlight" (Picken, 2011, p. 173).

Ibn Ajiba also notes:

> And know that the 'soul' and 'mind' and 'spirit' and 'secret' are the same thing, but the subtitle is different from the different orbits; what was from the orbits of the 'soul', what was from the lawful rules, what was the concept of 'mind', and what was from your orbits of divisions and the

'spirit,' and so on One of the circles of investigations and machinery was the concept of 'secret', and one shop.

In general, Muslims agree that the *ruh* contains divine, angelic qualities. Murata (1992) writes that, similar to Ibn al 'Arabi's teachings, Nasafi's contemplations also examine the spirit and its divine attributes. In his work, God is described as absolute and limitless Light, while the essence of the angelic or spiritual realm is characterized as the light that is created. This created light's attributes can be understood through incomparability or similarity perspectives. When viewed from an incomparable standpoint, angelic light is completely distinct from the uncreated Light of God, with no common ground that can be comprehended by humans. It remains a mystery why God and His Prophet used the same term for two entirely different realities. However, from a perspective of similarity, if the Prophet referred to angels as "light," it signifies their direct reflection of the true essence of "light," which is God Himself. Therefore, the attributes of God are prevalent in their essence, embodying unity, life, knowledge, and more, unlike earthly beings made of clay, which are numerous and inherently devoid of life, knowledge, and other qualities.

Nafs (Soul)

The purpose of *muraqabah* is to help the soul be mindful of certain inclinations and impulses. In the Qur'an, references to the *nafs* (singular) and *anfus* (plural) number approximately 266. In the English translations of the Qur'an, *nafs* is translated as person, self, personality, psyche, or soul; however, these translations have some limitations. For example, the term psyche in secular psychology refers to human psychology, which does not accommodate the religious or spiritual meaning of soul (Abu-Raiya, 2012).

Naseer Ahmed (2017) states that, out of thirty-four translators, only six have translated "nafs" as conscience, while the majority have rendered it as soul. Some suggest that the word *nafs* should not be translated into English and that it is best to use *nafs* rather than its suggested English translations. Alternatively, one could translate *nafs* as person, personality, or human being based on al-Ghazali's theory of personality structures (Abu-Raiya, 2012). The following are sample references to *nafs* in the Qur'an:

> They seek to deceive God and those who believe in Him: but they deceive none save their anfus.
>
> (2:8)

> They cannot help them, nor can they help their anfus.
> (7:192)
>
> There has now come to you an apostle of your anfus...
> (9:128)
>
> Such are those who shall forfeit their anfus...
> (11:21)
>
> The king said: 'bring him before me. I will choose him for my own nafs.'
> (12:52)
>
> And when you slew a nafs and then fell out with one another...
> (2:72)
>
> No nafs dies unless God wills.
> (2:145)
>
> Thereupon each nafs will know what it has done...
> (10:30)
>
> ... He has decreed mercy for His nafs, and will gather you all in the Day of Resurrection...
> (6:12)

Discussing the Qur'anic references to the *nafs*, Abu-Raiya (2012) asks what implications can we draw from these verses? Does this suggest that God possesses a "personality" or is a psychological entity? *Nafs* can be understood as the equivalent of the psyche, unconscious, or id in Freudian psychoanalysis, or as personality in self-psychology and Jungian psychology. The nature of *nafs* is associated with a person's animal nature (Saniotis, 2012). In al-Ghazali's (1995) seminal works, *nafs* refers to the lower part of humans, which is the seat of desires, emotions, and undesirable personal qualities, or refers to the self or the person.

Some Sufis locate the *nafs* in different bodily organs and the circulatory system; *nafs* has also been described as "emitted from the heart" and spread to the interior organs via blood circulation, as it is believed that these carry feelings, emotions, desires, cravings, and impulses (Saniotis, 2012). Some even locate *nafs* in the lower part of the body (i.e., male semen or a woman's womb). *Nafs* is bound to the body and the spirit.

In Sufi psychology, it is generally accepted that a human being possesses both their father's and mother's *nafs*; however, Saniotis (2012) states that women's *nafs* are more powerful and stronger than men's *nafs*. In Islamic psychotherapy, the term *nafs* usually refers to "the lower self, similar to the ego, in that it is part of the soul that inclines toward the *dunya* through desires, distracting a person from Allah and opening them to the influence of *shaytan* (the devil)" (Rothman & Coyle, 2020, p. 1736).

Stages of the *Nafs*

Al-Ghazali notes that human qualities include ascending (angelic), descending (demonic), and dispersing (animal). Which qualities are dominant depends on the stages of development of the *nafs*. The Qur'an encourages spiritual development. In this respect, al-Ghazali compares the spiritual journey to *jihad* (struggle) due to the challenges on the path. He states:

> To know the reality of the heart is difficult, and permission to explain it has not been given. At the beginning of walking on the path of religion, there is no need for knowledge of it. On the contrary, the beginning of the path of religion is spiritual struggle [mujahada]. When a person performs the spiritual struggle as he should, then he will himself actualize this knowledge, without hearing it from anyone. This knowledge is part of the "guidance" to which God refers in His words, "Those who struggle in Us—surely We shall guide them on Our paths" [29:69]. If a person has not yet finished his struggle, it is not permissible to tell him of the reality of the spirit. However, before struggle one must know the army of the heart, since he who does not know this army cannot undertake the holy war [jihad].
>
> (Cited by Murata, 1992, p. 232)

The Development of the Soul

In Islamic psychology, when someone engages in spiritual/soul development, the *nafs* goes through the following developmental stages:

1 *an-nafs al-'ammāaah* (the inciting *nafs*)
2 *an-nafs al-luwwamah* (the self-accusing *nafs*)
3 *an-nafs al-mulhamah* (the inspired *nafs*)
4 *an-nafs al-muṭma'innah* (the *nafs* at peace)
5 *an-nafs ar-raḍīyyah* (the pleased *nafs*)
6 *an-nafs al-marḍiyyah* (the pleasing *nafs*)
7 *an-nafs aṣ-ṣāfīyyah* (the pure *nafs*)

These concepts have been evaluated from different psychological and theological perspectives. There were attempts to find similarities between the Islamic understanding of *nafs* and psychological theories. For example, according to Stefania Pandolfo (2018), the unconscious self, or the Freudian concept of the unconscious is *la shu'ur* in Arabic. A famous Sufi Shaykh, Ibn 'Arabi, also used the term "to refer to the incommensurability and alterity of God" (Pandolfo, 2018, p. 3).

Muslim spiritual masters inspired by the Qur'an and the Prophetic tradition encouraged and designed techniques for soul development. Al-Ghazali noted:

> Know that the key to knowledge of God is knowledge of one's own soul. That is why it has been said, "He who knows his own soul knows his Lord." That is also why God said, "We shall show them Our signs upon the horizons and within their souls, until it is clear to them that He is the Real".
>
> [41:53]
>
> In short, nothing is closer to you than you. If you do not know yourself, how will you know the other? Moreover, you may think that you know yourself and be mistaken, for this kind of knowing is not the key to the knowledge of the Real. The beasts know this much of themselves—since of yourself you know no more than the outward head, face, hands, feet, flesh, and skin. Of the inward dimension you know that when you are hungry, you eat bread, and when you are angry, you fall on the other person, and when appetite dominates, you make for the marriage act. All the beasts know that much.
>
> Hence you must seek your own reality. What thing are you? From whence have you come? Where will you go? For what work have you come to this dwelling place? Why were you created? What and where is your felicity? What and where is your wretchedness?
>
> (Cited by Murata, 1992, p. 230)

In this section, we will review three stages of *nafs*, which I consider more "tangible," or at least can be grasped by the human psyche in psychotherapeutic work. However, we should also keep in mind that many people, including religious and spiritual leaders, usually wrestle or "journey" between the first and second stages of *nafs*.

Nafs al-Ammara: The Qur'an refers to *nafs al-ammara* as an evil-commanding *nafs*. It is the seat of desires, or the state of *nafs* which is "... succumbed to forbidden passions and Satan's seduction" (al-Ghazali, 1995, p. 5). In the Qur'an, these desires and passions are "forbidden ones, prone to evil, hidden-secretive and obsessive in nature" (Abu-Raiya, 2012, p. 224).

> Whatever good befalls you, it is from God, and whatever ill from your nafs...
>
> (Q. 4:79)
>
> His nafs prompted him to slay his brother...
>
> (Q. 5:30)
>
> Your nafs has tempted you to evil...
>
> (Q. 12:18)
>
> His master's wife attempted to seduce his nafs...
>
> (Q, 12:23)
>
> ...Their anfus became arrogant...
>
> (Q. 25:21)
>
> We created man and know what bad things his nafs whispers to him and we are closer to him than his jugular vein.
>
> (Q. 50:16)
>
> ...the unbelievers follow but vain conjectures and the whims of their anfus.
>
> (Q. 53:23)
>
> But he that feared to stand before his Lord and curbed his nafs's desire.
>
> (Q. 79:40)

At the stage of *nafs al-ammara*, untamed and untrained *nafs* show the symptoms *al-mashaqqa, al-diq* (anxiety), and an excessive inclination to *al-haraj* (distress). Treating the soul and improving the relationship with both the self and the sacred results in *al-ittisa'* (relaxation) and *al-inshirah* (tranquillity). Moreover, the *nafs* has its problems and needs, or *al-hajat/al-matalib* (demands and needs). A neglect of these needs causes dissatisfaction and leads to acquiring negative qualities.

The Sufi tradition recognizes that desires are natural inclinations in all humans and does not deny the importance of fulfilling earthly needs. According to al-Muhasibi, uncontrolled desires for worldly possessions can lead to spiritual ailments through excessive indulgence in forbidden pleasures, resulting in physical, emotional, psychological, and spiritual harm. In Sufi teachings, appetites are divided into "hidden appetites" or *al-shahawat al-khafiyya* and "manifest appetites" or *al-shahawat al-zahira*. Al-Muhasibi distinguished between the two, explaining that desires for food, drink, and clothing are not inherently sinful. However, these desires can become destructive when they are unbridled and excessive, such as the craving for power, status, recognition, and praise for virtuous acts. Additionally, ingratitude, a common human trait, can lead to various mental and emotional burdens (Q. 100:6). The Quran attributes ingratitude to the pursuit of material wealth (Q. 17:83) and to feelings of discontent and irritation, often stemming from material and psychological needs (Q. 10:12).

These are the spiritual problems and diseases of the *nafs* according to the Sufi interpretations of the Qur'an: *al-kibr* (conceit), *al-ghill* (malice), *al-hasad* (envy), *al-riya'* (ostentation), *su' al-zann* (having a bad opinion [of someone]), *i'tiqad su' al-damir* (believing in the evil of the conscience), *al-mudahana* (fallacious flattery), *hubb jam' al-mal* (the love of accumulating wealth), *al-takathur* (excess), *al-tafakhur* (bragging and the love to hear praise), and *hubb al-sharaf mahmada* (the love of rank). "These spiritual diseases of the animal soul are products of ignorance, ungratefulness, the lack of *hubb and wudd* (love), *al-ghafla* (heedlessness), al-*sahw* (forgetfulness), extreme adherence to *ittiba' al-hawwa* (the desires), and a*l-shahawat* (sexual appetites)" (Isgandarova, 2018, p. 125).

According to Sufi psychology, one needs to practise a strict regimen of spiritual practices such as fasting, chanting, and prayers to train and control the *nafs*; otherwise, it tends to distract the mind and leads to wrongful and sinful acts.

Nafs al-Lawwama is the self-reproaching conscience, the reproachful *nafs*, or the cognitive dissonance. It is the state where the human soul achieves peace, but still can be influenced by the impulses of *nafs ammara*. Nevertheless, if it has a strong foundation, then it can direct the person towards right or wrong (Haque, 2004, p. 367).

> I do call to witness the Resurrection Day; And I do call to witness the self-reproaching conscience: (Eschew Evil). Does man think that We cannot assemble his bones? Nay, We are able to put together in perfect order the very tips of his fingers. But man wishes to do wrong (even) in the time in front of him.
>
> (Q. 75:1–5)
>
> "To the persons whose Nafs or consciousness is at peace and satisfied (Nafs al-Mutma'inna) will be said" Come back thou to thy Lord, - well pleased (thyself), and well-pleasing unto Him! Enter thou, then, among My devotees! "Yea, enter thou My Heaven!"
>
> (Q. 89:27–30)

At this stage, the person experiences cognitive, spiritual, and moral dissonance and engages in constant reflection to reduce dissonance in terms of attitudes, beliefs, or behaviours. When a person realizes that their conflicting attitudes, beliefs, or behaviours are causing moral, spiritual, and cognitive dissonance, they attempt to change the element that conflicts with their religious or spiritual view.

Nafs al-Mutma'inna is the *nafs* that is content and at peace, the tranquil *nafs* (Abu-Raiya, 2012; al-Ghazali, 1995; Haque, 2004). According to Abu-Raiya (2012), attaining this state is difficult because it means the human soul has successfully attained the state of tranquillity and returned to the divine.

In addition to *'aql*, *ruh*, and *nafs*, in *muraqabah* practice, we also pay attention to *jism* or *badan* (body), *ihsaas* (feelings, emotions), and *nafas* (breath). In Sufi psychology, *badan* is a temporary temple where *ruh*, *'aql*, and *nafs* are "grounded in the body" (Saniotis, 2012, p. 74). Al-Ghazali (2015) noted that the body and its organs, such as the eyes, ears, tongue, stomach, hands, and feet, serve the soul to live a righteous life, not to sin in earthly life.

Murata (1992) summarizes the differences between *ruh* and *badan* as "the spirit is near to God, the body far from Him. The spirit is knowing, the body ignorant. The spirit is alive, the body dead. The spirit is desiring, the body without desires" (p. 236).

Regarding the soul, Murata (1992) highlights the difference between body and soul, stating:

> If the spirit is light and the body clay, the soul is fire. It is a mixture of light and clay, both one and multiple at the same time. It is subtle and luminous enough to establish a link with the spirit, but dense and dark enough to maintain contact with the body.
>
> (p. 237)

The body depends on the soul in terms of its activities because "The spirit fecundates the soul, and the soul gives birth to bodily activities in the visible world" (Murata, 1992, p. 238). As Rumi outlines, "The poor body will not move until the soul moves. Until the horse goes forward, the saddlebag stands still" (Murata, 1992, p. 229).

Nevertheless, the *ruh* in the human body has the capacity to evolve. In this respect, spiritual purity is connected to physical purity, which should not be limited to a simple understanding of body wash and hygiene products. Physical purity also refers to living a proper way of life, such as eating a pure and halal diet. In this respect, it is important to take care of the body as it is, a divine trust. Taking care of this trust is important, as it is susceptible to different kinds of attacks, including spiritual attacks.

In Sufi psychology, *ihsaas*, or emotions, are important to building relationships not only with fellow human beings, but also with God. Emotions are adaptive, maladaptive, and endogenous (Keshavarzi & Khan, 2018). The Qur'an praises courage, patience, and mercy as emotional responses in the face of adversity and difficulties; however, the Qur'an also encourages avoiding extremes. Sufi psychology invites followers to always keep their emotions under control through the '*aql*. In *muraqabah* practice, breath, or *nafas*, is of significance. In Sufism, *ruh* is directly associated with the breath. According to Sufis, when we inhale and exhale, we do so in the form of the "hu" sound. They encourage us to take every breath with mindfulness and in a state of *muraqabah*. Saniotis (2012) reports that one Sufi at Nizamuddin shrine in India told him, individuals with "good breath" are considered blessed as they speak positively. They possess good *nafas*. Conversely, those who speak negatively are often associated with bad *nafas*, as their words carry a foul scent. Therefore, breathing practices are important to Sufi rituals and healing practices to improve personal shortcomings.

Thus, the purpose of *muraqabah* is to transform the cravings and demands of *nafs al-ammara* and lead it to become a *nafs al-mutma' inna* (self-atpeace). *Muraqabah* aims to decrease psychological and spiritual conflict and disorders by increasing *iradah*, or determination. In some Sufi orders, Sufi masters achieve this result by fostering the disciple's love and devotion for the spiritual guide. After reaching the desired level of attachment, the Sufi master helps the disciple purify the self from the commanding ego's harmful passions, demands, and attachments. They prepare the heart for the Divine Attributes (Amini, 1999). Similarly, in clinical settings, the therapist provides a therapeutic environment based on empathy, compassion, genuine regard, and congruency. The therapist then provides psychoeducation on the nature of thoughts, feelings, and emotions that can cause emotional pain and suffering.

Questions for Discussion

1 Generally, what is your understanding of the Islamic and Western concepts of soul and spirit? What are the differences and similarities? If the soul is absent, what is the essence of being a human?
2 What was the understanding of the stages of the soul? Discuss the stages of the soul in the Qur'an and other sources of the Islamic tradition. How might reflecting on the stages of the soul help an individual to become a spiritual person?
3 Do you think all humans have the capacity to achieve the most advanced developmental levels in the stages of soul? Why or why not? How does *muraqabah* help the person to start and continue the journey of spiritual development? Reflect and explain the process.

4 How does the practice of *muraqabah* help one in soul treatment? What would be the experience(s) of the person practicing *muraqabah*? Discuss the role of *muraqabah* in Islamic psychotherapy that aims to help the person become spiritually and emotionally mature.

Note

1 A detailed account of this information can be found at: https://ibnarabisociety.org/suffering-compassion-and-atonement-james-morris/.

4 The Relevance of *Muraqabah* in Islamic Psychotherapy

There is no direct work in Islamic psychotherapy literature that demonstrates the application of *muraqabah* in psychotherapy with clients; however, we are witnessing an emergence of rich discussion in the field on the benefits of incorporating spiritual tools in treating emotional and spiritual health problems. Some of these discussions have focused on historical traditions that explicitly demonstrate the diversity of approaches in Islamic psychotherapy. The present relevant literature on *muraqabah* also focuses on this modality and technique as a heart-based therapy rather than only a mind-focused mindfulness technique. This is not a new approach in Islamic psychotherapy, but rather a steadfast continuation of the previous counselling and psychotherapy approaches in Islamic tradition.

Many research studies (al-Balkhī, 2014; al-Razī, 2007; Haque, 1998; Hatim, 2017; Isgandarova, 2018; Keshavarzi et al., 2020; Moffic et al., 2019; Ragab, 2015; Rahman, 1987; Utz, 2011; York, 2018; Younos, 2017) outline how Muslims in the past and present view taking care of body, mind, and soul as a religious vocation. Fazlur Rahman (1987) notes in his introduction to his book, *Guide for Students (Hidayat al-Muta 'allimin)*, that Abu Bakr Rabi' ibn Ahmad al-Akhwani al-Bukhari (10th century), the student of famous Muslim physician Abu Zakariya al-Razi, stated:

> Wise men have said that it is incumbent upon every person to learn [the basics] of the Sacred Law, for when a person knows the Sacred Law, he is immune from going astray. Second, he must know some [basic] medicine in order to preserve his health so that quack doctors will not be able to destroy him. Third, he must learn some art to earn his livelihood by lawful means.
>
> (Rahman, 1987, p. 39)

Some of these discussions led to the emergence of certain contemporary models, such as the Islamically integrated psychotherapy proposed by Carrie York al-Karam (2018) and the traditional Islamically integrated

DOI: 10.4324/9781032631387-5

psychotherapy proposed by Hooman Keshavarzi, Fahad Khan, Bilal Ali, and Rania Awad (2020). Almost all new frameworks claim to work within the paradigms of Islamic psychology. Rothman (2018) defines Islamic psychology as "an indigenous approach to the study and understanding of human psychology that is informed by the teaching and knowledge from the Quran and the Prophetic tradition..." (p. 26). The primary focus of Islamic psychology and psychotherapy is the assessment and treatment of the soul, and more specifically, "the heart rather than the mind as the center of the person" (p. 26). The therapist's role is to help clients live a psychologically balanced life in accordance with *fitrah*.

From the diagnostic and assessment perspectives, Subandi et al. (2023) suggest the DOTSH (diseases of the spiritual heart) concept derived from Islamic spirituality, but in the context of the relationship and significance to mental disorders diagnosed in the DSM-5. For them, based on al-Ghazali, Muslim mental health providers can identify and assess six DOTSH categories, which are: (1) appetence, (2) evil of tongue, (3) anger, (4) envy, (5) greed for wealth, and (6) arrogance. With respect to psychological manifestations, DOTSH corresponds with: (1) desire (appetite, lust), (2) verbal and physical behaviour (lie, curse, violence), (3) feeling (anger, hate, envy), and (4) attitude or character (miserliness, greed, stinginess, pride). In the DSM-5, we also find the following patterns: "lust, appetence, lie, curse, falsehood, deception, dispute, mockery, anger, violence, bitter, temper, outrage, resentment, revenge, irritation, envy, dislike, aversion, suspicious, spite, resentment, hostility, antagonism, longing, miserliness, stinginess, arrogance, haughty, pride, superiority, and grandeur" (p. 10). For example, the DOTSH category Evil of Tongue can be observed in cases of Bipolar I Disorder Manic Episode (talkative), Conduct Disorder and Gambling Disorder (deceitfulness, lying), Antisocial Personality Disorder (deceitfulness), and Factitious Disease (falsification). Lust relates to symptoms of abnormal sexual behaviours in the DSM-5, such as, Paraphilic Disorders, Voyeuristic Disorder, Exhibitionistic Disorder, Frotteuristic Disorder, Sexual Masochism Disorder, Sexual Sadism Disorder, Pedophilic Disorder, Fetishistic Disorder, and Transvestic Disorder. Anger is considered a crucial criterion in the following disorders from the DSM-5: Intermittent Explosive Disorder, Oppositional Defiant Disorder, Disruptive Mood Dysregulation Disorder, Borderline Personality Disorder, and Bipolar Disorder (p. 18). Being inspired by al-Ghazali's classification of diseases, Subandi et al. (2023) suggest understanding the Islamic Diagnosis Manual by investigating the DOTSH concept.

Along with contemporary psychotherapeutic practices, Muslim psychotherapists suggest employing certain vigilant and ongoing spiritual practices to gain control over *nafs* and empower the mind and soul. For example, Rasool (2016) states that combining MBCT and *dhikr*, Dhikr-Based

Cognitive Therapy (DBCT), can create a programme that is more congruent with Islamic values and practices. Some Muslim therapists work within the Islamic model of the soul-mind-body. In a grounded study by Rothman and Coyle (2020), for example, the goal of therapy is to help the client understand the *nafs* and its different levels through psychoeducation based on Islamic teachings; to control harmful inclinations coming from the *nafs*; to develop compassion towards the *nafs*, as it also suffers from its harmful inclinations; and to develop self-awareness and watchfulness. In this respect, Ibrahim Rüschoff and Paul M. Kaplick (2018) note that the therapist should "aid the patient in coming closer to the state of *al-nafs al mutmainna*" (p. 135) through the 99 Names of Allah.

Rothman (2018), however, suggests a framework that helps the process of self-growth. He invites us to think that this growth is "neither linear nor sequential" (p. 35). Such an approach reflects the developmental stages of the *nafs*: "*nafs-al-ammarah* (commanding self; 12:53), *nafs-al-awwamah* (reproaching self; 75:2), and *nafs-al-mutmainnah* (contented self; 89:27)" (p. 35). In this developmental process, the role of the therapist is to help the client focus and engage with the process by attuning to their self, as well as equipping them with the necessary tools using both the Islamic tradition and western psychotherapeutic techniques. For example, Rothman uses cognitive restriction by suggesting concepts such as *'aql* and *dhikr*. He sometimes uses *dhikr* "perhaps out loud in session with clients to calm them if they are having an anxiety attack, for example—the way I use it more often at the level of the *aql* is as assigned homework outside of a session" (Rothman, 2018, p. 42). The following is an example of how to implement these phrases in a session with a client, as suggested by Rothman (2018), the 99 names of Allah, each highlighting a distinct attribute, can address specific needs. In addition, it is suggested saying and practicing *astaghfirallah* (seeking forgiveness from God), *salawat* (praises) on the Prophet, Allahu Akbar (God is the greatest), *subhanallah* (glory to God), or merely repeating the word "Allah." This simple practice is often recommended to Muslim clients as a starting point because it is familiar and directly impactful.

Farah Lodi (2018) presents the HEART model. This model is also based on CBT and the following concepts from the Islamic tradition: (i) *taqwa* (God consciousness) and *tawwakul* (trust in God), (ii) compassion, (iii) acknowledging and accepting difficult emotions, (iv) reframing thoughts in the context of belief in the hereafter, (v) communication with God through a variety of religious and spiritual tools, and (vi) having a lifestyle founded upon the Qur'anic code of conduct (pp. 79–80). For example, Lodi presents a compassionate scheme using the Prophetic tradition that encourages forgiveness, mercy, and compassion, as well as the compassion-based CBT proposed by Paul Gilbert. She uses role playing and the Gestalt empty-chair technique to encourage the client to reflect on questions, such as "What do you think it must be like to be in the other person's shoes?"

In her sessions with clients, Lodi also discusses the benefits of reading the Qur'an and chooses specific verses that communicate security, safety, peace, relaxation, tranquility, comfort, connection, sympathy, contentment, and reliance on God; encourage optimism and confidence in the Creator as well as the self; and discourage anything that is not beneficial to the self. She states that these Islamic teachings echo "the CBT principle that adaptive thinking leads to positive emotions and actions, while maladaptive thinking can lead to negative emotions and actions…" (p. 80). Lodi uses clinical measuring tools such as the Beck Depression Inventory, self-report scales, and client feedback forms at regular intervals "to make sure that therapy goals and expectations are being met. When setting and tracking these goals, we keep in mind the Quranic verse, God will not change the condition of a people until they change what is in themselves" (p. 78).

Lodi also suggests meditation based on Islamic tradition and Easwaran's Eight Point Program (EPP), which is acknowledged as a social cognitive meditation programme with cross-cultural validity consisting of major spiritual and religious rituals. Based on the research findings of Oman et al. (2009), she suggests these eight meditation practices for empathy, forgiveness, and self-efficacy:

1 Passage meditation: The Prophet spent many hours meditating upon Qur'anic verses.
2 Repetition of a holy word: The Prophet engaged in *dhikr*, which is focused meditation upon and repetition of holy words, such as the 99 Divine names of God. Repeatedly focusing on a word linked to patience, forgiveness, compassion, or gratitude supports retention of its meaning and integration of it into behavior (Oman & Borman, 2015).
3 Slowing down: The Prophet set priorities and spent time on inner reflection.
4 Focused attention: He spent much time in seclusion in the Cave Hira, meditating with deep concentration.
5 Training the senses: He filtered everything according to *taqwa, tawakul*, and compassion.
6 Putting others first: He taught that humans are God's vice-regents on earth, responsible for selfless goals.
7 Spiritual association: He encouraged people to spend time with others on a spiritual path.
8 Inspirational reading: The first words of the Quranic revelation are, "Read, in the name of your Lord." Seeking knowledge is a core value taught by the Prophet.

Lodi (2018) also recommends that her clients sit in a quiet, comfortable spot with sincere intention and breathe deeply and slowly for a clear mind.

She notes that when mindfulness is done properly, it can help to attain a transformational cognitive shift. Unlike secular mindfulness, this kind of mindfulness aims "toward an enlightened awareness of divine support" (p. 94). For example, the client is encouraged to read *surat al-Fatiha*, which is the first chapter of the Qur'an, with focused attention and comprehension. For this, the client needs to recite the chapter slowly and absorb and reflect on its meaning. Such reading might help the client focus on God's majesty, mercy, forgiveness, and gratitude, which can form new and optimistic neural pathways.

Based on al-Ghazali's thoughts, Keshavarzi and Khan (2018) suggested that two modalities can help a person achieve an awareness of self and improve their relationship with God and others. The first is traditional Sufism, wherein one commits himself/herself to the Sufi order, and the second is the TIIP which stands for *Traditional Islamically Integrated Psychotherapy*. They state that the theoretical principles of change are *inkishaf* (introspective self-awareness), *i'tidaal* (psycho-spiritual equilibrium), and *itihaad* (integrative wholeness). Furthermore, the therapeutic strategies and session outlines aim to pursue two main goals, ultimately leading to the final aim of *ittihaad* (integrative unity). This concept seeks to unify the interconnected aspects of the psyche to create a cohesive whole that functions harmoniously in pursuit of connecting with God and realizing one's spiritual capabilities. By attaining this unified state, individuals also harmonize their entire being with God's intentions, aligning their actions with His will.

Keshavarzi and Khan (2018) suggest that the six goals of the first session are: (1) building the therapeutic alliance, (2) assessment of religiosity, (3) diagnosis and conceptualization, (4) assessment of internal and external psycho-spiritual functioning, (5) psychoeducation and setting therapeutic goals, and (6) assessment of stage of change (p. 183). The following tests are suggested to measure the religiousness of the client: Psychological Measure of Islamic Religiousness (PMIR) or Muslim Experiential Religiousness (MER). The treatment plan uses elements of the psyche. For example, on the *aqlani* (cognitive) level, the therapist helps clients to shift "toward a positive attribution bias—balancing fear (*khawf*) with hope (*rajaa*)," differentiate "personality (*shakhsiyyah*) from character attributes (*akhlaq*)," practise *tawakkul*, or see "behaviors as a manifestation of God's perfect will and ultimate plan for the client" (p. 190).

With respect to *muraqabah*, Keshavarzi and Khan (2018) place it under the category of *ruhani*, or soul-related interventions, which are:

1 *Muraqabah*: Islamic contemplative exercises
2 *Dhikr*: remembrance of God
3 *Hajj/Umrah*: religious pilgrimage
4 Spiritual mentorship
5 Regular *salat*: five prayers on a daily basis

6 Prescribed *duas* or prayers with a concentration on the meanings that challenge faulty cognitions (p. 191)

The following is a brief sample session on *muraqabah* with the client called Kareem (not his real name) outlined by Keshavarzi and Khan (2018). First, during the session, the therapist utilized empathic following and exploration to assist the client in determining whether the client preferred a formal or personalized approach to spirituality. After contemplation, the client chose to join the Naqshbandi order formally, the therapist discussed practicing *muraqabah* for 15 minutes daily. The therapist recommended incorporating diaphragmatic breathing and focusing on inhaling the name "Allah" and exhaling "hu." To start, the therapist guided Kareem to close his eyes and concentrate on his heart. He instructed Kareem to visualize light entering his heart with each breath, cleansing him of anxieties, worries, and concerns, and fostering *tawakkul* (trust in God). With each inhalation, the light expanded in his chest, while each exhalation purged negative energies. Kareem tried this method during the session, experiencing a sense of calm and peace. The therapist suggested this self-soothing technique for moments of anxiety.

In addition, Keshavarzi and Khan (2018) discuss the importance of spiritual preparation for the sessions. Other Muslim psychologists and psychotherapists also highlight this. In general, preparing the client for *muraqabah* in Islamic psychotherapy starts with consent to certain rules. The Muslim psychotherapist needs to explain the rules first, as the effectiveness of *muraqabah* depends on the level of preparatory work done with the client. In traditional Sufi practice, these rules are called *adab* (manners or etiquette), which are compulsory to follow.

Adab "means at once comportment, courtesy, culture, refined speech, literature, correct ethical attitude…" (Nasr, 2007, p. 89). For Muslims, *adab* should be practised in all aspects of life. One's *adab* is evident in the way they greet people, talk to people, sit to eat, or enter places of worship. In Islamic terminology, *adab* is also about "controlling the passions, which affect and often originate human actions" (Nasr, 2007, p. 89). In this respect, *adab* is the foundation of harmony rather than disorderliness in human behaviours. Otherwise, poor *adab* is associated with the lower self. Perhaps many have heard how Mawlana Jalal ad-Din Rumi coined the importance of *adab* by stating, "Edeb Ya Hu!" (a proper translation can be "Manners, please!").

The Prophetic tradition also emphasized learning and following good manners. Hadith collections, including Sahih al-Bukhari, include a special chapter called *Kitab al-adab*. From these collections, we learn that it is the Prophetic tradition to treat people with respect, be honest, and avoid all harmful manners, such as backbiting and swearing. In *Sunan Abi Dawud* (4776, Book 43, Hadith 4), it is noted, "Good way, dignified good bearing and moderation are the twenty-fifth part of Prophecy."

The spiritual masters and disciples also do not accept what is considered *haram* or unlawful, such as "non-sharing of food, farting and burping aloud, laughing and eating in such a manner that exposes the inside of the mouth to another person's sight, drunkenness and uttering obscenities…" as all these "exhibit the *nafs* in one way or another" (Saniotis, 2012, p. 73). Some Sufi schools also encourage disciples to pay attention to their appearance, as it "portrays an aura of respectability, refinement and sophistication. A Chisti pir's life reflects his constant observance of the edicts of Indo-Muslim etiquette (*adab*)…" (Saniotis, 2012, p. 71).

Based on the Qur'anic emphasis on *adab* and the prophetic examples, Muslim intellectuals and spiritual masters developed the concept of *adab* in *muraqabah*. The first step is the physical preparation for *muraqaba*, called *tahara*, which can include one of *ghusl* (complete ablution with bathing), *wudu* (minor ablution with washing face, arms, hands, feet, ears, and wiping the head), or *tayammum*, which is performed by those who cannot perform either *ghusl* or *wudu* and involves touching clean sand with both palms and gently sweeping them over the face and back of the hands.

In Islamic tradition, *tahara* is an important religious and spiritual ritual of purification performed before one starts reading the Qur'an, performing a daily prayer, or visiting the Holy Kabah. A complete obligatory ablution, or *ghusl*, is required for certain bodily impurities after sexual relations, ejaculation, menstruation, giving birth, and washing a corpse. There are also certain days when a complete bath is recommended. For example, both Sunnis and Shias prefer to take a complete bath on special religious days, such as on Fridays, on Muslim festival days, and before entering the holy

> You who believe, when you are about to pray, wash your faces and your hands up to the elbows, wipe your heads, wash your feet up to the ankles and, if required, a wash your whole body. If any of you is sick or on a journey, or has just relieved himself, or had intimate contact with a woman, and can find no water, then take some clean sand and wipe your face and hands with it. God does not wish to place any burden on you: He only wishes to cleanse you and perfect His blessing on you, so that you may be thankful. Remember God's blessing on you and the pledge with which you were bound when you said, 'We hear and we obey.' Be mindful of God: God has full knowledge of the secrets of the heart.
> (Q. 5:6–7)

city of Mecca. Even "those who have never performed *ghusl* cannot enter a mosque. Muslims believe a person cannot encounter God without maintaining a *ghusl* level of purity" (Esposito, 2009).

Along with the Qur'an, the Prophet Muhammad's words regarding physical purification permanently imprint on any Muslim's mind. For example, in one of the hadith narrations, physical purity is considered half of the faith. In this respect, Rothman (2018) also brings attention to the importance of specific practices from the Prophetic tradition, those that "are essential for establishing constancy and increasing internal balance" (Rothman, 2018, p. 47). He states that behavioural commitments are important and begin with *niyyah* (intention) and *aml* (action). In therapy, we use these concepts to "help maintain a connection to the rope of Allah amid the ever-changing state of our *nafs* and the constant ups and downs of life" (Rothman, 2018, p. 46). In Islamic tradition, as noted before, a proper way of life does not only mean being committed to five daily *fard* (obligatory) prayers and fasting during Ramadhan. As a therapist, Rothman considers non-obligatory and recommended spiritual practices are also important, practices such as "fasting two days a week, waking up in the middle of the night for *tahajud* (night prayer), eating halal (permissible) *wa taib* (healthy), daily *nawafl* (optional) prayers, reciting Quran, doing *dhikr*, and exercising" (Rothman, 2018, p. 47). He also encourages his clients to adopt some of these self-disciplinary practices in daily life.

For Muslims, purification means not only maintaining physical cleanliness and proper hygiene, but it also has a specific sacred value as a sign of respect for God. Thus, purification starts with a proper declaration, such as "Bismillah ir-Rahman ir-Raheem" (In the name of Allah, Most Gracious, Most Merciful). A ritual of physical purification dictates that one's clothes and body must be free from any amount of urine, stool, vomit, or blood, if at all possible. The ritual washing of the face, forearms, and feet is a prerequisite for performing prayers or other rituals.

Once a person completes the ablution, they can then recite the following prayer: *ash-hadu 'an laa 'ilaaha 'I'll allaah wahdahu laa shareeka lahu wa 'ash-hadu 'anna Muhammadan 'abduhu wa Rasooluhu.Allaahumma-j'alnee minat-tawwaabeena waj'alnee minal-mutatahhireen.Subhaanaka Allaahumma wa bihamdika, 'ash-hadu 'an laa 'ilaaha 'illaa 'Anta, 'Astagh firuka wa 'atoobu 'ilayk*. This prayer means:

> I testify that there is no one worthy of worship besides Allah. He is all by Himself and has no partner and I testify that Muhammad is Allah's servant and Rasul (Messenger). O Allah, count me (include me) among those who seek forgiveness and amongst those who stay clean. O Allah, You are pure, I praise You and testify that only You are worthy of worship and I seek forgiveness from You. I turn to You for repentance.

The Relevance of Muraqabah in Islamic Psychotherapy

Some Muslims also follow the Prophetic tradition of being in a state of ablution at bedtime, as follows:

> The Prophet said to me, "Whenever you go to bed perform ablution like that for the prayer, lie or your right side and say, "Allahumma aslamtu wajhi ilaika, wa fauwadtu `Amri ilaika, wa alja'tu Zahri ilaika raghbatan wa rahbatan ilaika. La Malja'a wa la manja minka illa ilaika. Allahumma amantu bikitabika-l-ladhi anzalta wa bina-biyika-l ladhi arsalta" (O Allah! I surrender to You and entrust all my affairs to You and depend upon You for Your Blessings both with hope and fear of You. There is no fleeing from You, and there is no place of protection and safety except with You O Allah! I believe in Your Book (the Qur'an) which You have revealed and, in Your Prophet, (Muhammad) whom You have sent). Then if you die on that very night, you will die with faith (i.e. or the religion of Islam). Let the aforesaid words be your last utterance (before sleep)." I repeated it before the Prophet and when I reached "Allahumma amantu bikitabika-l-ladhi anzalta (O Allah I believe in Your Book which You have revealed)." I said, "Wa-rasulika (and your Apostle)." The Prophet said, "No, (but say): 'Wanabiyika-l-ladhi arsalta (Your Prophet whom You have sent), instead."
> (Sahih al-Bukhari, Vol. 1, Book 4, Hadith 247)

In therapy, it might be easier to request a client take a proper *wudu* (in Arabic) or *destemaz* (in Persian) (ablution) if the facility has a special area for clients. If not, then *tayammum* would be sufficient. Such preparatory work has benefits, as ablution activates the sympathetic nervous system, releases neurotransmitters that can help the client concentrate, calms a stressed-out mind and racing thoughts, and provides mental satisfaction.

With respect to spiritual purification, in Sufi tradition, the master reminds the disciple that telling lies is considered a great sin. The Prophet (pbuh) said, "the signs of a hypocrite are three: whenever he speaks, he tells a lie; whenever he promises, he breaks it; and if you trust him, he proves to be dishonest." Healthcare professionals may expect smooth interactions with patients and families during the process of breaking bad news. Nevertheless, these patients and families should not be denied the sensitive application of professional truth-telling techniques. This is in congruence with the ethical principles of truth-telling and full disclosure in a clinical setting.

Saniotis (2012) reports that this spiritual practice:

> not only permits a Sufi to enter into different 'domains of experience' but allows him to develop a personalized repertoire for understanding his practices, experiences and the sensations invoked by them. The mystical practice of retreat conveys the inter-relationship between mystical mastery and a sensuous awareness of knowing the corporeal.
> (p. 74)

Similarly, Saloumeh Bozorgzadeh and Lana Ruvolo Grasser (2022) suggest Sufi psychotherapy be based on Sufism and common psychotherapeutic modalities such as cognitive behavioural therapy (CBT), dialectical behavioural therapy (DBT), motivational interviewing, and positive psychology. They define the goals of Sufi psychotherapy as: "to help patients recognize their reactivity, understand experiences of daily life as being more than the patient's reaction to them, and become a master of those reactions" (Bozorgzadeh & Grasser, 2022, p. 408). For the purpose of assessment and treatment of psychosocial, emotional, and mental health problems, they suggest certain Sufi and general counselling techniques such as discussing and addressing spiritual well-being, exploring personal history and ancestral heritage; promoting curiosity and spiritual growth through various activities and non-linear approaches; incorporating Sufi-based practices for spiritual well-being; encouraging inner exploration, purpose alignment, and expression through spiritual artwork; helping clients differentiate between heart-driven and mind-driven values; using Socratic questioning and silent prayer for introspection and therapy; empowering individuals to trust their inner voice and cultivate self-discipline; and inspiring hope in spiritual journeys (Bozorgzadeh & Grasser, 2022).

In a few studies, the role of *muraqabah* was also explored in clinical settings. In one study (Husain & Hasan, 2021), *muraqabah* is defined as "an intentional practice of the *qalb* (heart) which man has yet to learn how to meditate" (p. 134). Some research studies use qualitative and quantitative data to demonstrate *muraqabah's* benefits in treating procrastination, emotion regulation (Bytamar et al., 2020), depression, and other mental health problems (Dwidiyanti et al., 2021). According to Susanty and Hawadi (2019), *muraqabah* did not have a significant correlation with academic dishonesty in graduate students in the context of the relationship between self-regulated learning and academic dishonesty among graduate students; however, *muraqabah* can "negatively correlate with academic dishonesty if Muslim graduate students have a perception that the behavior includes acts that violate religious values and are not in line with the rules of Allah SWT" (p. 249).

In clinical settings, *muraqabah* is translated as Islamic spiritual mindfulness based on three concepts: mindfulness, spirituality, and Islam. It refers to "a state of mind, a process of keeping one's mind in the present moment, on purpose, non-judgmentally, fully observe and accept what is experienced in life from a place of calm objectivity, and detached from potentially destructive thoughts and feelings" (Dwidiyanti et al., 2021, p. 220).

Unlike other mindfulness techniques used in clinical settings, *muraqabah* is God-centred. Husan and Hasan (2021) state that "During the practice of *muraqabah*, saints and the learned, and common people keep vigil of the holy essence of Allah, or His attributes, or some other aspect in the mind with devotion" (p. 132). This means that at the foundation of this technique lies the:

> conscious of the awareness of God (Allah) over their soul, innermost thoughts/feelings, and action. In other words, it is comprehensive self-knowledge and self-awareness that Allah is always watching us at all times, which consequently will change our actions, feelings, thoughts, and inner states of being to be better. It can also be described as a mutual awareness, while we are of Allah, and Allah is aware of us.
> (Dwidiyanti et al., 2021, p. 220)

Piraino (2021) gives an example from Mandel, a traditional Italian Jerrahiyya-Halvetiyya Shaikh at the Milan mosque in Padova, who not only "strongly influenced the development of Italian Sufism and Islam as a whole," but also integrated psychoanalysis and Sufism, "often calling the dhikr (ritual that consists in the repetition of God's names) 'a collective session of therapy,' and tracing Freudian, Jungian, and Adlerian theories with the history" (p. 196).

Dwidiyanti et al. (2021) propose the DAHAGA (*Deteksi Sehat Bahagia/Happy Healthy Detection*) application with its eight features: (1) problem, (2) bad behaviour, (3) early detection, (4) independent health target, (5) pretest, (6) post-test, (7) mindfulness exercises, and (8) information. In their previous works, they also proposed the following steps and methods to apply *muraqabah*: (1) intention-generating based on focusing the needs of the heart in prayers and with an awareness that God watches and supervises us; (2) self-evaluation or self-introspection by accepting shortcomings and accepting without judgement, but with an aim to improve these shortcomings; (3) body scan with a focus on the conditions of the heart's, or feelings', affect on body, such as feeling tightness in the chest, neck, pounding of the heart, and accepting them completely with relaxation; (4) repentance; (5) prayer with a focus on God; (6) surrendering the self to God with sincerity; and (7) relaxation with a focus on holding the body that is in pain, taking a deep breath, and then coughing (p. 220).

In clinical applications, *muraqabah* should also be integrated with psychoeducation, intention, and self-evaluation techniques. For example, in the case of depression, based on Yapko's (2016) recommendations, a Muslim therapist teaches the client about:

> (1) the ability to make effective decisions, (2) effective coping or stress management skills, (3) skills to build and maintain positive relationships, (4) problem-solving skills, and (5) building a realistic and motivating future. Such abilities are taught at each stage of Islamic spiritual mindfulness.
> (Dwidiyanti et al., 2021, p. 224)

Mirdal (2012) uses the Rumi concept of mindfulness and suggests the following principles for mindfulness practices: unlearning and looking at the world with "A Beginner's Mind"; decentring; meditation while breathing and walking; and attuning the body and mind through music, dance, and "flow," then letting go. At the stage of unlearning, the client aims to identify unrealistic thoughts, feelings, and expectations and tries to go beyond the previous emotional boundaries and mental concepts that were not helpful. In decentring, the client is encouraged to divert attention from themself to others and "to act from tranquility and love" (Mirdal, 2012, p. 1209). Meditating while breathing and walking is one of the suggested activities in Rumi's concept of mindfulness. This is explained with traditional Sufi walking practices, as they increase "the ability to distinguish various states of awareness and control them…. bridge the gap between the seemingly divine and seemingly commonplace… be aware of the rhythm of the breath" (Mirdal, 2012, p. 1210). Mirdal further notes that, after trying this meditative practice, the client can try "a different rhythm by comparison, a different direction or intensity of breathing, or a different intention of feeling (for instance, walking toward a goal)" (p. 1210). The purpose is to notice changes in inner state, thoughts, and feelings.

Mirdal (2012) suggests that the experience of flow is comprised of the following elements:

- Clear goals (expectations and rules are discernible, and goals are attainable and align appropriately with one's skill set and abilities).
- Concentrating and focusing (a high degree of concentration in a limited field of attention. A person engaged in the activity will have the opportunity to focus and to delve deeply into it).
- Losing the feeling of self-consciousness (the merging of action and awareness).
- A distorted sense of time—one's subjective experience of time is altered.
- A balance between ability level and challenge (the activity is neither too easy nor too difficult).
- Control over the situation or activity.
- Effortlessness of action (p. 1211).

My previous works also present the Sufi understanding of *muraqabah* as a meditation-based therapy in Islamic psychotherapy. I suggested that some mental, emotional, and spiritual problems can be treated through practicing *muraqabah*, as it provides an opportunity for *inskishaf* (personal development), *i'tidal* (psycho-spiritual equilibrium), and *ma'rifah* (enlightenment). I outlined some frameworks through which this spiritual practice can be incorporated into mindfulness-based stress reduction (MBSR), mindfulness-based cognitive therapy (MBCT), dialectical behaviour therapy

The Relevance of Muraqabah in Islamic Psychotherapy

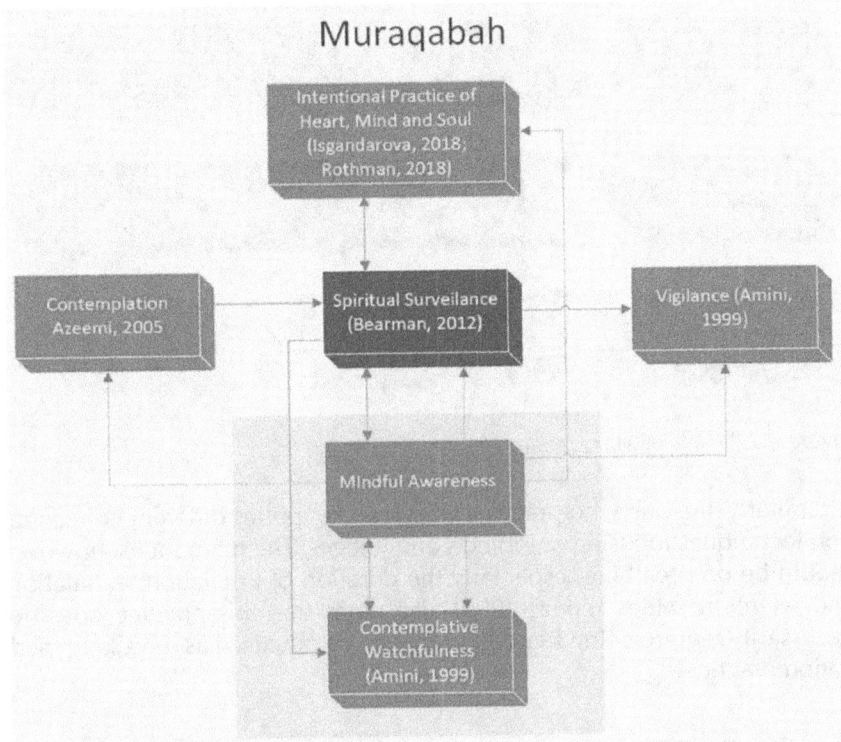

Figure 4.1 Summary of definitions of *Muraqabah*.

(DBT), acceptance and commitment therapy (ACT), and mindfulness-based relapse prevention (MBRP). I came to this conclusion after reviewing mindfulness practices from different spiritual and religious traditions. Of course, there are a variety of meditation styles and techniques; however, the classical techniques in *muraqabah* can be used to achieve therapeutic goals such as spiritual, mental, and emotional well-being. For example, when Sufi followers practise *muraqabah* at different levels, they aim to complete each level with certain goals. Overall, *muraqabah*, or mindfulness in contemporary Islamic psychotherapy, would help the client be more flexible in their feelings and thinking and free the mind and soul from their strongest conditioning, which could either be attachments to certain worldly things, unhelpful feelings, or temptations of the soul. It aims to increase mental, emotional, and spiritual agility. In other words, to set the mind, body, and soul free from being prisoner to a certain framework of thinking and feeling and stilling the mind. It can be compared to yogic concentration and breathing practices in Hinduism and Buddhism (Miles-Yépez, 2009).

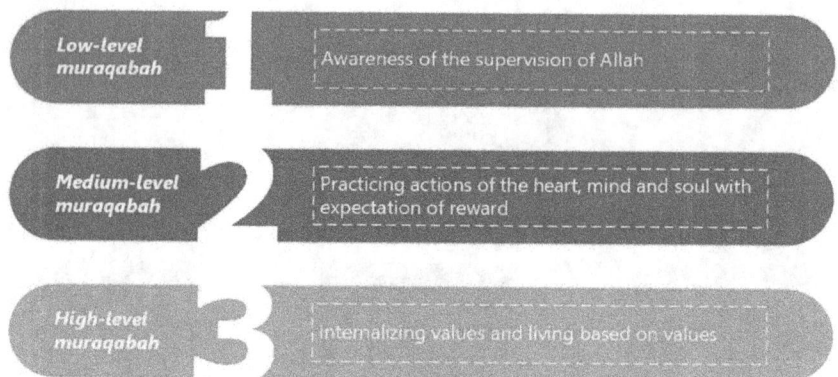

Figure 4.2 Levels of *Muraqabah*.

Similarly, the one who practises *muraqabah* applies different concentration techniques focusing on objects and images. The main focus, however, should be on breathing, especially the duration of inhalation, exhalation, and retention. Miles-Yépez (2009) also notes that this practice does not necessarily require being seated; it can also be practised as a walking meditation practice.

Questions for Discussion

1. Discuss the differences and similarities of various approaches in Islamic psychotherapy literature. In your view, which modality or approach in Islamic psychotherapy might be more helpful than other approaches?
2. How would you characterize different approaches? Which one is more important in the psycho-spiritual domain in professional work?
3. Discuss the importance of integrating Islamic psychotherapy approaches with contemporary psychotherapy theories and modalities.

5 The Techniques of *Muraqabah* in Islamic Psychotherapy

We have mentioned that, like other mindfulness techniques, *muraqabah* also helps to improve one's ability to concentrate and focus through techniques such as *mushahadah, tasawwur, tafakkur,* and *muhasabah*. Azeemi (2005), for example, wanted his followers to use "the force of perception concentrates on an object or idea, whether it is Divine Attributes or on the separation of body and soul or any other topic" (p. 71). Syed Ghauth Ali Shah (d. 1880) noted that traditional *muraqabah* encourages to attain "a point where the person himself becomes the meaning and becomes unaware of self" (Ali Shah, cited by Azeemi, 2005, p. 70).

In this regard, Azeemi (2005) compared *muraqabah* to other natural states of mind. For example, in a sleeping state, the brain is disconnected from outer senses such as whims, imagination, thoughts, feelings, and external distractions. This allows the brain to rest and relax. Similarly, *muraqabah* is "a way of imposing a state of sleeping without going to sleep" (Azeemi, 2005, p. 4). This allows the disciple to be free from Time and Space but in an awakened state.

In a clinical setting, the Muslim therapist wants the client to achieve the desired level of mindfulness by paying attention to the whims of undesired thoughts and controlling them during the process of *muraqabah*. In this section, we will highlight different techniques used during *muraqabah*.

Mushahadah

For ibn 'Arabi, this aspect of *muraqabah* is the stage of *mushahada* (witnessing, observing), when "the individual self is annihilated" (Chittick, 2007, p. 72). Ali Shah used to say that disciples believed that when "the heart is attentive to God or anything other than God then all internal organs follow its command because they are all obedient to the heart" (Azeemi, 2005, p. 70). During *mushahada*, an increased awareness or mindfulness of the Creator helps the disciple. Ibn 'Arabi's student, Muhammad ibn Ishaq

Sadr al-Din al-Qunawi (d. 1273) (1949), likened this process to achieving total emptiness. This understanding of emptiness is similar to contemporary ideas of optimal states of mindfulness. Both require freeing the mind from unnecessary thoughts and being aware of the moment by observing. To that end, the follower first learns how to apply decentring in order to remove the focus of attention from the self towards others. In cognitive therapy, it is expressed in terms of "cognitive shifting," which refers to "re-directing one's focus of attention away from a fixed idea or recurring thought, and toward a different focus of attention" (Mirdal, 2012, p. 1209).

In classical *muraqabah*, the disciple chooses an object for observation. These objects can represent symbols such as the face of their Sheikh, the prophet Muhammad, the Qur'an, or God. These objects and symbols aim to prevent the mind from wandering. Similarly, a Muslim psychotherapist can use various objects, such as elements of nature, to help the client focus on and observe the flow of emotions, feelings, and thoughts without being stuck, reactive, or distracted. When in the state of *mushahada*, the client remains still and motionless and can endure the burden of emotions without being reactive (Isgandarova, 2019a). The client lets these emotions, whims, and unwanted thoughts go in order to feel more positive feelings and thoughts. After three to five minutes of *mushahada*, the therapist invites the client to describe the experience of both pleasant and unpleasant bodily sensations, feelings, and emotions in a non-judgemental manner. Of course, being realistic, we understand that there might be times when unwanted thoughts, whims, and memories are out of control. These experiences should not discourage us. The therapist can use stories of well-known and master Sufis, who are also realists with whole ranges of spiritual and emotional mental states, or *hal* (plural *ahwal*) (Ernst, 20011, p. 115), which we will describe later. For example, Mevlana Jalal-ad-Din Rumi (d. 1273), talked about "acceptance and acknowledgement of both positive and negative experiences; unlearning of old habits and looking at the world with new eyes; decentering, changing one's focus from Self to Other; and attunement of body and mind…" (Mirdal, 2012, p. 1208). In this regard, Rumi emphasized "experiential approach" versus "experiential avoidance" (Mirdal, 2012). Therefore, at this stage, the Muslim psychotherapist can help the client accept whatever comes to them during the process of *muraqaba* and reflect on it to gain insight.

Tasawwur

In classical *muraqabah*, the stage of *tasawwur* (imagination) usually involved feeling the presence of God, but since the 18th century, it has also included the spiritual presence of the Prophet Muhammad and the Sheikh (Esposito, 2010). Amini (1999) notes that Ibn 'Arabi considered "creative imagination as a transformative force has the power to bring the angelic side of human beings out into manifestation. In doing so, it creates a dual movement" (p. 69). In this respect, creative imagination "causes invisible spiritual realities to descend to the reality of the Image" (Amini, 1999, p. 69). Ibn 'Arabi also gave an example from the Prophetic tradition, which used to say, "Love God as if you saw Him." This is possible only through imagination, which becomes a "place where the Divine and the sensible reality meet" (Amini, 1999, p. 69), which Ibn 'Arabi calls a fusion of the invisible, visible, spiritual, and physical. The main function of imagination, as per Ibn 'Arabi, is to comprehend the Divine by putting God at the centre of the imagination and directing the senses of perception to allow sensory facts to transform into symbols. In this process, Ibn 'Arabi invites the disciple to suspend all biases in order to let God reveal Himself through the 99 Names. In Rogerian therapy, this is called an "unconditional positive regard" for the client that "creates the container necessary for the client to begin to open up to the difficult process of therapy" (Rothman, 2018, p. 33). At this level, the imagination becomes active. Amini (1999) states that, like an active imagination, this kind of awareness emerges in a space that lies between Heaven and Earth which is also called "alam al-mithal." This area is comparable to what Jung has called "psychic reality."

The disciple uses signs or symbols, which, as noted by Jung, are "the best possible expression for something unknown" (Amini, 1999, p. 72). Ibn 'Arabi expressed this as *ta'wil*, which is translated as "interpretation through symbolism," as the disciple needs to use it in the process of active imagination to make new theophanies.

Amini (1999) uses Jung's concept of "coniunctio" to interpret the role of *ta'wil*. The term coniunctio signifies:

> the conjunction of the opposites within the psyche by understanding and integration of archetypal symbols of the collective unconscious. This process of understanding prepares the ground for the person to reconstruct everything experienced into a symbol, thus discovering the analogy between the concealed and the revealed.
> (Amini, 1999, p. 72)

However, it is also important to remember that Muslims, including Sufis, strongly believe that humans cannot comprehend and directly know the essence of God. The Qur'an repeatedly notes that God is Transcendent and Hidden.

> Whatever you may differ about is for God to judge. [Say], 'Such is God, my Lord. In Him I trust and to Him I turn, the Creator of the heavens and earth.' He made mates for you from among yourselves—and for the animals too—so that you may multiply. There is nothing like Him: He is the All Hearing, the All Seeing. The keys of the heavens and the earth are His; He provides abundantly or sparingly for whoever He will; He has full knowledge of all things.
>
> (Q. 42:10–12)

As previously discussed, some Indo-Muslim Sufi disciples, for example, use the image of the holy Ka'ba located in Mecca as a symbol in their imagination during *muraqabah*. The masters of the Sufi orders, such as Nakhshibandi, trained their disciples to "let the Shaykh enter the heart." In Sufi terminology, this exercise is still called *fana fi Shaikh*, which means "becoming One or being annihilated in or with the Master." With gradual training, the disciple also learns how to practise *fana fi Rasul* (Become One and Annihilated in or with Muhammad), *fana fil Qur'an* (Become One and Annihilated with or in the Qur'an and its commandments), and *fana fillah* (Become One and Annihilated in or with God).

As we can see, a variety of symbolic elements in the Sufi traditions are used in *muraqabah*. The main idea for their application is to place them at the centre or use them as a ritual or symbol for intensive concentration. In psychoanalysis, this can be labelled as applying archetypal imagery and relating it to the sacred. In the contemporary practice of *muraqabah*, it is not necessary to imagine the master, but the person can imagine a light that spreads to the whole body instead (Azal, 2015). That being said, the Muslim psychotherapist in clinical settings still plays the role of guide, teacher, and leader. Sufi and contemporary psychology emphasize the therapist's role in the therapeutic relationship. For example, when al-Ghazali prescribed intervention in cases where the patient rejects or is unable to stick to the opposite behaviour, he suggested that the "shaykh should lead him from that greatly undesirable habit to another one, less desirable" (al-Ghazali, 1993, pp. 56–59). Similarly, Mirdal (2012) outlines that "attainment of these psychological and spiritual states requires a facilitator or a teacher just as mindfulness training necessitates a person in authority to whom the patient turns for help..." (p. 1207). Keshavarzi and Haque (2013) also intensively discuss the critical role of the therapist and compare it to the role of *shaikh* (master, guide, leader, spiritual healer). They state:

> A shaykh, or spiritual doctor of sorts, has acquired and incorporated this experiential form of education (*tassawuf*) in the spiritual practices.

They have been given permission to initiate others into the spiritual path by their shaikh. These spiritual healers have been the source of treating mental illness for generations in the Muslim community.

(Keshavarzi & Haque, 2013, p. 236)

The role of a Muslim psychotherapist in *muraqabah* is to help the client practise contemplation or mindfulness—more precisely, to help the client practise being aware of one's thoughts, feelings, and sensations, as well as inspire the client to seek spiritual knowledge. In the context of therapy, *muraqabah* becomes a valuable psychotherapeutic tool for self-reflection and personal growth because it encourages the client to develop a deeper understanding of their experiences, gain insight, and find meaning in these experiences through the lens of the heart. Of course, this is not possible without connecting with one's feelings, emotions, beliefs, and values on a deeper level. By doing so, clients can gain insight and find meaning in their struggles or challenges.

In *muraqabah*, the therapist uses the power of *tasawwur*, or imagination, to learn, acknowledge, and explore their internal states, thoughts, sensations, and emotions in a safe and supportive environment. The role of the therapist is to create an atmosphere where the client feels open to experiencing and exploring all aspects of their inner world in a respectful and culturally sensitive manner. Thus, the therapist should know about the client's faith and cultural background and work collaboratively with the client to incorporate images and symbols of the client's beliefs and practices.

Tafakkur *and* Tadabbur

Next, the therapist uses *tafakkur* and *tadabbur*, translated as contemplation and theological reflection, "to think or to focus on a given object" (Azeemi, 2005, p. 66). In *muraqabah*, *tafakkur* involves thinking on a subject deeply, systematically, and in great detail; *tadabbur*, however, means contemplation, remembrance of God, and thoughts of God. Both words are used often in the Qur'an. *At-tafakkur wat-tadabbur* (remembrance of God, thought of God) (Q. 3:191, 4:82) establishes the process of meditation. Imam Ahmad al-Haddad, the author of *the Key to the Garden*, defines *tafakkur* as the focus and movement of the heart and mind through the meaning of things to reach the underlying intention. He also stated that "Knowledge comes from *tafakkur*…" Along with the key sources of Islam, the Qur'an and the prophetic narrations, the therapist can also use the social sciences to instruct the client to reflect and contemplate at this stage. The following quote from the Qur'an, for example, is often interpreted as an invitation to reflect on the creation for meditation.

> There truly are signs in the creation of the heavens and earth, and in the alternation of night and day, for those with understanding, who remember God standing, sitting, and lying down, who reflect on the creation of the heavens and earth: 'Our Lord! You have not created all this without purpose– You are far above that! – so protect us from the torment of the Fire. Our Lord! You will truly humiliate those You commit to the Fire. The evildoers have no one to help them. Our Lord! We have heard someone calling us to faith– "Believe in your Lord"– and we have believed. Our Lord! Forgive us our sins, wipe out our bad deeds, and grant that we join the righteous when we die. Our Lord! Bestow upon us all that You have promised us through Your messengers– do not humiliate us on the Day of Resurrection– You never break Your promise.
> (Q. 3:190–194)

For example, in one of the narrations, the prophet Muhammad (pbuh) encouraged his followers to engage in reflection. Ibn 'Abbas and Abu Darda reported that he said, "*Tafakkur* for an hour is better than a whole nights salah." Muslim scholars and Sufi practitioners use various methods to enhance *tafakkur* and *tadabbur*. For example, Muhammad ibn Zakariya ar-Razi (Rhazes) (d. 925) considered *naz'ar*, or theological reflection and speculation, as *wa' jib* (obligatory). For Razi, theological reflection is the process of acquiring knowledge with the purpose of achieving happiness, or *sa'ada*, and perfection, or *kamal*. For this purpose, the person who tries this method affirms: (a) the existence of the rational human soul, separate from the body; (b) an intellectual pleasure that man may experience at the spiritual level rather than the bodily level; and (c) a spiritual afterlife in addition to the physical one (Shihadeh, 2005). For al-Ghazali, *kalam* (theology) was speculation with the intention of recognizing the validity of Revelation and religious belief; therefore, he considered it obligatory upon everyone. For him, theology was not a critical enquiry, or *tahqiq*, but was a means to seek true knowledge of God, or *ma'rifah*. 'Ibn Arabi also mentioned methods of practicing it, such as praying, which should not be understood as regular communal recitation, but rather as theological reflection and a spiritual union and conversation with the Divine Beloved. Al-Suhrawardi (d. 1191) stated that theological reflection occurs in the heart, which goes beyond basic anatomical functions. It becomes a pure soul and is illuminated by a shining light.

According to Malik Badri (2000), a contemporary Sudanese Muslim psychologist, the Islamic concept of *tafakkur* differs from Eastern contemplation or meditation and requires conscious and rational thinking during meditative practice. In this respect, *tafakkur* is a cognitive and spiritual activity focusing on the mind, emotions, and spirit. Furthermore, *tafakkur* is "a refined form of worshipping God by appreciating His creating in this vast Universe" (Badri, 2000, p. xiv) and involves "a mixture of thought, cognition, imagination, sentiment, emotions and above all, spirituality" (Badri, 2000, p. 29). For example, the therapist invites the client to select a story from the Qur'an or hadith, such as the story of Yusuf (Joseph), to reflect on themes of adoption, loss, and depression in a clinical context.

The process of *tafakkur* in *muraqabah* involves, as Nūrbakhsh (1979) outlined, first, contemplation "upon oneself, to know oneself." This is cited in the Qur'an as: "Do they not reflect upon themselves?" (30:8). Second, it is to reflect upon God's creation. Nasr (2007), in this respect, notes that contemplating nature, "seeing in its forms, life, and rhythms spiritual realities… are for the greatest importance not only in themselves, but also for us as wayfarers on the path to spiritual perfection…" (p. 47). For example, in this kind of contemplation, a tree becomes "a reflection of the tree of Paradise" (p. 47). Each mountain mirrors the Tree of Paradise, with every summit representing transcendence. The flowing stream embodies Divine Mercy, while the wind symbolizes the Spirit. An eagle flying above signifies the human spirit striving for perfection through spiritual pursuits, reaching out towards the Divine throne. A fish swimming in the deep symbolizes the soul immersing itself in the boundless ocean of Infinity.

Lastly, it is to "contemplate upon God" (Amini, 1999, p. 106). This process requires a few steps: (1) knowledge (via sight, hearing, touch, smell, and taste); (2) inspection of aesthetic aspects and qualities of data that yield fine appreciation, delicate feelings, and powerful passion; (3) crossing the boundary beyond or relating the object of contemplation to the Creator; and (4) spiritual cognition or *shuhud* (Badri, 2000, pp. 30–31). The therapist can introduce the work of Abu Zayd Ahmed ibn Sahl al-Balkhi (d. 934), a Muslim psychologist and author of *Masalih al-Abdan wa al-Anfus* (Sustenance for Body and Soul). In this book, al-Balkhi discusses common mental disorders such as fear, depression, and anxiety. For example, the client is invited to contemplate how their anxiety aligns with the four main categories of anxiety discussed by al-Balkhi: *al-ghadab* (anger), *al-jaza'* (sadness and depression), *al-faza'* (fears and phobias), and *wasawes al-sadr* (obsessional disorders). Ibn Qayyim al-Jawziyah (d. 1350) also invited his followers to pay attention to the cognitive processes of the mind because they become drives and incentives that lead to habits (al-Jawziyyah, 1981). These cognitive processes, or *khawatir* (the plural of *khatirah*), are translated "as an inner thought, a concealed speech or an internal dialogue" or as "a fast, inner, concealed reflection, notion or unvocal thought, which may come fleetingly" (Ibn Qayyim al-Jawziyah, cited by Badri, 2000, p. 22) and are considered automatic thoughts. Even while sleeping, they are active and uninterrupted (Badri, 2000, p. 22). These inner thoughts are the basis of human actions that can be harmful, sinful, and lead to strong emotions.

A Sufi master, Najm al-in Kubra (d. 1221), divided thought-impulses into four categories: *shaytani* (diabolic), *nafsani* (coming from the ego), *malaki* (angelic), and *rahmani* (divine). The disciple needs to differentiate between positive and negative thought-impulses for the purpose of strict self-discipline. The processes of being aware of and watching these thought-impulses mindfully are important; otherwise, the disciple might gratify the sensual and psychic desires of the ego, and this will hinder his/her ability to recognize divine, angelic thoughts. Watchfulness and mindfulness help the disciple to clean the heart as a polished mirror, which in turn helps the disciple to "see the presence of different thought-impulses and can thus discriminate between them" (Amini, 1999, p. 106).

In this regard, Ibn Qayyim al-Jawziyah (1981) stated:

> You should know that the beginning of any voluntary act is *khawatir* and *wasawis* (an inner temptation of Satan or whims) these *khawatir* and *wasawis* lead to conscious thinking. Next, thinking will be transferred to or stored in the memory and the memory will transform into volition and a motive that will be acted out in real life as an action. Repeating the action leads to a strong habit. So, eliminating an emotional or lustful habit is easier at an early state before it gains strength.
>
> (p. 173)

The client is then asked to reflect on how intrusive and persistent these thoughts are and how they hinder the individual from enjoying life, performing daily activities, and focusing on other aspects of life. For instance, al-Balkhi suggests that, under the influence of such thoughts, a person may constantly anticipate the worst outcomes for the near future. As a countermeasure, we can ask the client to reflect on these perceived outcomes. The client might start by experiencing fleeting thoughts that are difficult to resist; however, as Ibn Jawziyah recommended, the client is encouraged to navigate and manage these thoughts by accepting positive and beneficial thoughts while exerting control over harmful ones. Malik Badri (2000) compares this practice with cognitive-behavioural therapy, specifically a technique called systematic desensitization (p. 25). Systematic desensitization in psychotherapy is used to help the client relax and imagine themselves in a peaceful and serene environment, gradually replacing the anxiety-inducing feelings with a sense of tranquility.

In this regard, al-Ghazali recommended a gradual approach when stimulating the opposite in internal cognition. He suggested that:

> illness can only be treated with its opposite, like treating heat with cold, and cold with heat… the malady of ignorance is treated with learning,

that of avarice with generosity, pride with humility, greed with abstinence and all by assuming the contrary.

(al-Ghazali, 1993, pp. 56–59)

Muhasabah

The term *muhasabah* is an Arabic word meaning "introspective examination" and refers to the process of taking account of the soul or self. It is known to have been referenced in the Islamic tradition as far back as Umar ibn al-Khattab, a companion of the prophet Muhammad, and was popularized by Harith al-Muhasibi, whose name became synonymous with the practice (Picken, 2011).

One of the best and most comprehensive definitions of *muhasabah* as a technique is attributed to al-Harith al-Muhasibi (d. 857); his significant contributions to the concept even earned him the nickname "al-Muhasibi." By using this technique, the disciple can identify and gain control over the positive and negative aspects of the human soul. Classical Sufi masters particularly paid attention to *dhamm al-nafs*, which refers to the criticism and dispraise of the soul for its evil actions, intentions, and pursuit of desires. Al-Muhasibi described how one engages in accusation of the soul, known as *ittiham al-nafs*. It is also important to consider that the nature of the lower self is deceitful; it can even be described as an "enemy within." Therefore, Sufis introduced punitive measures on the soul, known as *inkisar al-nafs* (the "broken soul"), which are ultimately beneficial.

In a clinical setting, therapists can assist their clients in identifying weaknesses within the soul and exploring ways to reform them. Additionally, therapists can help clients identify compulsive and unhelpful coping mechanisms, which may prevent them from engaging in effective *muraqabah*. In their groundwork, Rothman and Coyle (2020) described how to use this technique. For example, participants could explore ways to enhance self-awareness can be cultivated. For instance, when assisting a client coping with anxiety and struggling with sleep due to racing thoughts and negative self-assessments, a therapist may propose the following: "Why not take five to seven minutes to reflect on your day, holding yourself accountable, going through it from morning to night."

Miles-Yépez (2009) notes that *muhasabah* refers to intentions and behaviours of "balancing accounts" and "precise calculation" in two senses: "self-examination, or taking account of one's own personal thoughts and actions; and a thorough examination of spiritual ideas and ideals, contemplating them in a discursive meditation." It is not a simple reflection but requires a comprehensive analysis that delves deeply into the subject, encompassing all related thoughts and emotions. This approach can successfully be integrated with the popular Western psychological therapeutic

96 *Mindfulness Techniques and Practices in Islamic Psychotherapy*

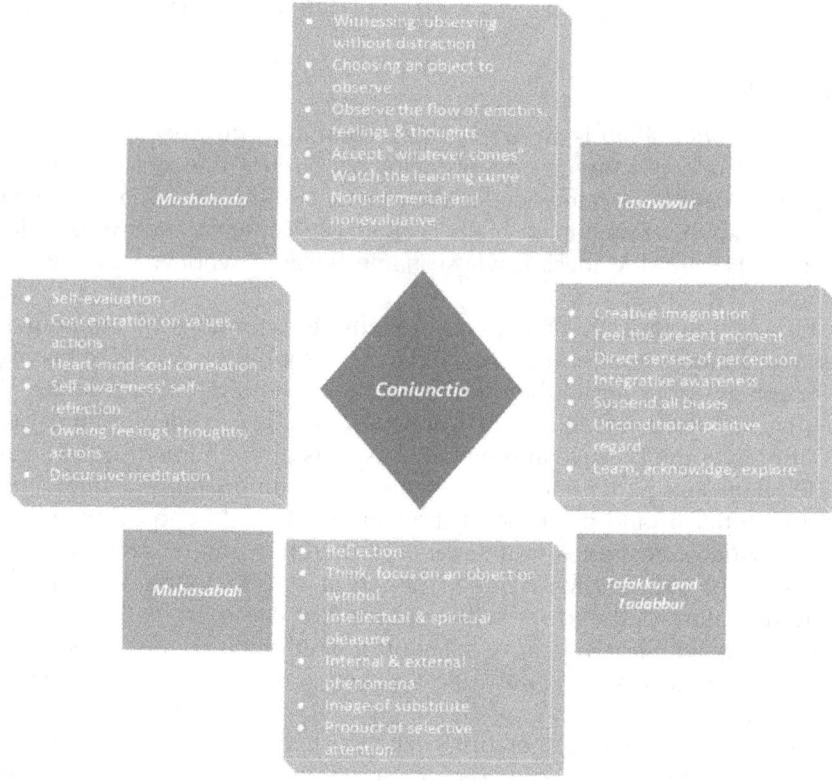

Figure 5.1 Muraqabah techniques.

practice of keeping a journal of thoughts and activities throughout the day, week, or even months (Ronan & Kazantzis, 2006).

Stages of the Human Condition during *Muraqabah*

Emotional and spiritual states or conditions, or *hal* (pl. *ahwal*), and transient stations, or *maqam* (pl. *maqamat*), based on divine manifestations in human nature are crucial to spiritual or inner transformation. Not only in a clinical sense but also from a spiritual aspect, it is not easy to translate the words *hal* and *ahwal*, as they have many subtle layers and meanings. In general, these concepts relate to spiritual conditions or states of the heart and, therefore, refer to the "phase" or "mood" of the heart (Rice, 2017).

Sufi literature is again our main reference, as it is the best primary resource that outlines the disciple's emotional states and conditions during the spiritual journey (Nurbakhsh, 1981). These states include *gabz* (contraction), *bast* (expansion), *fana* (annihilation), and *baqa* (subsistence) (Amini, 1999). According to Jurjani,

> these conditions are not artificially produced, not induced or acquired, of joy or sorrow, contraction or expansion, and so on. Such a state passes away on the emergence of the attributes of the self. If it lasts and becomes a habitus or fixed quality, it is called a *maqam*...
> (Cited by Rice, 2017, p. 56)

The source of contraction and expansion is God. Some spiritual masters, like Jurjani, argued that these conditions and stages are permanent, but some, like Junayd al-Baghdadi, accepted them as transient and temporary.

And God contracts and expands, and to Him you shall be returned.
(Q. 2:245)

Moses said, 'Lord, lift up my heart and ease my task for me. Untie my tongue, so that they may understand my words, and give me a helper from my family, my brother Aaron–augment my strength through him. Let him share my task so that we can glorify You much 34 and remember You often: You are always watching over us.
(Q. 20:25–35)

Did We not relieve your heart for you [Prophet], and remove the burden that weighed so heavily on your back, and raise your reputation high? So truly where there is hardship there is also ease; truly where there is hardship there is also ease. The moment you are freed [of one task] work on, and turn to your Lord for everything.
(Q. 94:1–7)

For example, when the Divine Beauty is manifested, it causes expansion; however, the manifestation of the Divine Majesty leads to heart contraction. Of course, each manifestation leads to certain emotions and feelings. One who experiences expansion feels happy and joyful, but when the heart feels contraction, it becomes sad and depressed. Bayazid Bistami (d. 848–9) used to say that "the contraction of the heart lies in the expansion of the ego (*nafs*), while the expansion of the heart lies in the ego's contraction" (Amini, 1999, p. 63). Although the source of contraction and expansion sometimes cannot be controlled, on the spiritual path, the disciple can examine and control the ego's responses to these states. In this respect, the role of states such as *jam* (gathering, referring to unity and meditation upon God) and *tafraqah* (dispersion/differentiation between God and creation) are important, as these experiences lead to unification and separation. Unification is possible through mindfulness. Distraction causes inattention to Unity (Nurbakhsh, 1981).

Finally, another level of the human condition, *fana* (annihilation) and *baqa* (subsistence), is explained in the context of spiritual states. Amini (1999) notes that:

> annihilation indicates the annihilation of human traits and their transmutation into Divine Attributes. Contrary to annihilation is subsistence; it is after annihilation that the disciple attains subsistence in the Divine Attributes. These spiritual states occur as the disciple practices invocation, self-examination and meditation.
>
> (p. 64)

Nurbakhsh (1981) also stated, "When ignorance is annihilated, knowledge subsists" (p. 103). In this respect, spiritual practices are important as they help to annihilate forgetfulness. This then helps the disciple experience annihilation in God.

> [Prophet], when you recite the Qur'an, seek God's protection from the outcast, Satan. He has no power over those who believe and trust in their Lord; his power is only over those who ally themselves with him and those who, because of him, join partners with God.
> (Q. 16:98–100)

Questions for Discussion

1. What are the elements of *muraqabah* in classical Sufi psychology? Discuss which one can be used in contemporary Islamic psychotherapy practice.
2. Discuss stages of the human condition during *muraqabah*. How do you understand the following statement: "The practice of *muraqabah* helps the disciple to be free from Time and Space but in an awakened state"?
3. How can a Muslim therapist use *muraqabah* to help the client achieve self-awareness and insight that might lead to change in a positive meaning? Discuss some techniques and practice and notice them in yourself.
4. How can use of *muraqabah* be helpful for the assessment and treatment of various emotional, mental, and spiritual problems in Islamic psychotherapy? What would be some cautions about its use?

6 Incorporating Dhikr, Music, and Physical Movement in *Muraqabah*

Dhikr is the most prescribed and irreplaceable spiritual practice in *muraqabah*. Great Sufi masters always connect *muraqabah* with *dhikr*, either explicitly or indirectly. As one of the most popular, easy, and manageable spiritual practices, the word *dhikr* literally means remembrance or recollection (Schimmel, 1975). In the Islamic tradition, *dhikr* can be a simple, single phrase such as "God is one." Most *dhikr* practices involve repetitions "until they become virtually a part of the utterer's inner constitution" (Wolf, 2006, p. 252).

It is important to note that some Sufi *tariqahs* developed or compiled *dhikr* under the ritual of *wird* (pl. *awrad*), which means "watering place," "access or arrival" at specified times for devotion to God, and "rose" (Padwick, 1961, pp. 20–22). It can also mean "set, supererogatory personal devotions observed at specific times, usually at least once during the day and once again at night" (Denny, 2012). J.S. Trimingham (1971) noted that in the Sufi context, *wird* refers to: (1) the *ṭarīḳa* itself; (2) a special prayer or litany; and (3) the "office" of the *ṭarīḳa*, meaning its distinctive doctrines and devotional-meditative discipline. He states, "Each *ṭarīḳa* and each order derivative has its own *awrad* composed by its leaders. These form the 'theme' of the order" (p. 215). *Wird* can be obligatory and supererogatory, as noted by Abu Hamid al-Ghazali. These Ṣufi devotions usually refer to standard litanies and repeated formulae (e.g., *takbir*, *tahlil*, *tasbiḥ*, and *taṣliya*) and start with a recitation of the Qur'an. Sufi Sheikhs reported the origin of *wirds* as authentic; they claimed to receive these specific instructions from prophets or saints in spiritual encounters or dreams.

Unlike *dhikr*, however, Sufis require special training or to get permission from the Sheikh to recite *wirds* in *muraqabah*. For example, Omar et al. (2017) note that *dhikr* is used as a pre-condition practice at different levels of *muraqabah*. The recitation, wording, and terminology of the *dhikr* might include the proclamation "Allah, Allah" or "la ilaha illa Allah." At the beginning and intermediary levels, it is important to follow the practice of *suhbah* (gathering or association); discussion; conversation and *bay'ah* (allegiance); commitment to the practice; and the procedures of *tahlil*, or

DOI: 10.4324/9781032631387-7

analysis; and *wuquf qalbi*. The number of "Allah, Allah" proclamations can range from 1,000 to 3,000 times, and "la ilaha illa Allah" can be 111–1,300 times, depending on the Sufi order.

The Khalwati-Ushshaki leader, Ahmed Jahidi Efendi (d. 1659–1960), summarized four major types of *dhikr*: (1) *dhikr* of the tongue, with an effort to remove foul words from the tongue; (2) *dhikr* of the heart, contemplating only God; (3) *dhikr* of the *nafs* or soul by feeling and imaging; and (4) *dhikr* of the *ruh* or spirit, contemplating God's attributes in the universe.

For this purpose, they used the Qur'an and the Hadith literature to develop a complete set of *dhikr* practices. Either loudly or silently, the followers would read prescribed verses from the Qur'an, say the *Shahada* (the declaration of faith), *asma ul-husna* (the names of God), or *durud* (saying blessings for the Prophet Muhammad). Muslims usually use *tasbih* (prayer beads or a rosary), which can consist of 33 or 99 beads. These prayer beads are usually held in the right hand, between the forefinger and thumb, to chant Divine Names or Attributes (i.e., The Merciful, The Compassionate, The Truth, and The Light) hundreds or tens of thousands of times over the course of days or weeks, while hoping to activate a certain spiritual quality associated with a specific Divine Name or Attribute or to be protected from evil spirits. Nevertheless, almost all spiritual traditions in Islam agree that the highest form of *dhikr* is *la ilaha illa Allah*.

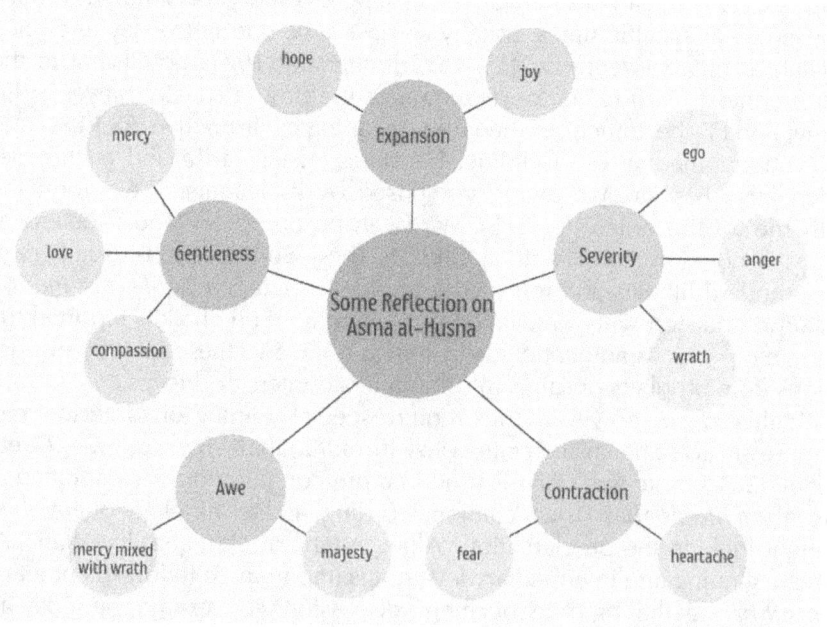

Figure 6.1 Asma ul-Husna.

Incorporating Dhikr, Music, and Physical Movement in Muraqabah

Of course, we also need to mention that some Muslims ascribe a magical power to *dhikr*. I have seen some chanting special *dhikr* to gain worldly power or control certain invisible spirits. In this respect, McCreery (1995), Skorupski (1976), and Foster (1974) provide examples to help us understand the mindset of people who use "magical" words and chants in various contexts. For example, McCreery explores exorcism in Taipei, or the practice of *che'ngo'-kiu* (controlling/propitiating the Five Ghosts), and notes that this practice should also be understood as a speech act, metaphor, poetic form, or all three (McCreery, 1995, p. 144). This tendency has also been recorded by Saniotis (2012), who observed the *dhikr* practices in Chishti *tariqa* in India and noted:

> Sufis believe that their rosaries embody mystical power, rooted in their understanding of the spirit world. For instance, unlike the *sawwabhi* rosary, which is predominantly used for prayer, Sufis refer to their rosaries as 'taskhir-i-jinn' (*jinn* controlling rosary). Sufi rosaries are personalised items and are never shared. They are sometimes made by Sufis themselves. Unlike *Chisti pirs* who often are seen carrying their rosaries, Sufis do not use their rosaries in front of others.
>
> (p. 76)

However, many Muslims engage in *dhikr* as an important *wazifa* (duty) or spiritual practice. Nūrbakhsh (1979) noted that through remembrance of God and reciting Divine Names, *dhikr* helps the average person purify the heart. The benefit of this purification is that it helps the person gain insight into the spiritual realm and experience a decrease in harmful inclinations of the ego (Amini, 1999).

In his *Tartib al-Suluk*, al-Qushayri describes three types of *dhikr*, which are *dhikr al-lisan* (the *dhikr* of the tongue), *dhikr al-qalb* (the *dhikr* of the heart), and *dhikr al-sirr* or *ruh* (the *dhikr* of the spirit) (Mulyati, 2003). Some divide *dhikr* into *jalali* and *jamali*, referring to the nature of the wording, which can focus on either divine power or majesty and divine beauty. In Naqshbandi orders, for example, the *dhikr* is recited silently, but in the Qadiri sect, it is verbal. Some Sufi sects believe that *jalali* and *jamali wazifa* have certain meanings and purposes. For example, Saniotis (2012) notes that:

> *Jalali wazifa* are recited to give spiritual power which a Sufi uses for controlling *jinn*, while *jamali wazifa* are recited to make a Sufi more compassionate and less intemperate. Here, notions of *jalali* and *jamali* are intertwined with Indian concepts of 'heating' (*garmi*), and 'cooling' (*sardi*), which are also used to classify foods. Abstinence from 'heating' foods is deemed essential when practicing *jalali wazifa*. These include onions, meat, garlic and hot spices because these foods are believed to 'heat' the mind and cause excessive passion. The analogy between

jalali and heating was pointed out to me. Shams, for instance, concerned by my impulsive nature had given me a *jamali wazifa* to recite so that I would 'cool down'. I was taught that the alleged harmonising effects of doing *jamali wazifa* counterbalanced irate tendencies.

(p. 77)

There is also a special prescribed technique to say *dhikr*. Many Sufis believe this technique should be followed and correctly implemented. For example, while performing *jalali wazifa*, one should follow the exact recitation technique because "incorrect recitation and careless preparation can have serious psychological ramifications" (Saniotis, 2012, p. 77). This is explained by the nature of the power of *jalal*, as it refers to "notions of excessiveness, ambiguity, danger and ebullition" (Saniotis, 2012, p. 77). The metaphor "fever" is also used to describe the power of *jalal*. For example, like the way a fever weakens the body, "*jalali wazifa* can make 'the mind boil', a metaphor for becoming overtly intemperate, if done to excess, or incorrectly" (Saniotis, 2012, p. 66).

Dhikr can be recited individually or in groups. Different Sufi orders have developed various practices and ethics of practicing *dhikr* to help their followers remember, concentrate, and unite with and be aware of God and the truthfulness of intention.

For example, when *dhikr* is performed in a group setting in the Naqshbandi order, the spiritual master sits in the circle and his disciples sit around him. After reciting the Qur'an, the spiritual master leads the congregants in an hour-long remembrance session by repeating *la ilaha illa Allah*. When *dhikr* is recited loudly, the master and disciples breathe quickly at four breaths per second, or in a four-per-beat pattern. Kugle (2012) notes:

> This meditation of "observing the breath" (*pas-i anfas*) is sometimes taught such that one only recites the name Allah. The method of doing this is to recite the name Allah while extending the final letter "h" with a long "u" so that it takes on the sound of "hu." While inhaling, one recites Allah and when exhaling, one recites -hu. Doing this does not employ the voice; rather one lets the breath expresses the language of the heart… One does this with each breath exhaled and inhaled while keeping one's concentration upon the navel as it is drawn in and extended out during breathing. After one does this meditation continuously and extensively, the meditation continues with one's breathing even if one is asleep or awake.
>
> (p. 88)

They also move their heads and bodies to the right and left. The remembrance session usually ends with a recitation of the Qur'an and praise for the Prophet. In the Khalwati order, the spiritual master and disciples sit in a circle and gently move their heads to the right, left, forwards, and backwards while performing *dhikr* such as *la ilaha illa Allah*, *hu*, and *hayy*. The master assigns special spiritual exercises, such as contemplative practices, to his disciples, who should complete them before and after the morning prayer. This is considered an important practice for training the ego.

Kugle (2021) quotes Chishti master Sheikh Kaleemullah Shahjahanabadi, who said:

> One should sit cross-legged with the back straight, the eyes closed, and the hands resting on the thighs. One then uses the big toe and the next toe of the right foot to firmly grip the sciatic nerve (*rag-i kimas*) that runs behind the left knee. Putting pressure on this will produce enough warmth in the heart to generate purity (*tafsya*). This warmth will melt and remove the fat that surrounds and constricts the heart, which is known as the dwelling place of the tempter (*khannas*). This will reduce the temptations and pollutions that plague the heart. Taking up this position, one should perform the meditation with single-minded heart and with assertive voice, either saying the words aloud or keeping silent as is suitable to one's situation and disposition.
>
> (p. 5)

Some *dhikr* was "believed to be so spiritually powerful that a person could go mad from reciting them without proper spiritual protection and preparation" (Hoffman, 1995, p. 132–133). Stoller (1994) reports that certain prayers are so profound that a Sufi devotee employs to access various embodied states are deeply interconnected. In numerous cultures worldwide, words are regarded as a source of energy, valued for their inherent significance rather than simply as symbols representing other concepts. (p. 562). Some Sufis even claim that different objects also praise God: "As the old Sufi Baba Ali once pointed out to me, 'If you listen carefully to the cars or when the trains pass, you will hear in their rhythms *la ilaha illa Allah* (There is no god but Allah)'" (Saniotis, 2012, p. 78). So, "sacred words contour their awareness of the lifeworld as pulsating with the name of Allah" (Saniotis, 2012, p. 78).

The regular recitation of certain *dhikr* enhances spiritual discernment, verging on clairvoyance, through visions and other forms of spiritual revelation. *Wirds* should be spoken as communal prayers after the evening prayer, rather than alone (Hoffman, 1995, p. 133). Ahmad Sirhindi (d. 1624) recommended reciting *Subhan Allah* (Glory be to God), *Allahu Akbar* (God is great), and *Alhamdu lillah* (God be praised) 100 times before falling asleep.

A correct recitation of prayers and *dhikr* is believed to have *barakat*, or a blessing effect, and of course, the first blessing is counted as purification of the heart and entire body. Therefore, Sufis strictly follow the etiquette of reciting *dhikr*. They sit "on the ground, either in a cross-legged position or sitting on their heels" (Saniotis, 2012, p. 77). Both closing and opening the eyes are allowed. They also pay attention to or develop a sensuous awareness of bodily rhythms. They believe this would allow the person to gain bodily mastery, such as breath control.[1] For example, when the disciple recites the *dhikr*, he/she needs to properly breathe in and out. Sufis believe that this helps the disciple develop a better concentration and improve their focusing abilities. This is possible through training the body to breathe properly.

Saniotis (2012) states that Sufis emphasize that some words possess mystical power and are not simply neutral reference for communication. Words in the form of chants, spells, incantations, talismans, prayers, and stories inform Sufis' understandings of mystical power and body awareness. The body can consume sacred words and mystical incantations. Talismans written with "Allah" were often placed in water by Sufis and then given to patients to drink. In addition, mystical designs called *puleeta*, which Sufis wrote for people suffering "spiritual afflictions," would be burned, with the fumes being inhaled by the patient. Sufis also used mystical words in combination with breathing on patients as a part of their therapy. In this way, within Sufis' therapeutic and mystical practices, words created a sensual kaleidoscope. Sufis stated that words were felt inside the body and moved within the body's viscera, blood, and breath.

Some Sufi leaders developed healing breath techniques based on the *dhikr* breathing techniques. In some countries, this is called *dum*, a popular healing practice of blowing on a patient (Saniotis, 2012, p. 81).

An Italian Sufi master, Mandel and his disciples described the practice *dhikr* as "the emotional state" that even becomes more "powerful and reinvigorated by movements and by breathing techniques" (p. 206). Mandel states that:

> This is everything that is needed for synchronic events to happen. This is why [during the dhikr] there are leaps of perception, rich personal symbols to interpret: visions, colours, images, and sounds. This is why leaps of space-time happened, due to the relativity of space-time, peculiar to synchronicity.
>
> (p. 206)

Muslims also count the number of *dhikr* by using either their finger joints or *tasbih* (prayer beads or a rosary). It is also called *misbahah*, subhah, or *sibḥa* in Egyptian pronunciation, *tasbih* in Persian and Muslim Indian usage, and *tesbih* in Turkish. *Tasbih* is a string with 33 or 99 beads made of wood, bone, or pearl. In the Shia tradition, *tasbih* is also made from the clay of Karbala, where Imam Hussain, the Prophet's grandson, was murdered by his enemies. In some Sufi orders, it is preferred to use *tasbih* made of sandalwood because it is believed that it "has the effect of curtailing the nafs…" (Saniotis, 2012, p. 81). Sandalwood is also used in Muslim aromatherapy and burned as incense in homes and shrines.

The beads of the *tasbih* are usually separated by two larger-sized beads called *imam*. Although the history of the *tasbih* is unknown because many religious and spiritual traditions across the world used and continue to use it in spiritual and religious ceremonies and rituals (early Christians have used it since the 3rd century, and it is popular among Hindus and Buddhists), Muslims have used it since the 9th century, when its appearance is attributed to Sufis, and later on to lower classes (Wensinck, 2012). Scholars such as Mez, Goldziher, and Vorlesungen argue that the first reference to the word *masabih* (pl. of *misbaha*) was made in the 800s (Wensinck, 2012).

Although some Muslims are against the usage of *tasbih* because they see it as *bid'ah* (a harmful innovation in religion), it is normal to see *tasbih* used by many pilgrims when they go on pilgrimage. While some argue that the following hadith only refers to the finger-reckoning of *dhikr*, the use of *tasbih* is also mentioned in the Prophetic tradition:

> on the authority of Saʿd b. Abi Waḳḳaṣ…. that he accompanied the Messenger of God, who went to visit a woman, who counted her eulogies by means of kernels or small stones lying before her. He asked her, 'Shall I tell you what is easier and more profitable?' 'Glory to God' according to the number of what he has created in the earth; 'glory to God' according to what he has created in the heaven; 'glory to God' according to the number of what is between these; 'glory to God' according to what he will create. And in the same way *Allah akbar, al-ḥamdu lillahi* and 'there is no might nor power except in God'.
> (Abu Dawud, Witr, bab 24; al-Tirmidhi, Daʿawat, bab 113)

The Prophet Muhammad's wife Safiya also reported:

> The Messenger of God entered while there were before me four thousand kernels which I used in reciting eulogies. I said: I use them in reciting eulogies. He answered: I will teach thee a still larger number. Say: 'Glory to God' according to the number of what he has created.
> (al-Tirmidhi, Daʿawat, bab 103)

Contemplating on Asma al-Husna—99 Names of Allah

Reflecting on the 99 Names of Allah is the most practised stage in *muraqabah*. For example, in many Sufi orders, like the Naqshbandi and Mevlevi orders, the disciples engage themselves in daily recitation of the word *Allah* 3,000 times. The hope is that the tongue of the heart engages itself only with Allah alone, emptying the mind and the heart from names other than Allah. In this respect, it would be helpful to highlight the theology of the 99 Names of Allah and its place in *muraqabah* practice in Islamic psychotherapy.

In her masterpiece work, *The Tao of Islam*, Sachiko Murata (1992) uses the primary works of no less than 48 Muslim sages, including original works attributed to the Shi'i Imams, Ibn Sina and Mulla Sadra, poetry from Hafiz, 'Attar, and Rumi, and various *'irfani* or Sufi works, such as those by Ibn al-'Arabi, to provide a comprehensive picture of Islamic theology and cosmology with respect to the Divine Names and Attributes, which are 99. Both Murata (1992) and Amini (1999) provide insights from spiritual psychology to help understand the earliest reflections on these 99 Names of Allah in the context of God, the cosmos, and human beings. In addition, Murata (1992) presents insight into the differences between the theological, or *kalam*, tradition and the spiritual tradition of Islam, and her stance is helpful to our discussion of the 99 Names of Allah in *muraqabah*.

In Islam's spiritual tradition, the image of God, as ibn 'Arabi observed, was a God who was distant, remote, and incomprehensible. However, as Murata (1992) demonstrated in her work using selections from spiritual masters in the Islamic tradition, God is a Higher Being, but also supremely lovable and caring. This love is mutual, as the divine love for His creation gives birth to love for the divine.

The spiritual tradition of Islam teaches that God's compassion and love for His creation are not remote and incomprehensible. Yes, some divine works invite us to reflect on mysteries that are, in general, visibly and clearly demonstrated in nature and the universe. The Qur'an and the Prophetic tradition suggest using the 99 Names of Allah as a means to grasp and understand God's love and compassion. For example, the Qur'an states, "Wherever you turn, there is the face of God" (2:115) and "We are nearer to man than the jugular vein" (50:16). These names *tashbih*, or "similar," can be observed in God's creation, specifically in human attributes.

In this respect, as Amini (1999) states:

> The universe is the manifestation of God's immeasurable creative power accompanied by His desire to reveal Himself. As mentioned in the prophetic tradition "I (God) was a Hidden Treasure longing to be known, so I created creation in order to be known" (Koran). Every being in its form (surat) and essence (ma'na) manifests God, regardless if she is conscious of being a Divine manifestation or not. In Islamic belief, a difference is made between the Divine Essence (dhat) and the Divine Attributes (sifat). The Divine Essence is what He alone knows of Himself. The

Divine Attributes are the Names (asma) of God manifested in creation or in the Holy Koran.

(pp. 50–51)

Understanding and reflecting on human attributes that include mixed feelings—joy, happiness, anger, and wrath—can help us understand God's names, including positive and negative feelings. Murata (1992) states:

> These names are frequently divided into two categories known as the names of mercy and wrath, or gentleness and severity, or beauty and majesty, or bounty and justice. The contrast between these two groups is constantly kept in view by our authors. When God establishes a relationship with creatures in terms of either group, specific results are found in the cosmos. In brief, names of beauty demand that God be near to creatures and that they feel intimacy (*uns*) with Him. Names of majesty demand that He be far from them and that they feel awe (*hayba*) of Him. The first category of names pertains more to the receptive or yin side, since they are connected with such "feminine" qualities as love, beauty, and compassion. In contrast, the second category pertains more to the dominating, controlling, and forceful side of things, the yang dimension. Both sides are essential to existence, and neither side can be completely separated from the other. Beauty has its majesty, and majesty has its beauty.
>
> Wrath is certainly merciful, while mercy may not always be free from wrath. A smaller mercy now may prevent a greater mercy later.
>
> (p. 56)

Categorizing the 99 Names into two groups, such as Divine Attributes of the Essence and Attributes of the Acts, Amini (1999) states that the "Attributes of the Essence are all the Names whose opposites are not pertinent to God" (p. 51). Furthermore, Amini gives examples to comprehend God's uniqueness. Let's take the example of God's name, *al-Hayy*, which can be translated as the Living, and *al-Guddus*, meaning the Holy. When we discuss these qualities and attributes in human life, Muslims believe that the 99 Names are manifested in human nature. Understanding and being mindful of these manifestations, or *tajalli*, are important as they are crucial to the path of spiritual transformation. In this respect, Rumi stated, "by their contrasts things are made clear" (Amini, 1999, p. 52). He also stated, "Behind every nothingness, the possibility of existence is concealed; in the midst of Wrath, Mercy is hidden like the priceless cornelian in the midst of dirt" (Amini, 1999, p. 52).

However, in the context of the 99 Names, "death" and "unholy" are simply not among God's attributes. In the Attributes of the Acts, God is indeed *al-Muhyi* (the Life-giver) and *al-Mumit* (the Slayer). Amini (1999) quotes Jalal ad-Din Rumi, who said, "The positive attributes signify God's kindness and compassion (lutf) and negative attributes indicate His wrath or harshness (gahr)" (p. 51).

Murata notes that Muslims who emphasize God's names with negative attributes, such as wrath, and constantly reference hell and punishment are like Muslim "Confucianists," who see God primarily as *yang*. However, those who focus more on God's love, compassion, and mercy and use examples from the Prophetic tradition, such as "God's mercy precedes His wrath," see God as primarily *yin*. In this respect, Amini (1999) quotes various Sufi masters who strongly believed that the whole universe, including humans, was created with love. For example, Shibli (d. 945) stated that:

> an individual's love for God has two sources: God's love was imprinted on us before we were born, in pre-eternity, and an individual loves God because she knows God. Shibli sees love as innate in all of us, but it must be awakened if the Sufi wishes to advance on the spiritual path.
>
> (Amini, 1999, p. 58)

Ibn 'Arabi also noted that "Divine love" (*hobb ilahi*) has two aspects: the longing of God for His creatures and the longing of the creatures for God, or the yearning of God Himself epiphanied in beings who want to return to Him. The being who longs with nostalgia is simultaneously the being towards whom God's nostalgia yearns. These two, man and God, are in fact one; they form a bi-unity, the unity of being, or *wahdat-e wujud*. The same longing is the basis on which the desire to return to God manifests (Amini, 1999, p. 58).

Murata's explanation helps us comprehend this further. She gives examples from God's names, such as Mighty, Inaccessible, Great, Majestic, Compeller, Creator, Proud, All-High, King, Wrathful, Avenger, Slayer, Depriver, and Harmer, stating that these names reflect *yang*, but divine names such as Beautiful, Near, Merciful, Compassionate, Loving, Gentle, Forgiving, Pardoner, Life-giver, Enricher, and Bestower, known as the "Names of Beauty" or "Gentleness" are *yin* (Murata, 1992, p. 55). However, *yin* and *yang* "can be seen as a replica of the Tao, with the two fundamental principles, *yin* and *yang*, harmoniously present" (Murata, 1992, p. 18). It is wrong to assume these two principles, or two different names, work against each other; instead, they work in harmony. In this respect, famous Sufi poet Rumi states, "Severity and gentleness were married, and a world of good and evil was born from the two" (Rumi, 1925–1940, II 2680, quoted in Chittick, 1983, p. 101).

Incorporating Dhikr, Music, and Physical Movement in Muraqabah

Reciting, reflecting on, and watching the vibrations and revelations of the divine names in *muraqabah* have many benefits. Again, I find Murata's reflection very powerful:

> A simple calculation of the number of divine names that occur in the Koran shows that the names that imply God's closeness to and concern for human beings, such as Merciful, Compassionate, Kind, Generous, and Forgiving, far outnumber names that speak of Him in terms of distance and transcendence. These names of proximity demand that God be concerned with the intimate details of everyday human life. God is "with you wherever you are" (57:4). He is "nearer to you than the jugular vein" (50:16). "Wherever you turn, there is the face of God" (2:115). Islamic spirituality has been concerned with this perspective from earliest times. Especially in texts that have to do with the intimate relationships between God and human beings—such as prayers and supplications—appeals to God's kindness, mercy, forgiveness, and generosity have always played a central role.
> (Murata, 1992, p. 53)

In *muraqabah*, as Ibn 'Arabi suggested, contemplating and reflecting on the 99 Names can only be achieved through a personal experience of God: "We can typify Him and take Him as an object of our contemplation, not only in our innermost hearts but also before our eyes and in our imagination, as though we saw Him" (Amini, 1999, p. 58).

Thus, in Islamic belief systems, the nature of God is usually not discussed[2]; however, it is important to remember that the four most fundamental relational qualities of God, particularly vis-a-vis humans, can be reflected in *muraqabah*. These qualities are: (1) creation, (2) sustenance, (3) guidance, and (4) judgement (Rahman, 1987, p. 12). In the context of these qualities, and as demonstrated before, Muslims believe that God shows unbounded, limitless mercy to His creations. From this perspective, the Qur'an denies chaos in the universe and in human life. Various verses in the Qur'an emphasize that the creation of the universe in balance (cosmos) is proof of God's primordial love (see Q. 31:20; 2:29; 45:12).[3]

In the light of this, it would be helpful to provide an example from the *Mathnawi* by Jalal al-Din al-Rumi (d. 1273) and summarize this discussion here:

> Moses saw a shepherd on the way, crying, 'O Lord who choosest as Thou wilt. Where art Thou that I may serve Thee and sew Thy clothes and kill Thy lice and bring milk to Thee, O worshipful one; That I may kiss Thy little hand and rub Thy little feet and sweep Thy little room at bed-time.' On hearing those foolish words, Moses said, 'Man, to whom are you

speaking? What babble! What blasphemy and raving! Stuff some cotton into your mouth! Truly the friendship of a fool is enmity, the High God is not in want of such like service!' The shepherd rent his garment, heaved a sigh, ad took his way to the wilderness. Then came to Moses a revelation: 'Thou hast parted my servant from Me. Wert thou sent as a Prophet to unite, or wert though sent to sever? I have bestowed on everyone a particular mode of worship; I have given everyone a peculiar form of expression. The idiom of Hindustan is excellent for Hindus, the idiom of Sind is excellent for the people of Sind'.

(Rahman, 1987, p. 32)

> Say, "I seek refuge with the Lord of people, the Controller a of people, the God of people, against the harm of the slinking whisperer—who whispers into the hearts of people—6 whether they be jinn or people."
>
> (Q. 114:1–6)

The following verses by famous Muslim thinker and poet Muhammad Iqbal (1875–1938) also resonate very well with our understanding of God:

You created the night and I created the lamp.
You produced the clay and I fashioned the drinking cap.
You made jungles, meadows, and hills,
And I turned them into flower-beds, lawns, and gardens.[4]

In *muraqabah*, the disciple is supposed to contemplate the divine attributes:

in such a way that the existence of all things disappears and only Allah remains in the mind. When one is able to hold on to the thought, forgetting the self in such a way, attaining the state of annihilation (fana) for a given time.

(Husain & Hasan, 2021, p. 132)

Physical Movements in *Muraqabah*

When performing *muraqabah*, especially reciting *dhikr*, the follower may stay still, lean to the right and left, or turn their head from right to left. In some Sufi orders, the followers may also move or dance in circles, kneel, or stand motionless.

Incorporating Dhikr, Music, and Physical Movement in Muraqabah

A few writers in the field of psychotherapy explored spiritual dance and movement practices that could benefit Muslim clients. Harel et al. (2021) have studied integrating Sufi whirling practices in psychotherapy with the intention to:

> gain a vicarious empirical understanding of Sufi whirling dervishes' (SWDs') experiences during the spiritual ritual of whirling to benefit understanding the experience of clients expressing themselves through free whirling and to improve the cultural competence of dance movement therapists and psychotherapists working with Muslim Sufi clients.
>
> (p. 1)

They also identified certain physical benefits of Sufi whirling, such as:

- expanding our "understanding of phenomena such as psychic experiences or morbidities such as vestibular disorders that have been linked with psychiatric disorders" (Eckhardt-Henn et al., 2008; Nizamie et al., 2013, as cited in Harel et al., 2021, p. 2);
- "focusing the mind in a present-centered awareness, focusing on breath, witnessing the self in an accepting and compassionate way, physical discomfort, and the mystical experience" (Lewis, 2014, as cited in Harel et al., 2021, p. 2);
- using meditation as a holistic practice to improve "attention, sensitive awareness, concentration, and mindfulness" because such techniques "include active/dynamic meditations, in which the body is in an active posture with different goals (e.g., self-regulation, harmony with nature, self-transcendence, higher states of consciousness, and the experience of God)" (Iqbal et al., 2016; Kabat-Zinn et al., 1986, as cited in Harel et al., 2021, p. 2);
- encouraging "altruistic behaviors, such as prosociality, greater levels of generosity, empathic arousal, and social bonding, have been found in highly stressful rituals that evoke powerful emotions, especially those with empathic experiences of pain" (Xygalatas et al., 2011, 2013, as cited in Harel et al., 2021, p. 2).

Wolf (2006) gives an example of the ceremony of the Madho Lal Husain:

> In his passion (jazbah), the dancer raised his out-stretched arms and slowly whirled, his hair billowing out. Facing the burning chiraghdān, he crouched low to the ground and shook his head right and left, synchronizing his shallow footsteps and the vertical movements of his bent forearms with the drum pattern's duple meter. A break. Then, facing the drummers, his back briefly to the flame, he swirled his hair,

which seemed to propel his torso around. His feet followed with tiny steps, tracing narrow circles. A dhol player followed suit, spinning with increased intensity and velocity, his heavy drum visibly tugging at his neck; he did not miss a single beat… These forms of musical and kinesthetic synchronicity, coming together, are critically valued from the artistic perspective of some participants.

(p. 251)

The body movements in Islamic spiritual practices have a deep meaning, and such bodily practices integrated with spiritual and philosophical themes are common in many Muslim countries. For example:

When Panjabi drummers spin while playing, they may reinforce the Sufi theme of cyclicity and, more importantly, achieve transcendence in a manner consistent with the process of reciting dhikrs. Such virtuosity has the potential to resonate with poetic images when contextualized in a Sufi setting such as the 'urs of Madho Lal Husain…

(Wolf, 2006, p. 252)

The benefits of dance movements in psychotherapy have also been recorded in multiple research studies. Jung (1935), for example, stated that the body is essentially a manifestation of the mysterious force that creates both the psyche and the body. The distinction we make between the psyche and the body is superficial and aimed at aiding understanding them better. In reality, there is only a living body; the psyche and body are intricately connected. They are essentially one and the same, both embodying a living essence (Sassenfeld, 2008, p. 6).

In psychotherapy, there is also a psychotherapeutic modality based on dance called Dance Movement Psychotherapy (DMP). DMP is "the psychotherapeutic use of movement to promote emotional, social, cognitive, and physical integration of the individual" (American Dance Therapy Association, 2020). In general, DMP has benefited from verbal, somatic, and creative arts therapies, but integrates psychotherapeutic concepts in a uniquely enactive way (Streater, 2022). Different DMPs aim to release negative thoughts and emotions through body movements. Sharon J. Mijares (2022) notes:

The psyche travels through the depths of our bodies meeting, becoming entrapped by, and being freed from the inner and outer obstacles blocking the path to the jewel—authenticity of self. Our bodies are engaged in this journey. If we ignore hidden ego-states, sub-personalities, and archetypal forces, we fail to grow.

(p. 353)

Incorporating Dhikr, Music, and Physical Movement in Muraqabah   113

DMPs have been effective in treating substance abuse (Day, 2023), somatic disorders (Mijares, 2022), behavioural problems in children (Moschos & Pollatou, 2022; Mochos et al., 2023), trauma (Streater, 2022), increasing social functioning (Veid et al., 2023), and helping clients with intellectual disabilities (Dawson et al., 1998; Takahashi & Kato, 2023). Different movements and techniques, such as "circle dances, improvisation, performance, drumming, gestural exploration, imagery work, movement analysis, education, teaching and learning" (Streater, 2022, p. 44), are used in DMP to observe and assess feelings through breathing and sensing.

Questions for Discussion

1 Discuss the elements of *muraqabah* practice in Islamic psychotherapy. What would you consider the most helpful or controversial?
2 Choose a challenging experience and think about it using some *muraqabah* elements.
    How did you feel? Did you feel compassion and kindness to yourself? If yes, can you use it in a clinical context? If not, discuss the internal construction of emotions.
3 Discuss skills and knowledge base in using *muraqabah* in Islamic psychotherapy.

Notes

1 Some researchers reported the influence of Sufi practices, including *dhikr* and breathing during the *dhikr*, on other non-Muslim religious/spiritual traditions. In his book titled *Western Sufism: From the Abbasids to the New Age* (Oxford University Press), Mark Sedgwick (2016) talks about the Jewish Sufis in Egypt. Feldman (2019) also talks about the Sufi practices among the followers of Shabbtai Tzvi in Ottoman Salonica, who converted from Judaism to Islam during the 1680s and renamed themselves as Ma'aminim, which literally meant faithful, and were later known as the Dönme (those who converted). Feldman describes how they implemented *dhikr* in their ritual singings. It was a very natural and organic addition during this time period in the Ottoman Empire, when *ilahi* (a devotional hymn glorifying the divine) singing was part of religious and spiritual gatherings. Ma'aminim also kept a strong linkage to their Sabbatian tradition and messianic theology, and gradually created a hybrid faith and practice unique to their context. In this respect, they appropriated the important *dhikr* ritual along with other Sufi practices and ideas. Overall, since the late 1700s, the spiritual leaders of Ma'aminim compiled more than 100 devotional songs written in Judeo-Spanish (Ladino) combined with Hebrew, Aramaic, and Ottoman-Turkish. Most of these devotional songs were compiled in five manuscripts. The common *dhikr* in these devotional songs were "La Ilaha Illa Hu" (there is no God but Hu) and *Illallah Hu'* (there is no Allah but Hu, meaning that Allah is Hu). According to Feldman (2019), Ma'aminim appropriated the component Hu as a common name of God because it was also

accepted as a sacred name in the Sabbatian tradition which consisted of the Hebrew letters hei (ה), vav (ו), and alef (א). The Psalms (150:6) also states: "let everything that has breath praise Yah, praise Yah" (Psalms 150:6). According to Feldman (2019), "The word 'Yah' in Hebrew is a name of God, while in the Ottoman Turkish used in the Sufi *dhikr* phrases, 'ya' is an interjection (translated above as 'Oh'). In combining the biblical verse with the Sufi phrase, the poet is able to integrate the Jewish meaning of the word 'Yah' with the interjection 'ya' of the Muslim tradition in a remarkable way…" (p. 48). In general, Ma'aminim followed certain Sufi physical movements. such as breathing techniques, with the purpose of attaining an ecstatic state. Feldman (2019) states, "We see that the Islamic verse became part of the Sabbatian text without any changes, and combined with the following Hebrew words creates a parallelism between the divine Muslim name Allah and the Jewish divine name 'Adonai.' In the fourth line we can see another parallelism between Islamic and Jewish divine names, the Muslim Rabbena (ربّنا), in Ottoman Turkish, from Arabic: 'our Lord', and the Jewish 'Yah'" (p. 48). Boas Huss also noted that Islamic and Jewish mysticism influenced each other in many ways. For example, he stated that "Apart from the shared philosophic sources of Sufism and Kabbalah, and the acquaintance of Kabbalist with Sufi-inspired Jewish texts, and possibly with some Muslim Sufi writings, there were a few cases of direct encounters between Jewish Kabbalists and Muslim Sufis. Evidence of an acquaintance with Sufi doctrines and practices is found in the book Sharei Tzedek (The Portals of Justice) that was written in the land of Israel in the late thirteenth century, probably by Nathan ben Saadiah Harar, a disciple of Abraham Abulafia (1240–1291)" (p. 252). In medieval Muslim Spain, there were some famous Jewish sages such as Juda Halevi of Toledo, Moses ben Ezra of Granada, Josef ben Zadiq of Cordoba, Samuel ben Tibbon, and Simtob ben Falaquera who attended the Spanish Sufi schools (Shah, 1980, p. 37). Some researchers also noted the increasing interest in Sufism in the Roman Catholic Church (for details, see Cyprian Rice's (1969) work on the Persian Sufis). Rice was R.A. Nicholson's student. Nevertheless, Christian spiritual concepts also influenced Sufism, as some Muslim Sufis had relations with the Syrian monks who were documented by Adalbert Max, Arend Jan Wensinck, Margaret Smith, and Tor Andrae (Schimmel, 1975, p. 10).

2 We should note here that there is a general exception in the *kalam* (dialectical, discursive) tradition of Islam, where the nature of God is extensively discussed, even in the context of other faith traditions. It is generally accepted that God is the very basis of the Qur'an's entire doctrinal teachings; therefore, a detailed discourse should be provided to bring clarity to some questions and doubts. As a theological school known as supporters of rationalism and free will, the Mu'tazila put an extreme emphasis on human choice and freedom, natural reason, and justice that leaves no flexibility, because humans "are responsible for their actions, wherein God plays no role" (Rahman, 1987, p. 5). The Ash 'ari school, contrary to Mu'tazila, supports the ideas of absolute will and power of God, God as the decision-maker, no objective moral law, and that humans can acquire God's compassion and mercy. Sufism, the mystical tradition of Islam, however, started "as a reaction to the development of general worldliness in the Muslim community" and emphasized the inner life of the human being, with the "tendency of the soul," ecstatic ideal of love of God, seeking union with God, and tolerance (Rahman, 1987, p. 6).

3 It is no surprise that these verses awakened Muslims' interest in science. They were used by Muslim reformists in the 19th and 20th centuries to reawaken this

spirit. Nevertheless, the Qur'an also asserts a belief in miracles. Many stories of the prophets in the Qur'an point to the miraculous, mysterious nature of creation. However, the Qur'an also emphasizes that miracles should not be understood outside of their context. For example, when the Meccan disbelievers challenged the Prophet Muhammad to show miracles, God answered that the Qur'an is the greatest miracle; the miracles of the previous prophets "were never effective against disbelievers, so there would be no more of them, Qur'an, 17, 50" (Rahman, 1987, p. 12).

4 In some versions: You created the forest, the mountain, and the desert; I made the walk, the garden, the orchard. See Muhammad Iqbal, Kulliyyat (Collection of Persian Poems) (Lahore, n.d., 284).

Conclusion

Times have changed, and how we see and implement tradition in almost all aspects of life has changed with them. How Muslims engage with these changes and their effect on mental and spiritual health is subject to deep reflection and study; however, we definitely see a profound need and yearning for connecting to the divine in our health care by implementing the Islamic tradition. In terms of mindfulness, Islamic tradition is rich in many kinds of meditative practices. Cultural traditions have also shaped and formed most of these meditative practices. Among these meditative practices, *muraqabah* is rich and deeply rooted in Islam's spiritual mystic tradition, Sufism. There are various *muraqabah* practices, and each has been shaped by great Sufi masters, all of whom linked the *muraqabah* tradition to the prophetic tradition. Most of these mindfulness practices come in visual, auditory, or kinaesthetic styles, but sometimes they integrate all of them.

There is one truth: we are at the earliest stages of development in our understanding and implementation of *muraqabah* in health care. One important question from our inquiry into *muraqabah* and psychotherapy is how to proceed from here. What is the next step and direction? Second, when we reviewed Islamic mindfulness's historical narratives and contemporary applications, the question of their potential therapeutic effects arose. Of course, as can be discerned from Islamic psychotherapy literature, these practices can have many benefits; however, we need evidence-based research to find the best practices for implementing *muraqabah*. It is encouraging and inspiring to see how many Muslim psychiatrists, psychologists, psychotherapists, and others are deeply interested in and care about studying the effectiveness of *muraqabah* in Islamic psychotherapy.

As we know, in the past, as an Islamic mindfulness practice, *muraqabah* was recommended for spiritual purposes. The research being done by inspiring Muslim researchers and therapists, however, shows that *muraqabah* has many other benefits. For example, it is becoming a valuable tool in treating mental and emotional disturbances such as severe depression, anxiety, bipolar disorder, personality disorders, and attention-deficit disorders.

First, *muraqabah* can help with stress relief and relaxation. In this area, we need evidence-based research. Similarly, like the benefits of mindfulness in other areas, *muraqabah* also goes beyond simple relaxation. In some studies, the physical benefits of *muraqabah*, such as control of blood pressure, increase in life expectancy, improvement of vision, reduction of fat in the blood, improvement in the performance of the heart, increased immunity, growth of red blood corpuscles, and end of insomnia, have been reported (Azeemi, 2005, pp. 84–85). We also need evidence-based research in this direction. In general, *muraqabah* is a crucial technique to providing a framework for body-spirit-mind awareness. The therapist aims to teach the client how to practise it in daily healing. Like the traditional Sufi masters, the therapist chooses various techniques from the Islamic tradition, including *dhikr* texts, to reflect the mental, emotional, physical, and spiritual situation of a person. The therapist should keep in mind that the client may be "in a state of struggle against sources of uncertainty, instability and insecurity and reinforces the view that believers gain a sense of meaning, coherence and purpose from spirituality" (Hussein, 2018, p. 35). By learning how to practise it properly and accurately, the client may achieve psychological equilibrium. Like other mindfulness techniques, *muraqabah* also has the potential to produce a state of calmness. In this respect, it can alter states of consciousness; however, the ultimate purpose of *muraqabah* is to intensify the state of communion with the sacred.

There are also questions about whether *muraqabah* can be applied in a non-Muslim context. As we, and many Sufi writers, have noted, there are many benefits to Islamic meditation and contemplation. In the Western world, almost everyone is familiar with the teachings of Rumi, whose work is profoundly based on Islamic mysticism. As we have demonstrated in this book, his poetry is also used in *muraqabah* practices. This gives us a basis on which to claim that the concepts and practices in classical Sufi psychology have universal value and can easily be adapted to the challenges of clinical settings. This also applies to *muraqabah* practices. Therefore, the concept of *muraqabah* can be incorporated into mindfulness-based therapy with Muslim and non-Muslim clients, but with caution to avoid proselytization. In addition, more research is required to enhance evidence-based *muraqabah* in Islamic psychotherapy practice. The limited research we already have in this area demonstrates how the concept of *muraqaba* can be a source of inspiration for both Muslim and non-Muslim therapists.

Finally, as Pargament (2007) writes:

> Before any kind of treatment can be formally evaluated, it must be clearly articulated so practitioners can be trained in the method, so the method

itself can be implemented with a reasonable degree of standardization, and so others can replicate the findings of evaluative studies.

(p. 320)

Following his train of thought, it is important to highlight the importance of appropriate therapist training before applying *muraqabah*. This kind of training is embodied in both theological *and* psychological training.

The ethics of *muraqabah*, first and foremost, require respect for tradition. Similarly, to differentiate existing mindfulness practices from the doctrinal framework of traditional Buddhist mindfulness, some Sufi practices may not be separated from the Islamic mystical tradition. In this regard, Buehler (2016) notes that many modern observers attending this ritual in Turkey, often tourists, may not grasp the depth of the worship that once characterized it before it evolved into a popular tourist attraction. They simply purchase tickets and settle in to watch. Following the teachings of Mevlevi instructor Kabir Helminski, the whirling ritual, which involves turning towards God, is described as a way to honour and show respect for our connection with the Divine. It serves as a moving form of meditation, more demanding than traditional meditation since losing focus or presence can disrupt the turning's balance.

In past and contemporary Sufi schools, classical Sufi orders encouraged practicing *muraqabah* under the direct leadership of a *sheikh*. This was necessary to avoid not only spiritual misguidance, but also the improper application of *muraqabah*. Sufi masters who were trained in Islamic psychology were also skilled at managing unpredictable, unhealthy experiences such as *waswasa* (i.e., whispers, obsessions, etc.) and disturbing or frightening experiences. This example informs us that Muslim therapists should also watch over and guide the client to apply *muraqabah* ethically and properly. They should also be knowledgeable and skilled in managing negative feelings such as anger and resentment, or hallucinations. Therefore, Muslim therapists who want to integrate *muraqabah* practice in therapy should be adequately trained in Islamic studies such as the Qur'an, the history of Sufism, and Sufi psychology. Training in mindfulness-based therapies will also enrich their vision and experience. Thus, with proper training in classical Sufi psychology and one of the aforementioned mindfulness-based therapies, therapists can help their clients develop self-awareness, loving-kindness, compassion, and empathy in their healing journey.

Glossary of Key Terms

'aql. An Islamic term for intellect or "id." Theologically, it is a concept referring to natural human knowledge in Islamic. it is also associated with using reason as a source for Shari'ah.

al-tibb al-ruhani. In Islamic philosophy, it means the healing of the "spirit," or "spiritual health."

Bimaristan. Hospitals.

Caliph (khalifa). A representative or successor; the title adopted by the rulers of the Islamic community indicating that, as successors of Muhammad, they were both spiritual and temporal leaders. After the destruction of the Abbasid caliphate in 1258, the title was held by various rulers, including the Ottoman sultans. The office is referred to as the caliphate or khilafat.

Chakras. The "force centres" or whorls of energy on the physical body. Seven major chakras or energy centres are believed to exist, located within the subtle body.

Dawah. An Arabic word which denotes preaching of Islam. It means literally "issuing a summons" or "making an invitation."

Dervish. A Sufi Muslim who follows an ascetic path and known known for their extreme poverty and austerity. In Christianity, they are similar to mendicant friars or Hindu/Buddhist/Jain sadhus. Dervishes also practised wisdom, medicine, poetry, enlightenment, and witticisms.

Du'ah. Prayers of supplication for use in a range of situations.

Fard. An Islamic term which denotes a religious duty. In Persian, Turkish, and Urdu, it is pronounced as *farz*.

Fiqh. Islamic jurisprudence, or the science of interpreting the Shariat (q.v.). There are four orthodox schools: Hanafi, Hanbali, Maliki, and Shafii. The sources of fiqh are the Quran, hadith, ijma, and qiyas.

Fitrah. An Islamic term to express a human nature.

Fusion of horizons. Gadamer used it as a dialectical concept which results from the rejection of two alternatives. He defined the concept of "situation" by saying that it represents a standpoint that limits the possibility of vision.

Hadeeth. Sayings or reported actions of Muhammad that is not found in the Quran, but that is accepted as a source of fiqh.
Hajj. Annual pilgrimage made to Mecca; every Muslim is supposed to make the journey at least once in a lifetime.
Ihsan. An Arabic term meaning "perfection" or "excellence." As a concept, it means to obtain perfection, or excellence, in worship, such that Muslims try to worship God as if they see Him, or have a strong faith that He is constantly watching over them.
Ilm al-Nafsiat. The science of the nafs ("self"or "psyche") which flowered during the Islamic golden age (8th–15th centuries).
Irada. In Arabic, it is both a verb and a noun. As a verb, it means to choose between two things, to desire. As a noun, it means the "mental power" or "will."
Imam. A leader of the Islamic community. Among the Shias (q.v.), the descendants of Ali.
Iman. An Islamic term usually translated as "belief" or "faith." In Sunni Islam, the fundamentals of the Iman are: belief in One God, Angels, Prophets (including Adam, Abraham, Noah, Moses, Jacob, David, Solomon, and so on all the way until Jesus and Muhammad), Scriptures (the Torah, the Psalms, the Gospels, and the Qur'an), the day of Judgement and the Akhirah or afterlife, and Predestination. Shias also believe in the Imamate (a *divine* institution which succeeded the institution of Prophethood).
Khanqahs. A building designed specifically for gatherings of Sufi gatherings and is a place for spiritual retreat and character reformation.
Living human document. Andon Boisen considered suffering souls as the "living human documents" of theology. He taught that as we read the sacred texts and interpret them, the humans are also sacred texts and we need to read and interpret them.
Muraqabah. A Sufi word for meditation and means "to watch over," "to take care of," or "to keep an eye."
Mushrik. In Islamic theology, it is someone who commits shirk, or ascribes partners to Allah by his polytheistic beliefs or idolatrous practices.
Nasihah. Sincere advice.
Praxis. A process by which a theory, lesson, or skill is enacted or practised, embodied, and/or realized. It is a practical and applied knowledge to one's actions.
Pir. A title for a Sufi master.
Rifq. An Arabic word for "gentleness."
Shari'ah. The law of Islam, comprising all the rules that govern life.
Shaykh. In Arabic, it means an "old man." A term used for a Sufi who guides disciples. A Sufi who is authorized to teach, initiate, and guide aspiring dervishes. Also used to denote a head of the caste or class tribal Muslims.

Sunni. The Muslim sect that asserts the leadership of Islam must be elected.

Shia. The Muslim sect that asserts the leadership of Islam is hereditary in the descendants of Ali, the son-in-law of the Prophet. It is the dominant group in Iran, Azerbaijan, and is well represented in India.

Sufi. An Islamic mystic. Sufism, with its emphasis on the possibility of unity with the divine, was of special importance in winning converts to Islam in India.

Sadaqa. An Islamic term that means "voluntary charity."

Sunnah. An Arabic word that means habits or usual practices of Prophet Muhammad.

Tafakkur. In Islam the main practice of tafakkur is through recitation of the divine Names.

Tadabbur. An intellectual process to seek an explanation to the questions or problems in the world.

Tajweed. The word "tajweed" means to improve, make better. Tajweed of the Holy Qur'an is the knowledge and application of the rules of recitation so that the person recites every letter correctly, i.e., from its proper origin of pronunciation.

Taqwah. Arabic word which means "to guard against, preserve, shield, and prevent." In Islamic theology, it means "the fear of God" or "God-consciousness" and guarding against those things which bring Allah's displeasure.

Taraweeh. In Arabic, it literally means "to rest." In Islam, it is the special prayer performed during the Ramadan.

Tawhid. A theological term that refers to the oneness of God.

Tazkiat al-nafs. In Sufi practice, it is the purification of the soul from inclination towards evils and sins.

The Qur'an. For Muslims, the final Word of God. The fundamental source of *fiqh* and all rules governing human relationships.

Appendix
Overview of Sample *Muraqabah* Practices before Individual, Couple, or Group Sessions

These short, sample *muraqabah* exercises can be used as a preparatory stage for Islamic psychotherapy sessions. These sample meditations can be done in individual or group sessions, alone and/or silently. The purpose behind them is to help the client notice the breath and let go of all worrying or non-worrying thoughts in order to clear the mind. The benefit of such preparation is that it helps create space for connection, attachment, mindfulness against detachment and disconnection before the "talk therapy."

Session 1: Introduction to *Muraqabah*

This practice aims to introduce you to muraqabah.
  Practice:
  Sit in a comfortable position.
  Depending on your preferences, you can either open or close your eyes.
  Say slowly *Auzubillah minashaitan nirajeem*, or "I seek refuge in Allah from the outcast Shaitan."
  Slowly, say *Bismillahir Rahmanir Rahim*, or "In the name of God, the Lord of Mercy, the Giver of Mercy!"
  Consider yourself in God's presence.
  Focus your attention on your breathing.
  Take a deep breath in and out: Hoo!

Consider visualizing your *qalb* two fingers below your left breast. Its colour is red.
Visualize your *ruh* two fingers below your right breast. Its colour is white.
Visualize your *nafs* beneath your navel. Its colour is yellow.
Imagine your conscience, which we call *sirr*, at the centre of your breast. Its colour is green.
Visualize mystery, or *khafi*, above your eyebrows. Its colour is blue.
Visualize arcanum, or *akhfa*, at the top of your brain. Its colour is black.

Appendix: Overview of Sample Muraqabah Practices

Now, let's reflect together on the importance of emptying our minds. If we want to feel peace, joy, and happiness, we need to learn how to empty "the contents of our minds."
Let's read the following:

> If we want to attain peace of mind, we must know what *Muraqabah* is. Until we experience and observe the movement of mind within us from moment to moment, we will never understand the beauty of *Muraqabah*. When there is inner silence, then there is the possibility of contacting which is eternal and the essence of reality.
> (Husain & Hasan, 2021, p. 134)

Visualize that your heart and your mind are empty from worries and stress.

Your thoughts have left it for a moment.
Your emotions have left it for a moment.

If you have difficulty emptying your mind and your heart, reflect on where your obstacles to happiness and joy come from.

What are the inner conflicts, regrets, and frustrations?
Watch them. Observe them calmly. Let them go.

Reflect on what can quiet your mind.

Think about how you can learn not to define yourself with material things. Free your mind from all earthly things that give you suffering.

Observe your thoughts.

See your thoughts.
Allow your mind to be unconditioned and unburdened.
Let it be quiet and still.

Open your mind to the divine.

Let the true thoughts come in.
Let the positive emotions come in.

Repeat this verse from the Qur'an: "God is always watching over you" (Q. 4:1).

Take a deep breath in and out: *Hoo!*
Repeat five times.

Session 2: Spiritual Purification

The purpose of this practice is to introduce you to spiritual purification.
Practice:
Sit in a comfortable position.

Depending on your preferences, you can either open or close your eyes.

Say slowly *Auzubillah minashaitan nirajeem*, or "I seek refuge in Allah from the outcast Shaitan."
Slowly, say, *Bismillahir Rahmanir Rahim*, or "In the name of God, the Lord of Mercy, the Giver of Mercy!"
Consider yourself in God's presence.
Focus your attention on your breathing.
Now let's reflect together on the importance of preparation for spiritual purification using the story of Yusuf in the Qur'an.

> We tell you [Prophet] the best of stories in revealing this Qur'an to you. Before this you were one of those who knew nothing about them. Joseph said to his father, 'Father, I dreamed of eleven stars and the sun and the moon: I saw them all bow down before me,' and he replied, 'My son, tell your brothers nothing of this dream, or they may plot to harm you—Satan is man's sworn enemy. This is about how your Lord will choose you, teach you to interpret dreams, and perfect His blessing on you and the House of Jacob, just as He perfected it earlier on your forefathers Abraham and Isaac: your Lord is all knowing and wise.' There are lessons in the story of Joseph and his brothers for all who seek them.
>
> (Q. 12:3–7)

While your eyes remain closed, start reflecting on the trials of Jacob/Ya'qub and Yusuf's suffering. Remember that Ya'qub, Yusuf's father, was:

> subjected to the loss of two sons, and is treated as a fool for his visionary insight; and it is reflected in the ordeal of Yusuf himself, a child left to die in the desert by his envious brothers, rescued by a caravan

but then sold as a slave, again rescued and adopted by a noble of the king of Egypt, but then thrown in jail because of the false accusation of the courtier's wife, who desires him, and whom he desired but renounced to honor the law of his God; all the way to the promise, contained in the final disclosure of the unfathomable logic of the events, when a forgiving and thankful Yusuf is reunited with his father and brothers: "But at last—when those apostles had lost all hope and saw themselves branded as liars, our succor attained to them. (...) Indeed, in the stories [of these men] there is a lesson ("sign," 'ibra) for those who are endowed with insight (12:110–11)..."

(Pandolfo, 2018, p. 15)

Now let's reflect on:

... the "best of stories" is the story of the soul in its journey, whose nature is to be moved by desire, at once the signature of its carnal, violent, and vulnerable character and the imprint of its origin and final destination in God. Such is the desire of the courtier's wife (who remains unnamed in the Qur'an, but elsewhere is known as Zulikha), 43 who, as the poet Jami (d. 1492) suggested, should be read as an allegory of the nafs itself. It is a parable of the trials of the soul and its purification (tazkiya), as a result of the trials and battles of the embodied nafs and its passions. The erotic desire of Yusuf and Zulikha and the envy and greed of Yusuf's brothers are figures of the passions of the soul, the very ground on which the soul and the self can transform and learn to recognize the "signs" that can be a guidance in the world.

(Pandolfo, 2018, p. 16)

Take a deep breath in and out: *Hoo!*
Repeat five times.

Session 3: Introduction to Breathing Exercise

The purpose of this practice is to introduce you to nafas and its role in our survival, and to develop an appreciation for it.
  Practice:
Sit in a comfortable position.

Depending on your preferences, you can either open or close your eyes.

Say slowly *Auzubillah minashaitan nirajeem*, or "I seek refuge in Allah from the outcast Shaitan."

Slowly, say, *Bismillahir Rahmanir Rahim*, or "In the name of God, the Lord of Mercy, the Giver of Mercy!"
Consider yourself in God's presence.
Focus your attention on your breathing.
Let's reflect on what Azeemi (2005) said about breathing:

> In the emotional ups and downs and the overall nervous system, breathing has an essential role. During different emotional states, the rate of respiration fluctuates. In tragic circumstances, breathing could become a challenge as people often feel difficulty breathing after hearing the sad news. On the other hand, during anger, the rate goes up.
>
> During peaceful moments the style of breathing becomes different. During this state, breathing becomes balanced, and its rate goes down. However, when something suddenly comes as a shock, then we all simply gasp for air. Spiritual abilities and breathing are closely interrelated. According to Sufism, breath has two sides, ascending and descending, Inhaling is ascending movement while exhaling is descending.
>
> During ascending, our soul becomes closer to the spiritual state and, in the descending mode, moves towards the gravity. We are closer to our spiritual state when the inhaling is prolonged, and the breath is retained longer than usual. When respiration stops, then our link to the body is disconnected. That is why to enter he sub-consciousness senses, breathing does not have to be stopped, but is must be slowed down.
>
> (p. 61)

Now take another deep breath, in and out.

Consider visualizing your *qalb* two fingers below your left breast. Its colour is red.
Visualize your *ruh* two fingers below your right breast. Its colour is white.

Take another deep breath in and out.

Notice how your body becomes still.

Feel how your breath enters through your nose, then fills your chest and abdomen.

If you want, you can put your hand on your chest.
Remember, the Qur'an often locates the locus of change in our chest. In Arabic, the chest means "*sadr*," or *sudur* (plural), which the Qur'an mentions 44 times. The etymological root of the word *sadr* means "a beginning; to proceed or emerge from something."

Concentrate on how our chest is considered the seat of all ranges of emotions, feelings, and divine inspirations.

There is another word in the Qur'an that also means heart, which is *qalb*. However, *qalb* is considered the seat of human awareness of the divine and creative spirit, *ruh*. It is indeed in our chest, *sadr*, that transcendental transformation or purification begins.

Notice any *dayyiq* (tightness), *haraj* (oppressive burden or blindness), or transgression.
Notice how your mind becomes reactive. Allow yourself to focus back to your breath.

Remember what Moses asked God: *O my Lord, open up for me my heart!* (Q. 20:25).

Each time you breathe in and breathe out, say *Alhamdulillah* (Praise God), or simply say "Thank you, Allah."

A famous Sufi mystic Ibn 'Arabi also refers to *sadr* as the place where *ayat* or God's clear signs descend: *It (the revelation) is clear Signs in the hearts of those who have been given (divine) knowing...* (Q. 29:49).

Read Sura *Inshhirah* in Arabic if you can. If not, then read it in English:

> In the Name of God, the All-Compassionate, the All-Merciful
> Did We not open up for you your chest, [1]
> and lift off from you your burden
> which weighed down your back,
> and raise up for you your Remembrance?
> For surely with difficulty is ease;
> surely with difficulty is ease.
> So when you have finished, exert yourself to the utmost,
> and strive (only) to please your Lord.
>   (Q. 94)

Ibn 'Arabi says:

> Whatever depth there may be in the sea,
> the shore of the Heart is deeper!
> And if your Heart should be constricted from (knowing) Me,
> then the Heart of someone other than you is even tighter.
> Forget the ego-self (nafs) and accept

from a truthful One who speaks truthfully.
And don't oppose/diverge (from Me), lest you be pained:
for the Heart is suspended from Me.
Open It, and I will release it [iftahu, ashrahu], and do
that activity you've already realized!
Until when, O you of the hardened heart,
(will you keep) that heart of yours locked up?!

(cited by Morris, n.d.)

Notice any sensations or smells that accompany the breathing.

Feel a liberation that opens up our potential for illumination, compassion, and spiritual growth.

Take a deep breath in and out: *Hoo!*

Session 4: Introduction to '*Aql*

This practice introduces you to the role of 'aql.
Practice:
Sit in a comfortable position.

Say slowly *Auzubillah minashaitan nirajeem*, or "I seek refuge in Allah from the outcast Shaitan."

Slowly, say, *Bismillahir Rahmanir Rahim*, or "In the name of God, the Lord of Mercy, the Giver of Mercy!"

Let's reflect on breathing:

Exhale from both nostrils so that the lungs are free from air.
Slowly inhale through the nostrils.
When the lungs become full, exhale through the mouth without holding it in.
While exhaling, keep your lips round as if whistling.

> This exhaling and inhaling constitute one cycle. In the beginning, start with 11 cycles and gradually go up to 21. This exercise helps in controlling the muscles required for breathing, and it increases the duration of inhalation.
>
> The rate of respiration during meditation should be as low as possible; however, the rate of breathing must not be slowed intentionally. Otherwise, the focus would shift to breathing instead of meditation. The best way to avoid that is to inhale and exhale slowly for a while before starting meditation. That way, the respiratory rate will drop automatically (Azeemi, 2005, pp. 61–62).

Take a deep breath in and out: *Hoo!*

Say *Auzubillah minashaitan nirajeem*,[1] or "I seek refuge in Allah from the outcast Shaitan."

Slowly, say, *Bismillahir Rahmanir Rahim*, or "In the name of God, the Lord of Mercy, the Giver of Mercy!"

Now, close your eyes and think of your prefrontal cortex (PFC) as Allah's creation.

Remember that it is where we can find our *'aql*. Our PFC helps us to plan, organize, regulate our attention, make decisions, moderate and correct our behaviour, get motivation, and regulate our mood.

Observe the *'aql* located in your PFC and how it conducts your brain and its activities.

Challenge your PFC and observe the reactions of your *'aql*.

For example, you might feel angry, anxious, or sad when you make these challenges. Your PFC might lose control of the limbic system. Let the emotions come, but remember, your *'aql* still has the ability to control them.

Observe them again, and know that it is up to you to take care of your PFC, so it better controls such challenges.

Now focus on the role of the amygdala.

Say *Audhu Bismillah*.

Focus on your amygdala as Allah's creation.

You have heard of the body's Fight, Flight, and Freeze responses. It is the amygdala's role to trigger these responses.

Pay attention to the shape, location, and function of the amygdala.

Reflect on Allah's purpose in creating the amygdala.

Focus on the amygdala as your body's security guard.

It was created to alarm you and keep you safe. When the amygdala is out of control, what has Allah given us to calm it? Take a deep breath, in and out, to calm the amygdala.

Say *Athkuruni, athkurkum*... (Q. 40:60).

When you say *Athkuruni*, take a deep breath in and release as you slowly say *athkurkum*.

Now focus on the role of the insula.

Say slowly *Auzubillah minashaitan nirajeem*, or "I seek refuge in Allah from the outcast Shaitan."

Slowly, say, *Bismillahir Rahmanir Rahim*, or "In the name of God, the Lord of Mercy, the Giver of Mercy!"

Allah created your insula so you could have a subjective sense of self.

Focus on the location of the insula in your brain and its role in how you use your *'aql*.

It helps you to be mindful of your movements; have emotional, visual, and auditory awareness; identify risks; make decisions; and control your thoughts and attention. Your breath and pulse are also associated with the insula.

Now sit back down and relax.
Focus on your pulse by taking your pulse.

You can feel your pulse in your neck. Take your first two fingers (the index and middle fingers) and place them on your neck, just below your jaw and above your chest. Feel the pulse in your carotid artery.
The second way to feel your pulse is to place your index and middle fingers on the inside of your opposite wrist, just below the thumb.
A normal pulse, also known as your heart rate, should be 60–100 beats per minute; this rate can vary from person to person.

Breathe in and breathe out: *Hoo!*

Can you feel your heart rate? Is it slow or hard to feel? Is it fast?
What thoughts or feelings come up? Name them.

Slow down and count your pulse.

Take deep breaths while counting your pulse. Notice your pulse and bodily sensations.

Take a deep breath in and out: *Hoo!*
Repeat five times.

Session 5: Introduction to *Nafs*

This practice introduces you to the role of the nafs. We hope that this will help you develop an awareness of nafs.
Practice:
Sit in a comfortable position.
Say slowly *Auzubillah minashaitan nirajeem*, or "I seek refuge in Allah from the outcast Shaitan."
Slowly, say, *Bismillahir Rahmanir Rahim*, or "In the name of God, the Lord of Mercy, the Giver of Mercy!"
Let's reflect on breathing:

Inhale slowly from both nostrils.

When the lungs are full of air, hold the breath for five seconds.
Exhale through the mouth, similar to whistling. After a few moments of rest, repeat the process five times (Azeemi, 2005, p. 62).

Visualize your *nafs* beneath your navel. Its colour is yellow.
Reflect on Allah's creation of *nafs* and its role.

Having an idea of *nafs* helps you have a subjective sense of self.

Focus on the location of the *nafs* in your body, on its role in how the *nafs* is used, and on the relationship of the *nafs* to the *'aql*.

The role of *nafs* is to make decisions and to control and perform patterns of thought and attention.
Your breathing and pulse are also associated with *nafs*.

Now sit back and relax.
Focus on your pulse by taking your pulse.

You can feel your pulse in your neck. Take your first two fingers (the index and middle fingers) and place them on your neck, just below your jaw and above your chest. Feel the pulse in your carotid artery.
The second way to feel your pulse is to place your index and middle fingers on the inside of your opposite wrist, just below the thumb.
A normal pulse, also known as your heart rate, should be 60–100 beats per minute; this rate can vary from person to person.

Breathe in and breathe out: *Hoo*!

Can you feel your heart rate? Is it slow or hard to feel? Is it fast?
What thoughts or feelings come up? Name them.

Slow down and count your pulse.

Take deep breaths while counting your pulse. Notice your pulse and bodily sensations.

Now reflect on Yusuf's capacity "to receive the lesson" (Pandolfo, 2018, p. 17).

Remember that even prophets were encouraged to learn a lesson from their own trials.

Think about this Qur'anic verse: "indeed in the stories of these men, there is a lesson for those endowed with insight" (Q. 12:111).

Watch your thoughts and emotions: what would be your lesson in this process of *tazkiya*?

Observe them.
Name them.

Take a deep breath in and out: *Hoo*!
Repeat five times.

Session 6: *Badan/Jism,* Heart, and Chest

This practice introduces you to badan, qalb, and sadr. This can also be called a body scan. We aim to bring your attention to your body, chest, and heart and how they feel in the present moment.
Practice:
Sit in a comfortable position.
Say slowly *Auzubillah minashaitan nirajeem*, or "I seek refuge in Allah from the outcast Shaitan."
Slowly, say, *Bismillahir Rahmanir Rahim*, or "In the name of God, the Lord of Mercy, the Giver of Mercy!"
Let's read a sample provided by Young (2016, p. 31):

> Sight, Sound, and Body Are: Now Consider the following. You focus your attention on physical sights, physical sounds, and body sensations as they arise. If you get caught up in a thought, you let go of that thought and bring your attention back to a physical sight, physical sound, or a body experience.
>
> (Young, 2016, p. 31)

Now read:

> Breath Is Now You focus your attention on the sensation of breath at your nostrils. If your attention is pulled to anything else, you return to focusing on the breath. You try to detect each in-breath and each out-breath as a distinct event. You try to detect the very instant when each in-breath begins and when it ends, and likewise for each out-breath. In addition, you try to notice any tiny fluctuations that may occur during the course of the in- or out-breath.
>
> (Young, 2016, p. 31)

Let's reflect on our breath:

Try practicing the three-minute breathing space every day.

Take a mindful breath in and out: *Hoo!*
    Focus on your listening. Focus on God as All-Hearing.
    Focus on your sight. Focus on God as All-Seeing.
    Focus on smelling.
    Focus on touch.
    Notice how your body feels each time you breathe in and breathe out.
    You can place your hand on your stomach.
    Notice the gentle rise of your stomach as you breathe in, and the fall of your stomach as you breathe out.
    Now put your hand on your chest.

What do you notice when your chest moves as you take each breath?
What do you notice when your stomach gently rises and falls as you breathe in and out?

Notice how your heartbeat slows down as your mind slows down.
    Notice how your muscles relax. Feel relaxation beginning with your feet, legs, and thighs.
    Move your body, as we sometimes do during *dhikr*.
    On each exhalation, say the word "peace" out loud or to yourself.
    Take a deep breath in and out: *Hoo!*
    Feel peace in your mind and heart.
    Repeat five times.

Session 7: *Dhikr*

This practice introduces you to dhikr and its benefits. We aim to bring your attention to the majesty and beauty of the Divine.
    Practice:
    Sit in a comfortable position.
    Say slowly *Auzubillah minashaitan nirajeem*, or "I seek refuge in Allah from the outcast Shaitan."
    Slowly, say, *Bismillahir Rahmanir Rahim*, or "In the name of God, the Lord of Mercy, the Giver of Mercy!"
    Sit in a comfortable position.

    Remember that when performed individually, the setting is suitable, and the client feels comfortable, he/she can sit on the floor with crossed legs.

This is also known as *Kuudi dhikr* (you can lean towards the right and left or turn your head from right to left). Clients can also do it at home in *sajda* (prostration) or standing, which is also known as *Kiyami dhikr* (you can lean towards the right and left or turn your head from right to left).

Pay attention to your hands.

Our Prophet advised: "Engage in *tasebeeh, tahleel,* and *taqdees* (i.e. engage in various forms of *dhikr*) and keep count with the joints of the Fingers. On the Day of *Qiyaamah* these fingers will be questioned and they will be made to speak."

Let's reflect on the great masters' ways of doing the *dhikr*. They thanked Allah for their good acts and asked for mercy and forgiveness for their sins. They did not ask for forgiveness out of the desire to cover up their sins. They recited *Subhan Allah* with a humble request to eradicate their sins. When they recited *Alhamdu lillah*, they praised and thanked God for Himself and not for His forgiving nature.

There are two ways of doing *dhikr*.

Way 1: Counting *dhikr* with the finger joints.

> In everyday life, after prayers or on other occasions, Muslims say *dhikrs* while counting our fingers and the joints on our fingers.
> Focus on each finger; each has three joints. Notice that the thumb has only two joints.
> Focus on each joint. Each joint has an inner side, an outer side, and a point.
> Notice that each finger has three inner joints, three outer joints, and one point at the tip. Notice that the thumb only has two inner joints, two outer joints, and one point at the tip.
> Notice that when you count all the joints except the joints of the thumb, you get 28. Adding the two inner joints, two outer joints, and one point at the tip of the thumb will make 33.
> We say 33 for *tasbih* (subhanallah), 33 for *tahmid* (alhamdulillah), and 33 for *takbir* (Allahu Akbar).
> Take a deep breath, in and out, each time you gently press on each inner finger joint.

Way 2: Counting *tasbih* with the fingertips.

> Abu Dawood and Haakim have narrated from the Prophet that he, Rasulullah (sallallahu alayhi wasallam), came to them while they

had heaped in front of them 4,000 date stones. They were reciting *Tasbeeh (Dhikr)* with the date stones.

Now take a deep breath in and out: *Hoo!*
Repeat five times.

Session 8: Asma ul-Husna

This practice introduces you to the Divine Names and when to say them.
Practice:
Sit in a comfortable position.

Make sure there are no external or internal distractions.

Say slowly *Auzubillah minashaitan nirajeem*, or "I seek refuge in Allah from the outcast Shaitan."
Slowly, say, *Bismillahir Rahmanir Rahim*, or "In the name of God, the Lord of Mercy, the Giver of Mercy!"
Focus and choose one Name that bears emotional meaning to you.
Take a deep breath in and out: *Hoo!*
Reflect on this Name.
Using object relations theory, think about how you formed this emotional attachment to this specific Name.

For example, let's start with focusing on God's incomparability.

> Reflect how God's incomparability "is associated with qualities such as majesty (*jalal*), severity (*qahr*), wrath (*ghadab*), justice ('*adl*), anger (*sakht*), distance (*bu'd*), vengeance (*intiqam*), invincibility (*jabarut*), inaccessibility ('*izza*), holiness (*qudus*), magnificence (*kibriya'*), and so on."
>
> (Murata, 1992, p. 69)

Now, reflect on the human response to God's qualities such as awe (*hayba*), fear (*khawf*), and contraction (*qabd*).
Reflect on attributes such as beauty (*jamal*), gentleness (*lutf*), mercy (*rahma*), bounty (*fadl*), good pleasure (*rida*), nearness (*qurb*), forgiveness (*maghfira*), pardon ('*afw*), and love (*mahabba*).
Observe how your response or attachment to a specific name is related to intimacy (*uns*), hope (*raja'*), and expansion (*bast*).
See how awe is associated with majesty, or intimacy with beauty.

Find your own response to the connection between you and God.

Now, let's choose another Name using a reflection from Muhyiddin Ibn 'Arabi, who said:

> begin with a verse of Majesty, following it with its corresponding verse of Beauty, and then proceed to another verse of Majesty and so on, God willing. It may be that one verse will have two aspects—an aspect of Majesty and an aspect of Beauty. If so, God willing we will cite both its sources, in Majesty and in Beauty, because it contains the whole counterposition.
>
> (Ibn 'Arabi, 1989, p. 4)

> If God had so pleased, He could have made them a single community, but He admits to His mercy whoever He will; the evildoers will have no one to protect or help them. 9How can they take protectors other than Him? God alone is the Protector; He gives life to the dead; He has power over all things. 10Whatever you may differ about is for God to judge. [Say], 'Such is God, my Lord. In Him I trust and to Him I turn, 11 the Creator of the heavens and earth.' He made mates for you from among yourselves—and for the animals too—so that you may multiply. There is nothing like Him: He is the All Hearing, the All Seeing. 12 The keys of the heavens and the earth are His; He provides abundantly or sparingly for whoever He will; He has full knowledge of all things.
>
> (Q. 42:8–12)

After you read Q. 42:8–12, read the following reflection from Ibn 'Arabi:

You who are drowned in the sea of contemplation, that in the reading from Majesty, the likeness referred to in *laysa ka-mithlilihi shay'un* is literal likeness.

Reflect on God's blessings and love: *yuhibbuhum wa yuhibbunahu* (Qur'an 5:54), meaning, "He loves them, and they love Him."

Ibn 'Arabi (1989) says, "Since the Truth 'counts the number of everything,' you are among the things that are counted, and His protection and observation of you follow" (p. 16).

Feel "inspirations, glimpses, flashes, fragrances, and significances of the divine" (Ibn 'Arabi, 1989, p. 16) that come from counting the blessings.

Take a deep breath in and out: *Hoo!*

Repeat five times.

Session 9: Contemplating the Prophet

The purpose of this exercise is to reduce the suffering and stress associated with psychological, psychosomatic, and psychiatric disorders. By practicing this exercise, the aim is to develop an awareness of the present moment's experience of suffering and remind oneself of the limitless mercy, kindness, and compassion of God. The hope is that, at the end, one will reduce the negative impact of suffering and improve compassion and coping.
Practice:
Sit in a comfortable position.

Make sure there are no external or internal distractions.

Say slowly *Auzubillah minashaitan nirajeem*, or "I seek refuge in Allah from the outcast Shaitan."
Slowly, say, *Bismillahir Rahmanir Rahim*, or "In the name of God, the Lord of Mercy, the Giver of Mercy!"
Take a deep breath in and out: *Hoo*!
Pay attention to every small detail in this type of Sufi meditation as they form the basis of your practice. Make a kneeling position or sit cross-legged in the "Lotus Position." Close your eyes and mouth. Gently clench your teeth together and press your tongue against the roof of your mouth. Take a deep breath in and hold your breath to calm your heart rate and breathing.
Our hands hold significant mysteries. Therefore, their placement is crucial in this exercise. Through this meditation, you can begin to discover the secrets of the hands. Divine Codes are embedded on our hands by God. Rub them together to activate divine blessings. Our hands also act as receivers, capturing Divine Energies and positive vibrations. Position your hands comfortably and make the tip of your thumb touches the tip of your index finger, while extending the other fingers straight out. This hand gesture resembles the word "Allah" in Arabic script.
Now focus on your breath. Take a deep breath in through your nose and exhale through your mouth. As you breathe in through your nose, silently say "Hu-Allah." When you exhale through your mouth, pronounce "Hu." Imagine your heart as you inhale and visualize black energy leaving your body as you exhale.
When we exhale, imagine how the carbon monoxide leaving our bodies also takes out negative energy from our past. The Prophet (sas) advised, "When you drink (water), do not breathe into the vessel." Visualizing this expulsion of negative energy helps cleanse your soul of those past actions.[2]

Now, reflect on this verse:

> God and His angels bless the Prophet– so, you who believe, bless him too and give him greetings of peace.
>
> (Q. 33:56)

Slowly start reciting the *salawat* (blessing): *Allahumma Salli 'ala Sayyidina Muhammadin ninabiyyil-Ummiyyi wa 'ala aalihi wa Sallim tasleema.*

The meaning of this *salawat* is: "O Allah bless Muhammad *Sallahu walahi wasalam*, the unlettered Prophet, and his family and grant them best of peace."

Practise visualizing the Prophet or his prophethood.

Abd al-Karim al-Jili (d. 1408) called this the actual, waking vision of the Prophet, or *ru 'yat al-nabi yaqzatan*.

Now, focus on the Prophet's compassion and loving-kindness towards humans and animals.
Take a deep breath in and out: *Hoo!*
Repeat five times.

Session 10: Reflecting on Loving-Kindness

The purpose of this exercise is to reflect on loving-kindness in our lives and relationships.
Practice:
Sit in a comfortable position.

Make sure there are no external or internal distractions.

Say slowly *Auzubillah minashaitan nirajeem*, or "I seek refuge in Allah from the outcast Shaitan."
Slowly, say, *Bismillahir Rahmanir Rahim*, or "In the name of God, the Lord of Mercy, the Giver of Mercy!"
Take a deep breath in and out: *Hoo!*
Imagine God's love and mercy; it is unconditional and selfless.

Appendix: Overview of Sample Muraqabah Practices

Let's follow the Chishti Sufi master and scholar Muhammad Husaini Gisudiraz (d. 1422), and imagine our body and *nafs* as a tree (Kugle, 2021, p. 9).

Let's use the description by Nasr (2007) who inspired this reflection:

First, imagine Allah's love and your love for the sacred as a seed.
This seed is the basis of a growing tree. This tree represents your body.
Imagine your body as a tree growing from its roots. These roots are intellect, imagination, spirit, knowledge, and life.
Now imagine these roots as the divine reality, which we call *aqiqa*.
Imagine the first root, Intellect. Its branch is seeing.
Imagine the root of Imagination. Its branch is hearing.
Imagine the root of Spirit. Its branch is speaking.
Imagine the root of Knowledge. Its branch is understanding.
Now imagine the root of Life. Its branch is Doing.
Imagine leaves on the branches. If they are not taken care of, the leaves become dry, harming the branches and the tree. From the branch of Seeing, the dry leaf is Greed.
The branch of Hearing grows the leaf of Hatred.
The branch of Speaking grows the leaf of Anger.
The branch of Understanding grows the leaf of Pride.
The branch of Doing grows the leaf of Jealousy.
If the tree is taken care of properly, it will produce fruits.
Imagine these leaves as the *nafs*, or ego, and imagine that, if they are not taken care of, they can harm the heart.
If the *nafs* is taken care of with contemplation, it can give fruit to kindness, love, compassion, blessedness, and aspiration.
Imagine all of these fruits as Love.
This Love is divine. It is for the sake of God, through whom all that is comes into being.
Imagine the tree as "a Tree of Paradise."
Imagine "every mountain is a symbol of transcendence."
Imagine "the water of every flowing stream is a symbol of Divine Mercy."
Imagine "the wind is a mark of the Spirit."
Imagine "the eagle flying above" as a symbol of the human spirit flying towards the Throne of the Divine.
Imagine "'the fish swimming in the deep' as a symbol of the soul immersing itself in the ocean of Infinitude..." (Nasr, 2007, p. 47).

Take a deep breath in and out: *Hoo!*
Repeat five times.

Notes

1 It was narrated from Ibn Mas'ud that the Prophet (ﷺ) said: *Allahumma inni a'udhu bika minash-Shaitanir-rajim, wa hamzihi wa nafkhihi wa mafthihi* (O Allah, I seek refuge in You from the accursed Satan, from his madness, his pride, and his poetry)."
Grade: Hasan (Darussalam)
English reference: Vol. 1, Book 5, Hadith 808
Arabic reference: Book 5, Hadith 857
2 This section is a slightly modified version of meditation from *The Healing Power of Sufi Meditation* by Nurjan Mirahmadi (2005).

References

Abu-Raiya, H. (2012). Towards a systematic Qura'nic theory of personality. *Mental Health, Religion & Culture, 15*(3), 217–233. https://doi.org/10.1080/13674676.2011.640622

Ahmed, N. (2017). Islam and mysticism: Is 'nafs' soul? Part -1. Retrieved December 22, 2021, from https://www.newageislam.com/islamic-ideology/islam-and-mysticism--is-nafs-soul-part---1/d/111786

Al-Balkhī, A. i. S., & Badrī, M. (2014). *Abū Zayd al-Balkhī"s sustenance of the soul: The cognitive behavior therapy of a ninth-century physician*. Herndon, VA: International Institute of Islamic Thought.

Al-Ghazali, M. (1993). *Revival of religious learning (Ihya Ulum-id-Din)* (F. ul-Karim, Trans.). Karachi: Darul-Ishaat.

Al-Ghazali, M. (1995). *Al-Ghazali on disciplining the soul: Kitab riyadat al-nafs; & on breaking the two desires: Kitab kasr al-shahwatayn. Books XXII and XXIII of the revival of the religious sciences* (W. t. Ihya ulum al-din, Trans.). Cambridge, UK: Islamic Texts Society.

Al-Ghazali, M. (2015). *Al-Ghazali on vigilance & examination. Kitab a-muraqabah wa'l-muhasaba. Book XXXVIII of the revival of the religious sciences* (Translated with notes by A. F. Shaker). Cambridge: The Islamic Texts Society.

al-Jawziyah, Muḥammad ibn Abī Bakr Ibn Qayyim. (1981). *al-Fawa'id*. Beirut: Dar al-Nafa'is

American Dance Therapy Association. (2020). *American dance therapy association*. New York: American Dance Therapy Association.

Amini, F. (1999). *Sufi psychology and Jungian analytic psychology: Treatment of narcissistic personality disorder*. Michigan: ProQuest Dissertations Publishing.

American Psychiatric Association [APA]. (2013). *Diagnostic and statistical manual of mental disorders* (5th ed.). Arlington, TX: American Psychiatric Publishing.

Ano, G. A. (2005). *Spiritual struggles between vice and virtue: A brief psychospiritual intervention* [Unpublished doctoral dissertation]. Bowling Green State University, Bowling Green, OH.

Avants, S. K., & Margolin, A. (2003). *The spiritual self-schema (3-S) development program*. Retrieved September 25, 2023, from https://psycnet.apa.org/record/2015-27859-011

Azal, R. (2015). *Healing with Islamic meditation (Muraqaba)*. Retrieved form http://www.theartofislamichealing.com/healing-with-islamic-meditation-muraqaba/

References

Azeemi, K. (2005). *Muraqaba: The art and science of Sufi meditation.* Houston: Plato.

Badri, M. (2000). *Contemplation: An Islamic psychospiritual study.* Surrey: International Institute of Islamic Thought.

Bair, P. (1998). *Living from the heart: Heart rhythm meditation.* New York: Three Rivers Press.

Barnes, M. (1989). The body in the spiritual exercises of Ignatius of Loyola. *Religion, 19*(3), 263–273. https://doi.org/10.1016/0048-721X(89)90025-0

Bearman, P., Bianquis, T., Bosworth, C. E., Donzel, E. v., & Heinrichs, W. P. (2012). *Encyclopedia of Islam* (2nd ed.). Leiden: Koninklijke Brill NV. https://doi.org/10.1163/1573-3912_islam_DUM_3380

Bozorgzadeh, S., & Grasser, L.R. (2022). The integration of the heart-centered paradigm of Sufi psychology in contemporary psychotherapy practice. *Psychotherapy, 59*(3), 405–414. https://doi.org/10.1037/pst0000414

Brown, K. W., Ryan, R. M., & Creswell, J. D. (2007). Mindfulness: Theoretical foundations and evidence for its salutary effects. *Psychological Inquiry, 18*(4), 211–237. https://doi.org/10.1080/10478400701598298

Bstan-'dzin-rgya-mtsho, & Mehrotra, R. (2005). *The essential Dalai Lama.* Hodder Mobius.

Buehler, A. F. (2016). *Recognizing Sufism.* I. B. Tauris & Company, Limited.

Butcher, B. (2017). The martial as the mystical: Taekwondo as orthodox Christian contemplative practice. *Spiritus, 17*(2), 197–211. https://doi.org/10.1353/scs.2017.0027

Bytamar, M. J., Saed, O., & Khakpoor, S. (2020). Emotion regulation difficulties and academic procrastination. *Front Psychology, 11*, 524588. https://doi.org/10.3389/fpsyg.2020.524588

Cayoun, B. A. (2011). *Mindfulness-integrated CBT: Principles and practice.* Wiley-Blackwell. https://doi.org/10.1002/9781119993162

Chambers, R., Gullone, E., & Allen, N. B. (2009). Mindful emotion regulation: An integrative review. *Clinical Psychology Review, 29*(6), 560–572. https://doi.org/10.1016/j.cpr.2009.06.005

Chittick, W. C. (1983). *The Sufi path of love: The spiritual teachings of Rumi.* Translated by W. C. Chittick. New York: State University of New York Press.

Chittick, W. C. (2001). *The heart of Islamic philosophy: The quest for self-knowledge in the teachings of Afḍal al-Dīn Kāshānī.* Oxford University Press.

Chittick, W. C. (Ed.). (2007). *The inner journey: Views from the Islamic tradition.* Sandpoint, ID: Morning Light Press.

Choe, E., Jun, H., Na Suh, H., & Wang, K. T. (2021). Re-inventing the wheel: Re-adapting mindfulness practices for use with Asian/Asian American Christian clients. *Journal of Psychology and Christianity, 40*(2), 132–140. Retrieved from https://myaccess.library.utoronto.ca/login?qurl=https%3A%2F%2Fwww.proquest.com%2Fscholarly-journals%2Fre-inventing-wheel-adapting-mindfulness-practices%2Fdocview%2F2764526130%2Fse-2%3Faccountid%3D14771

Cohen, J. A., Mannarino, A. P., Kliethermes, M., & Murray, L. A. (2012). Trauma-focused CBT for youth with complex trauma. *Child Abuse & Neglect, 36*(6), 528–541. https://doi.org/10.1016/j.chiabu.2012.03.007

Dawson, J., Matson, J. L., & Cherry, K. E. (1998). An analysis of maladaptive behaviors in persons with autism, PPD-NOS, and mental retardation. *Research in Developmental Disabilities, 19*(5), 439–448. https://doi.org/10.1016/S0891-4222(98)00016-X

Day, C. (2023). Raving as healing: An autoethnographic study into how raving can inform the use of dance movement psychotherapy in clinical work with substance abusers in recovery. *Body, Movement and Dance in Psychotherapy, 18*(3), 162–177. https://doi.org/10.1080/17432979.2023.2205465

Denny, F. M. (2012). Wird. In P. Bearman, T. Bianquis, C. E. Bosworth, E. van Donzel, & W. P. Heinrichs (Eds.), *Encyclopaedia of Islam* (2nd ed.). https://doi.org/10.1163/1573-3912_islam_SIM_7914

Dewey, J. (1959). *Art as experience*. New York: Capricorn Books.

Drob, S. L. (2000). *Kabbalistic metaphors: Jewish mystical themes in ancient and modern thought*. New York: Jason Aronson Publishers.

Dwidiyanti, M., Munif, B., Santoso, A., Rahmawati, A. M., & Prasetya, R. L. (2021). DAHAGA: An Islamic spiritual mindfulness-based application to reduce depression among nursing students during the COVID-19 pandemic. *Belitung Nursing Journal, 7*(3), 219–226. https://doi.org/10.33546/bnj.1494

Eckhardt-Henn, A., Best, C., Bense, S., Breuer, P., Diener, G., Tschan, R., & Dieterich, M. (2008). Psychiatric comorbidity in different organic vertigo syndromes. *Journal of Neurology, 255*(3), 420–428. https://doi.org/10.1007/s00415-008-0697-x

Ernst, C. (2005). Situating Sufism and yoga. *Journal of the Royal Asiatic Society, Series 3, 15*(1), 15–43.

Ernst, C. E. (2011). *Sufism: An introduction to the mystical tradition of Islam*. Boston, MA: Shambhala.

Esposito, J. L. (2009). *The Oxford encyclopedia of the Islamic world*. New York: Oxford University Press.

Esposito, J. L. (2010). *Islam: The straight path* (4th ed.). New York: Oxford University Press.

Esposito, J. L. (2016). *Islam: The straight path* (5th ed.). New York: Oxford University Press.

Feldman, S. H. (2019). "Allahı Zikr Edilim" (Let Us Do Zikr for Allah): The Sabbatian appropriation of the Sufi practice of Zikr as religious renewal. *Zutot, 16*(1), 43–53. https://doi.org/10.1163/18750214-12161002

Ford, K., & Garzon, F. (2017). Research note: A randomized investigation of Evangelical Christian accommodative mindfulness. *Spirituality in Clinical Practice (Washington, D.C.), 4*(2), 92–99. https://doi.org/10.1037/scp0000137

Foster, M. K. (1974). When words become deeds: An analysis of three Iriquois longhouse speech events. In R. Bouman, R. Sherzer, & J. Sherzer (Eds.), *Explorations in the ethnography of speaking* (pp. 345–67). New York; London: Cambridge University Press.

Ford, K., & Garzon, F. (2017). Research note: A randomized investigation of evangelical Christian accommodative mindfulness. *Spirituality in Clinical Practice, 4*(2), 92–99. https://doi.org/10.1037/scp0000137

Frankl, V. (2003). *Man, in search of meaning*. Phoenix, AZ: Zeig, Tucker, and Theisen.

Freud, S. (1955). *Moses and monotheism*. New York: Vintage Book.

Frostadottir, A. D., & Dorjee, D. (2019). Effects of mindfulness based cognitive therapy (MBCT) and compassion focused therapy (CFT) on symptom change, mindfulness, self-compassion, and rumination in clients with depression, anxiety, and stress. *Frontiers in Psychology, 10,* 1099–1099. https://doi.org/10.3389/fpsyg.2019.01099

Fung, K., & Zhu, Z. (2018). Acceptance and commitment therapy and Asian thought. In R. Moodley, N. Zhu, & T. H.-T. Lo (Eds.), *Asian healing traditions in counseling and psychotherapy* (pp. 143–158). Thousand Oaks, CA: Sage Publications, Inc. https://doi.org/10.4135/9781071800768

Gilbert, P. (2009). *The compassionate mind: a new approach to life's challenges.* Oakland, CA: New Harbinger.

Gilbert, P. (2017). Compassion: Definitions and controversies. In P. Gilbert (Ed.), *Compassion: Concepts, research and applications* (pp. 3–15). London: Routledge. https://doi.org/10.4324/9781315564296

Frager, R. (1999). *Heart, self & soul: The Sufi psychology of growth, balance, and harmony.* Quest Books.

Glasse, C. (2008). *The new encyclopedia of Islam.* New York: Rowman & Littlefield Publishers, Inc.

Hamidullah, M. (1981). *The messenger of god: In the presence of the prophet.* Paris: Unesco Courier.

Harel, K., Czamanski-Cohen, J., & Turjeman, N. (2021). The spiritual experience of Sufi whirling dervishes: Rising above the separation and duality of this world. *The Arts in Psychotherapy, 75,* 101831. https://doi.org/10.1016/j.aip.2021.101831

Haque, A. (1998). Psychology and religion: Their relationship and integration from an Islamic perspective. *The American Journal of Islamic Social Sciences, 15,* 97–116.

Haque, A. (2004). Psychology from Islamic perspective: Contributions of early Muslim scholars and challenges to contemporary Muslim psychologists. *Journal of Religion and Health, 43*(4), 357–377. https://doi.org/10.1007/s10943-004-4302-z

Hatim, M. (2017). *Caregiving to Muslims: A guide for chaplains, counselors, healthcare and social workers.* Charleston: Createspace Independent Publishing Platform.

Hayes, S. C. (2004). Acceptance and commitment therapy and the new behavior therapies: Mindfulness, acceptance, and relationship. In S. C. Hayes, V. M. Follette, & M. M. Linehan (Eds.), *Mindfulness and acceptance: Expanding the cognitive-behavioral tradition* (pp. 1–29). New York: The Guilford Press.

Green, N. (2012). *Sufism: A global history.* Oxford: Wiley-Blackwell.

Hess, M. (2020). A Christocentric approach to mindfulness in healthcare chaplaincy (Order No. 28262394). Michigan: ProQuest Dissertations & Theses Global (2478602587).

Hoffman, V. (1995). *Sufism, mystics and saints in modern Egypt.* Columbia, SC: University of South Carolina.

Hoover, J. (2018). Can Christians practice mindfulness without compromising their convictions? *Journal of Psychology and Christianity, 37*(3), 247–255.

Howard, E. (2012). Lectio divina in the evangelical tradition. *Journal of Spiritual Formation and Soul Care, 5*(1), 56–77. https://doi.org/10.1177/193979091200500104

Husain, A., & Hasan, A. (2021). *Psychology of meditation: A practical guide to self.* Delhi: Psycho Information Technologies.

Helberg, N., Heyes, C. J., & Rohel, J. (2009). Thinking through the body: Yoga, Philosophy, and physical education. *Teaching Philosophy, 32*(3), 263–284. https://doi.org/10.5840/teachphil200932328

Hussein, J. W. (2018). The social–psychological and phenomenological constructs of spirituality in the culture of dhikr in eastern Ethiopia. *Culture & Psychology, 24*(1), 26–48. https://doi.org/10.1177/1354067X16672415

Jackson, M. (1989). *Paths toward a clearing: Radical empiricism and ethnographic inquiry*. Bloomington: Indiana University Press.

Jones, T. L., Garzon, F. L., & Ford, K. M. (2023). Christian accommodative mindfulness in the clinical treatment of shame, depression, and anxiety: Results of an N-of-1 time-series study. *Spirituality in Clinical Practice, 10*(2), 118–130. https://doi.org/10.1037/scp0000221

Jung, C. G. (2009). In M. Kyburz, J. Peck, & S. Shamdasani (Eds.), *The red book* (S. Shamdasani, Trans.). New York: Norton.

Isgandarova, N. (2018). *Muslim women, domestic violence, and psychotherapy: Theological and clinical issues*. New York: Routledge.

Ibn 'Ajībah, A. i. M., Aresmouk, M. F., Fitzgerald, M. A., & Ibn 'Ajībah, A. i. M. (2011). *The book of ascension to the essential truths of Sufism = Mi'rāj al-tashawwuf ilā ḥaqā'iq al-taṣawwuf: A lexicon of Sufic terminology*. Louisville: Fons Vitae.

Ibn 'Arabi, M. (1989). *On majesty and beauty (the Kitab Al-Jalal Wa-l Jamal)* (R. T. Harris, Trans.). Available at: https://archive.org/stream/IbnAlArabiOnMajestyAndBeauty19p/Ibn%20al%20Arabi%20-%20On%20Majesty%20and%20Beauty%20%2819p%29_djvu.txt

Iqbal, T., & Farid, M. (2017). Sufi practices as the cause of spiritual, mental and physical healing at Chishti shrines in Pakistan. *Mental Health, Religion & Culture, 20*(10), 943–953. https://doi.org/10.1080/13674676.2017.1372736

Isgandarova, N. (2019). Muraqaba as a mindfulness-based therapy in Islamic psychotherapy. *Journal of Religion and Health, 58*(4), 1146–1160. https://doi.org/10.1007/s10943-018-0695-y

Jung, C. (2014). *Analytical psychology: Its theory and practice*. New York: Routledge.

Kabat-Zinn, J. (1990). *Full catastrophe living: Using the wisdom of your body and mind to face stress, pain and illness*. New York: Delacorte.

Kabat-Zinn, J. (1994). *Wherever you go, there you are: Mindfulness meditation for everyday life*. New York: Hyperion.

Kamada, S. (1977). Sarraj's theory of mystical ladder. *Bulletin of the Society for Near Eastern Studies in Japan, 20*(1), 1–15, 261. https://doi.org/10.5356/jorient.20.1

Karimpour, G. (2020). *Cultural adaptation of Rumi's poetry for introducing mindfulness: An educational book for American Middle Eastern adults*. Michigan: ProQuest Dissertations Publishing.

Keshavarzi, H, & Haque, A. (2013). Outlining a psychotherapy model for enhancing Muslim mental health within an Islamic context. *International Journal for the Psychology of Religion, 23*(3), 230–249. https://doi.org/10.1080/10508619.2012.712000

Keshavarzi, H., & Khan, F. (2018). Outlining a case illustration of Traditional Islamically Integrated Psychotherapy (TIIP). In C. Y. Al-Karam (Ed.), *Islamically integrated psychotherapy: Uniting faith and professional practice* (pp. 175–207). Rutgers: Templeton Press.

Keshavarzi, H., Khan, F., Ali, B., & Awaad, R. (Eds.) (2020). *Applying Islamic principles to clinical mental health care: Introducing traditional Islamically integrated psychotherapy*. New York: Routledge. https://doi.org/10.4324/9781003043331

Kister, M. J. (1968). "Al-Taḥannuth": An inquiry into the meaning of a term (pp. 223–236).Retrieved November 4, 2018, from Kister.huji.ac.il.

Knabb, J. J. (2021). *Christian meditation in clinical practice: A four-step model and workbook for therapists and clients*. Downers Grove, IL: InterVarsity Press.

Kabat-Zinn, J. (2003). Mindfulness based interventions in context: Past, present and future. *Clinical Psychological Science Practice*, *10*, 144–156.

Koenig, H., King, D., & Carson, V. B. (2012). *Handbook of religion and health*. Oxford: Oxford University Press.

Koenig, H. G. (2018). *Religion and mental health: Research and clinical applications*. Academic Press an imprint of Elsevier.

Koenig, H. G., McCullough, M. E., & Larson, D. B. (2001). *Handbook of religion and health*. Oxford University Press. https://doi.org/10.1093/acprof:oso/9780195118667.001.0001

Kugle, S. (2012). *Sufi meditation and contemplation: Timeless wisdom from Mughal India*. New Lebanon, NY: Suluk Press.

Kugle, S. (2021). Islam and meditation. In M. Farias, D. Brazier, & M. Lalljee (Eds.), *The Oxford handbook of meditation* (Online ed.). Oxford Library of Psychology. https://doi.org/10.1093/oxfordhb/9780198808640.013.9. Accessed 29 August 2023.

Koenig, H. G., & Pritchett, J. (1998). Religion and psychotherapy. In H. G. Koenig (Ed.), *Handbook of religion and mental health* (pp. 323–336). Academic Press. https://doi.org/10.1016/B978-012417645-4/50089-4

Lee, B. (2018). Integrating Asian healing traditions into psychotherapy. In R. Moodley, T. Lo, & N. Zhu (Eds.), *Asian healing traditions in counselling and psychotherapy* (pp. 83–95). Thousand Oaks, CA: Sage.

Lee, J. (2020). The influence of Swami Satyananda's Meditation on John Main's Christian Meditation. *Journal of Hindu-Christian Studies*, *33*(1). https://doi.org/10.7825/2164-6279.1771

Lew, Alan. (2000). Prayer and the uses of meditation. *Judaism*, *49*(1), 93–103.

Leaman, O. (2006). *The Qur'an: An encyclopedia*. New York: Routledge.

Linehan, M. (1993). *Cognitive-behavioral treatment of borderline personality disorder*. New York: Guilford Press.

Lippard, P. V. (1988). The rhetoric of silence: The society of friends' unprogrammed meeting for worship. *Communication Quarterly*, *36*(2), 145–156. https://doi.org/10.1080/01463378809369715

Lobel, D. (2007). Awareness, love, and reverence (Murāqaba, Mahabba, Hayba/Yir'ah). In D. Lobel (Ed.), *A Sufi-Jewish dialogue* (pp. 219–242). University of Pennsylvania Press. https://doi.org/10.9783/9780812202656.219

Lodi, F. (2018). The HEART method: Healthy emotions anchored in RasoolAllah's teachings: Cognitive therapy using Prophet Mohammed as a psychospiritual exemplar. In C. Y. Al-Karam (Ed.), *Islamically integrated psychotherapy* (pp. 76–102). West Conshohocken, PA: Templeton Press.

Lee, J. (2020). The influence of Swami Satyananda's meditation on John Main's Christian meditation. *Journal of Hindu-Christian Studies*, *33*(1). https://doi.org/10.7825/2164-6279.1771

Lewis, F. D. (2014). *Rumi-past and present, east and west: The life, teachings, and poetry of Jalâl Al-Din Rumi*. New York: Oneworld Publications.

Long, I. J. (2014). Caring for the Muslim soul: Approaches to the spiritual care of Muslim patients. In T. S. O'Connor, K. Lund, & P. Berendsen (Eds.), *Psychotherapy: Cure of the soul* (pp. 49–58). Waterloo: Waterloo Lutheran Seminary.

Lutz, A., Slagter, H. A., Dunne, J. D., & Davidson, R. J. (2008). Attention regulation and monitoring in meditation. *Trends in Cognitive Sciences, 12*(4), 163–169. https://doi.org/10.1016/j.tics.2008.01.005

McCarthy-Jones, S., Waegeli, A., & Watkins, J. (2013). Spirituality and hearing voices: Considering the relation. *Psychosis, 5*(3), 247–258. https://doi.org/10.1080/17522439.2013.831945

McCorkle, B. H., Bohn, C., Hughes, T., & Kim, D. (2005). "Sacred moments": Social anxiety in a larger perspective. *Mental Health, Religion, and Culture, 8*, 227–238.

McCreery, J. L. (1995). Negotiating with demons: The uses of magical language. *American Ethnologist, 22*, 144–164.

Mijares, S. G. (2022). Archetypes, ego states and subpersonalities: An exploration of diversity within somatic awareness. *Body, Movement and Dance in Psychotherapy, 17*(4), 343–355. https://doi.org/10.1080/17432979.2022.2090436

Miles-Yépez, N. (2009). Sufi meditation. Available at: https://delumina.net/blog/2014/11/14/sufi-Meditation

Mirahmadi, N. (2005). *The healing power of Sufi meditation*. Detroit, MI: Islamic Supreme Council of America.

Madkur, I. (1983). *Fi al-Falsafah al-Islamiyyah*. Cairo: Dar al-Ma'arif.

Miu, T.-A. (2018). Hesychasm – the return to the peace of the spirit. *ICOANA CREDINTEI. International Journal of Interdisciplinary Scientific Research, 4*(7), 43–50. https://doi.org/10.26520/icoana.2018.7.4.43-50

Moffic, H. S., Peteet, J., Hankir, A. Z., & Awaad, R. (Eds.) (2019). *Islamophobia and psychiatry: Recognition, prevention, and treatment*. Springer International Publishing. https://doi.org/10.1007/978-3-030-00512-2

Morris, J. W. (n.d.). *Opening the heart: Ibn 'Arabi on suffering, compassion and atonement*. The Oxford, UK: Muyiddin Ibn Arabi Society. Available at: https://ibnarabisociety.org/suffering-compassion-and-atonement-james-morris/

Moschos, G., & Pollatou, E. (2022). The effect of a psychomotor intervention program in children 3-10 years of age: A systematic review. *Body, Movement and Dance in Psychotherapy, 17*(4), 294–309. https://doi.org/10.1080/17432979.2022.2078406

Moschos, G., Pollatou, E., Kambas, A., & Bekiari, A. (2023). The effect of psychomotor intervention program on emotional competence and behaviour problems in children four to five years of age. *Body, Movement and Dance in Psychotherapy, 18*(3), 187–200. https://doi.org/10.1080/17432979.2023.2227890

Moodley, R., Zhu, N., & Lo, T. H.-T. (Eds.) (2018). *Asian healing traditions in counseling and psychotherapy*. Thousand Oaks, CA: Sage.

Mulyati, S. (2003). *The educational role of the Tarīqa Qādiriyya Naqshbandiyya with special reference to Suryalaya*. Michigan: ProQuest Dissertations Publishing.

Murata, S. (1992). *The Tao of Islam: a sourcebook on gender relationships in Islamic thought*. New York: State University of New York Press.

Murata, S., & Chittick, W. C. (1994). *The vision of Islam*. Paragon House.

Nasr, S. H. (2007). *The garden of truth: The vision and practice of Sufism*. San Francisco, CA: Harper.
Netton, I. R. (2000). *Sufi ritual: The parallel universe*. Routledge. https://doi.org/10.4324/9781315028149
Neusner, J. (2020). *Neusner on Judaism. Volume 1: History*. New York: Routledge.
Maslow, A. H. (1970). *Motivation and personality* (2nd ed.). New York: Harper & Row.
Nūrbakhsh, J. (1979). *Murāqabāh*. New York: Khānaqāh-i Ni'mat Allāhī.
Nurbakhsh, J. (1981). *Sufism I. Meaning, knowledge and unity*. London: Khanigahi Nimatullahi Publications.
Mirdal, G. M. (2012). Mevlana Jalāl-ad-Dīn Rumi and mindfulness. *Journal of Religion and Health, 51*(4), 1202–1215. https://doi.org/10.1007/s10943-010-9430-z
Nizamie, S. H., Katshu, M. Z., & Uvais, N. A. (2013). Sufism and mental health. *Indian Journal of Psychiatry, 55*(Suppl 2), S215–S223. https://doi.org/10.4103/0019-5545.105535
Okamoto Caballero, P. E. (2017). *Tai Chi Chuan in psychotherapy: A phenomenological study*. Michigan: ProQuest Dissertations Publishing.
Nurbaksh, J. (1990). *Sufi women*. London: Khanigahi Nimatullahi Publications.
Omar, S. H. S., Rahimah, E., Adam, F, Othman, M. S., Basri, I., Ibrahim, E., Mohd Safri, A., Baru, R., Mohamad, M. Z., Shuaiba, O., & Padwick, C. (2017). *Muslim devotions, prayer-manuals in common use*. London: Oneworld Publications.
Orhan, K.Z. (2021). İmâm-ı Rabbânî sonrası Nakşibendiyye'de murâkabe murāqaba in the post-Sirhindī Naqshbandiyya. *Ondokuz Mayıs Üniversitesi İlahiyat Fakültesi Dergisi- Ondokuz Mayıs University Review of the Faculty of Divinity, 50*, 395–427. https://doi.org/10.17120/omuifd.885285
Nurbaksh, J. (1992). *In the tavern of ruin: Seven essays on Sufism*. Khaniqahi-Nimatullahi Publications.
Pandolfo. (2018). *Knot of the soul: Madness, psychoanalysis, Islam*. Chicago: The University of Chicago Press.
Pargament, K. I. (2007). *Spiritually integrated psychotherapy: Understanding and addressing the sacred*. New York: Guilford Press.
Persico, T. (2014). Hitbodedut for a new age: Adaptation of practices among the followers of Rabbi Nachman of Bratslav. *Israel Studies Review, 29*(2), 99–117. https://doi.org/10.3167/isr.2014.290207
Pickell, T. R. (2019). Gentle space-making: Christian silent prayer, mindfulness, and kenotic identity formation. *Studies in Christian Ethics, 32*(1), 66–77. https://doi.org/10.1177/0953946818808142
Picken, G. (2011). *Spiritual purification in Islam: The life and works of al-Muhasibi*. London: Routledge.
Piraino, F. (2021). The Sufi Shaykh and his patients: Merging Islam, psychoanalysis, and Western esotericism. In M. Sedgwick & F. Piraino (Eds.), *Esoteric transfers and constructions* (pp. 195–217). Palgrave Studies. https://doi.org/10.1007/978-3-030-61788-2_11
Ragab, A. (2015). *The medieval Islamic hospital: Medicine, religion, and charity*. New York: Cambridge University Press.
Rahman, F. (1979). *Islam*. Chicago: The Chicago University Press.
Rahman, F. (1987). *Health and medicine in the Islamic tradition*. New York: The Crossroad Publishing Company.

Rahmani, M., Gharamaleki, A. F., & Arif, H. (2018). Journey in Sufism. *Journal of Sufi Studies, 2018*(1–2), 125–139. https://doi.org/10.1163/22105956-12341310

Rassool, G. H. (2016). *Islamic Counselling: An Introduction to Theory and Practice*. New York: Routledge.

Oman, D., Thoresen, C. E., Park, C. L., Shaver, P. R., Hood, R. W., & Plante, T. G. (2009). How does one become spiritual? The Spiritual Modeling Inventory of Life Environments (SMILE). *Mental Health, Religion & Culture, 12*(5), 427–456. https://doi.org/10.1080/13674670902758257

Rice, C. (2017[1969]). *The Persian Sufis* (3rd ed.). London: Routledge. https://doi.org/10.4324/9781315113517-5

Padwick, C. E. (1961). *Muslim devotions: A study of prayer-manuals in common use*. London: S.P.C.K. Publishing.

Rahman, F. (1987). *Health and medicine in the Islamic tradition*. New York: The Crossroad Publishing Company

Rothman, A., & Coyle, A. (2018). Toward a framework for Islamic psychology and psychotherapy: An Islamic model of the soul. *Journal of Religion and Health, 57*(5), 1731–1744. https://doi.org/10.1007/s10943-018-0651-x

Rothman, A., & Coyle, A. (2020). Conceptualizing an Islamic psychotherapy: A grounded theory study. *Spirituality in Clinical Practice, 7*(3), 197–213. https://doi.org/10.1037/scp0000219

Rüschoff, I., & Kaplick, P. M. (2018). Integrating Islamic spirituality into psychodynamic therapy with Muslim patients. In C. Y. Al-Karam (Ed.), *Islamically integrated psychotherapy: Uniting faith and professional practice* (pp. 133–148). New Jersey: Templeton Press.

Rye, M. S., & Pargament, K. I. (2002). Forgiveness and romantic relationships in college: Can it heal the wounded heart? *Journal of Clinical Psychology, 58*(4), 419–441.

Saniotis, A. (2012). Attaining the mystical body: Indian Sufi ascetic practices: The mystical body: Sufi ascetic practices. *The Australian Journal of Anthropology, 23*(1), 65–83. https://doi.org/10.1111/j.1757-6547.2012.00165.x

Saniotis, A. (2018). Understanding mind/body medicine from Muslim religious practices of Salat and Dhikr. *Journal of Religion and Health, 57*(3), 849–857. https://doi.org/10.1007/s10943-014-9992-2

Sassenfeld, A. (2008). The body in Jung's work: Basic elements to lay the foundation for a theory of technique. *The Journal of Jungian Theory and Practice, 10*(1), 1.

Schimmel, A. (1975). *Mystical dimensions of Islam*. Chapel Hill, NC: The University of North Carolina Press.

Schimmel, A. (2011). *Mystical dimensions of Islam*. Chapel Hill: The University of North Carolina Press.

Rassool, G. H. (2016). *Islamic counseling: An introduction to theory and practice*. New York: Routledge.

Razi, A. B. M. ibn Z. (2007). *Razi's traditional psychology*. Translated by A. J. Arberry. Islamic Book Service.

Ritter, H. (2011). Abdal-Karīm, Ḳuṭb al-Dīn b. Ibrāhīm al-Jīlī. In P. Bearman, Th. Bianquis, C. E. Bosworth, E. van Donzel, & W. P. Heinrichs (Eds.), *Encyclopaedia of Islam* (2nd ed.). Brill: Augustana.

Shah, I. (1980). *The way of the Sufi*. London: Octagon Press.

Ronan, K. R., & Kazantzis, N. (2006). The use of between-session (homework) activities in psychotherapy: Conclusions from the Journal of Psychotherapy. *Journal of Psychotherapy Integration, 16*(2), 254–259. https://doi.org/10.1037/1053-0479.16.2.254

Schimmel, A. (2011). *Mystical dimensions of Islam*. Chapel Hill: The University of North Carolina Press.

Simkin, D. R., & Black, N. B. (2014). Meditation and mindfulness in clinical practice. *Child and Adolescent Psychiatric Clinics of North America, 23*(3), 487–534. https://doi.org/10.1016/j.chc.2014.03.002

Sedgwick, M. (2016). *Western Sufism: From the Abbasids to the new age*. New York: Oxford University Press.

Skorupski, J. (1976). *Symbol and theory: A philosophical study of theories of religion in social anthropology*. London: Cambridge University Press.

Segal Z. V., Williams J. M. G., & Teasdale J. D. (2002). *Mindfulness-based cognitive therapy for depression: A new approach to preventing relapse*. New York: Guilford.

Streater, O. K. N. (2022). Truth, justice and bodily accountability: Dance movement therapy as an innovative trauma treatment modality. *Body, Movement and Dance in Psychotherapy, 17*(1), 34–53. https://doi.org/10.1080/17432979.2021.2020163

Subandi, M. A., Derin, S., & Setiyawati, D. (2023). Al Ghazali's concept of diseases of the spiritual heart and its significance to the DSM-5-TR diagnosis. *Journal of Religion & Health*. https://doi.org/10.1007/s10943-023-01871-y

Susanty, R., & Hawadi, L. F. (2019). *Relationship between self-regulated learning and Muraqabah with academic dishonesty of Muslim graduate student* (pp. 239–248). ICRMH. https://doi.org/10.4108/eai.18-9-2019.2293321

Symington, S. H., & Symington, M. F. (2012). A Christian model of mindfulness: Using mindfulness principles to support psychological well-being, value-based behavior, and the Christian spiritual journey. *Journal of Psychology and Christianity, 31*(1), 71–77.

Takahashi, H., & Kato, T. (2023). Effectiveness of dance/movement therapy in individuals with intellectual disability: A systematic review. *Body, Movement and Dance in Psychotherapy, 18*(1), 56–74. https://doi.org/10.1080/17432979.2022.2101528

Trimingham, J. S. (1971). *The Sufi orders in Islam*. Oxford: Oxford University Press.

Utz, A. (2011). *Psychology from the Islamic perspective = 'Ilm al-nafs min manẓūr Islāmī*. English ed. 1. Riyadh: International Islamic Publishing House.

Valiuddin, M., & Khakee, G. (1980). *Contemplative disciplines in Sufism*. London: East-West Publications.

Veid, N., Pollari, A., Hyvönen, K., & Pylvänäinen, P. (2023). Dance movement therapy group improves social functioning and increases positive embodied experiences in social situations. *Body, Movement and Dance in Psychotherapy, 18*(3), 201–217. https://doi.org/10.1080/17432979.2022.2122563

Verman, M. (1992). *The books of contemplation: Medieval Jewish mystical sources*. New York: State University of New York Press.

Wensinck, A. J. (2012). Subḥa. In *Encyclopaedia of Islam* (2nd ed.) Leiden: Koninklijke Brill NV. https://doi.org/10.1163/1573-3912_islam_SIM_7113

Wilhoit, J. C. (2014). Contemplative and centering prayer. *Journal of Spiritual Formation and Soul Care, 7*(1), 107–117. https://doi.org/10.1177/193979091400700110

Wolf, R. K. (2006). The poetics of "Sufi" practice: Drumming, dancing, and complex agency at Madho Lāl Husain (and beyond). *American Ethnologist, 33*(2), 246–268. https://doi.org/10.1525/ae.2006.33.2.246

Worthington, E. L. Jr. (2004). Forgiveness is an emotion-focused coping strategy that can reduce health risks and promote health resilience: Theory, review, and hypotheses. *Psychology & Health, 19*(3), 385–405. https://doi.org/10.1080/0887044042000196674

Sells, M. A. (1996). *Early Islamic mysticism : Sufi, Qur'an, Miraj, poetic and theological writings*. Paulist Press.

Yasien, M. (1996). *Fitrah: The Islamic concept of human nature*. London: Ta-Ha.

Young, S. (2016). What is mindfulness? A contemplative perspective. In K. A. Schonert-Reichl & R. W. Roeser (Eds.), *Handbook of mindfulness in education: Integrating theory and research into practice* (pp. 29–45). Springer-Verlag Publishing/Springer Nature. https://doi.org/10.1007/978-1-4939-3506-2_3

Younos, F. (2017). *Principles of Islamic psychology*. Bloomington, IN: Author House.

Index

Note: **Bold** page numbers refer to tables; *italic* page numbers refer to figures and page numbers followed by "n" denote endnotes.

Abbadi (d. 1152) 39
Abd al-Karim al-Jili 35–37, 138
Abd-Al-Rahman Nur-Al-Din Muhammad Dashti 37
'Abd al-Wahid b. Zayd 33
Abu Bakr Rabi' ibn Ahmad al-Akhwani al-Bukhari 73
Abu Ja'far Muhammad ibn Jarir ibn Yazid al-Tabari 30
Abu-Raiya, H. 57, 60, 62, 65, 70
Abu 'Uthman al-Maghribi 33
Acceptance and Commitment Therapy (ACT) 13, 15, 16, 24; see also therapies
adab 11, 78, 79
Adam 36, 45, 46, 63
"addict self-schema" 25
Adham, I. 32
Ahmad al-Faruqi al-Sirhindi 57
Ahmed, N. 64
"Ain Sof" 31
akhfa 44, 122
akhlaq 77
"alam al-mithal" 89
al-diq 68
al-faza' 93
al-ghadab 93
al-Guddus 107
al-hajat 68
Alhamdu lillah 103, 134
al-haraj 68
al-Hayy 107
Ali, B. 74

'Ali ibn Muhammad ibn Ali al-Husayni al-Jurjani 97
Al-insan al-kamil fi ma'rifat al awakhir w-al-awa'il 37
al-inshirah 68
Ali Shah, S. G. 87
al-ittisa' 68
al-jaza' 93
"Allah, Allah" proclamations 99, 100
Allahu Akbar 75, 103, 134
al-mashaqqa 68
al-matalib 68
al-Muhyi 108
al-Mumit 108
alpha 45
Alpharabius 36
al-shahawat al-khafiyya 68–69
al-shahawat al-zahira 69
al-Zahir 3, 39, 44
Amini, F. 47, 54, 55, 62, 89, 98, 106–108; *Sufi Psychology and Jungian Analytic Psychology: Treatment of Narcissistic Personality Disorder* 7
aml 80
ancient Eastern practices 15; *see also* practices
Ano, G. A. 25
Antisocial Personality Disorder 74
Apophatic (negative) prayer 20, 24; *see also* prayers
Apostle Paul 19
'aql 2, 32, 56–59, 71, 128–130

154 Index

aqlani 77
aqrabiya 44
archetypal imagery 90
Ashkenazi Hasidim 17
asma ul-husna 100, *100,* 105–110, 135–137
associated Buddhist practice 12; *see also* practices
as-suf libas al-inam 31
astaghfirallah 75
ATLA Religion Database with ATLASerials 6
Attar: *The Conference of the Birds* 51
Attributes of the Acts 107
Avants, S. K. 25
Awad, R. 74
'Awarif al-Ma'arif 44
awliya 38
Azeemia order 47, 49; *see also* orders
Azeemi, K. S. 39, 41, 47–50, 87, 126
'Aziz al Din Nasafi 61

bada'ah 37
badan/jism 70, 132–133
Badri, M. 92, 94
al-Baghdadi, J. 97
Bair, P.: *Living from the Heart: Heart Rhythm Meditation* 50
Balayev, R. 5
al-Balkhi, A. i. S. 93, 94
baqa' 41, 97, 98
barakat 51
Barnes, M. 21
bast 97
batin 3, 39
bay'ah 99
Bearman, P. 2, 6
Beers, J. 13
bio-psycho-social-spiritual mental health framework 8
Bipolar I Disorder Manic Episode 74
Bishop, S. R. 13
al-Bistami, A. Y. 41, 97
body-spirit-mind awareness 117
borderline personality disorder 13
Bozorgzadeh, S. 82
Bratslav Hasidic Jewish community 18
breathing exercise 125–128; *see also* exercises
Brown, K. W. 13
Buddhist belief system 15

Buddhist/Buddhism 26; beliefs of nirvana and karma 15; doctrinal framework of 12; healing 15; key teaching of 15; meditation, as stress-reduction techniques 13 *see also* techniques; and mindfulness-based therapy 23; practices in contemporary Western psychotherapy 25; transcendent perfections 16; view of suffering and healing 15; worldview of self 15
Buehler, A. F. 25, 26, 118; *Sufi Varieties of Transformative Practice: Transformation of the Ego-Self* 25
al-Bukhari, S. 78
Butcher, B. 22

Cassian, J.: *The Conferences* 23
Cave Hira 30
Cayoun, B.: in MiCBT 13
"centering prayer" 24–25; *see also* prayers
CFT *see* Compassion Focused Therapy (CFT)
Chambers, R. 13
Chariot mysticism 17
Chishti, M. 52; order 45, 51; *tariqa* 101
Christian: Christian accommodative mindfulness programme 24; Christian-based mindfulness 23; Christian-based therapy 25 *see also* therapies; Christian-derived meditative practices 24; meditation and mindfulness 23; mindfulness practices in 19, 22; mindfulness techniques, unique psychospiritual benefits of 24 *see also* techniques; of sacred music 52; worship practices 20
classical: Islamic spirituality 6 *see also* spiritual/spirituality; *muraqabah* 88; Sufi psychology 11, 37, 117
clinical context, mindfulness in 13; *see also* context
The Cloud of Unknowing (Pickell) 20
cognitive-behavioural therapy 94; *see also* therapies
cognitive processes 93
cognitive shifting 88
cognitive therapy 88; *see also* therapies
common psychotherapeutic modalities 82; *see also* modalities

"compassionate mind" 14
compassion-based CBT 75
Compassion Focused Therapy (CFT) 14, 16; *see also* therapies
Conduct Disorder and Gambling Disorder 74
"coniunctio" 89
contemplative mindfulness practices, of "Eastern" religions **17**, 24, 26
contemplative prayer 25; *see also* prayers
contemporary models 73; Islamic psychotherapeutic practices 18, 31, 57, 74, 85; *see also* practices; western psychotherapy, mindfulness in 13–29
context: clinical context, mindfulness in 13; of *muraqabah* 28; Muslims 29; non-Muslim 117; psychotherapy 13; Sufi/Sufism 99; of therapy 91; *see also* therapies
"cosmic orchestra" 38
Coyle, A. 57, 58, 75, 95

DAHAGA application 83
Dance Movement Psychotherapy (DMP) 112–113
DBCT *see* Dhikr-Based Cognitive Therapy (DBCT)
DBT *see* dialectical behaviour therapy (DBT)
destemaz 81
Dewey, J. 51
dhamm al-nafs 95
Dharma Seals 15
dhikr 2, 10, 26, 43, 51, 74, 75, 80, 99–105, 110, 117, 133–135
Dhikr-Based Cognitive Therapy (DBCT) 74–75; *see also* therapies
Diagnostic and Statistical Manual (DSM)-5-TR 28, 74
dialectical behaviour therapy (DBT) 13; *see also* therapies
al-Din Naqshibandi, Baha 42, 43
diseases of the spiritual heart (DOTSH) 28, 74
Divine 18, 20, 27; concept of 3; love 108; perspective 20
Divine Attributes of the Essence 71, 87, 98, 100, 106–107
Divine Beauty 97
Divine Energy 50

Divine Majesty 97
Divine Names 100, 101, 106
DMP *see* Dance Movement Psychotherapy (DMP)
dojang 22
DOTSH *see* diseases of the spiritual heart (DOTSH)
"dry" and "rigid" religious system 5
duas 78
dum 104
durud 100
Dwidiyanti, M. 83

Eastern Orthodox: practices 22 *see also* practices; spirituality 22 *see also* spiritual/spirituality
"Eastern" religions, contemplative mindfulness practices of 24
Easwaran's Eight Point Program (EPP) 76
Efendi, A. J. 100
ego 3
Eightfold Path 15
emotion-regulation systems 14–15
evidence-based treatment modalities 1; *see also* modalities
Evil of Tongue, DOTSH 74
exercises: breathing exercise 125–128; Loyola's Exercises 21; spiritual/spirituality 8, 21, 48, 103
Ezekiel 17

Factitious Disease 74
fana 45, 97, 98; *fana fil Qur'an* 45, 90; *fana' fi'l-Shaikh* 45, 48, 90; *fana fi Rasul* 45, 90
fanaa' 41
al-Farabi, Abu Naṣr Muḥammad ibn Muḥammad 36
fard 80
fitrah 27, 74
Ford, K. 24
Foster, M. K. 101
Four Noble Truths 15
Frankl, V. 3
Freud, S.: concept of the unconscious 67; field of psychotherapy 3
fu'aad 61
Fung, K. 16

gabz 97
Garzon, F. 24

Index

ghafla 1
ghayb 3, 39
al-Ghazali, M. 28, 32, 33, 39, 44, 55–57, 59, 63, 65–67, 70, 74, 77, 90, 94, 99; *kalam* 92; *muraqabah* 7; theory of personality structures 64
ghusl 79, 80
Gilbert, P. 14, 75
glossolalia 20
Grasser, L. R. 82
Greenberg, M. 19
Gregorian chants 52
Guide for Students (Rahman) 73

haatif-e-ghabi 45
al-Haddad, I. A.: *Key to the Garden* 91
hadith 80, 105; collections 78; of *ihsan* 43; Qur'an and 1, 56; *taqwa* 55; traditions 56 *see also* tradition/traditional
halakhah 18
al-Hallaj, Husain ibn Mansur 36
Hanbal, Imam 32
Haqiqah 33
haqlqat-i-salat 45
Haque, A. 90
haram 52, 79
Harel, K. 111
al-Harith al-Muhasibi 32, 34, 63, 68–69, 95
Hasan, A. 2, 82
Hassan Ukhra Sayyed Muhammad Azeem Barkhiya 47
Hawadi, L. F. 82
Hayes, S. C. 13
The Healing Power of Sufi Meditation (Mirahmadi) 50
healing practices 27; *see also* practices
heart-based therapy 73; *see also* therapies
HEART model 75
Hebrew language 18
hekhalot literature 17
Helminski, K. 118
hesychasm 19, 24
high-level *muraqabah* 42
Hindu mantra meditation 23; *see also* meditation
hitbodedut 18
Holy Kabah 79
Howard, E.: *Lectio Divina* 22

Islamic psychotherapy; spirituality see spiritual/spirituality; and Sufi see Sufi/Sufism; tradition 1, 8, 26, 33, 35, 75, 80 see also tradition/traditional

Islamic psychotherapy 7–10, 28, 32, 54, 58, 61, 63, 73–86; meditation-based therapy in 84; mindfulness in 8, 25; *muraqabah* in 116; perspective 10; techniques see *muraqabah,* in Islamic psychotherapy techniques; see also psychotherapy; therapies

i'tidal 77, 84
itihaad 77
itminan 7

Jabal al-Nur 30
jalali wazifa 101
jam 98
jamali wazifa 101–102
Jami' at-Tirmidhi 61
al-Jawziyah, Ibn Qayyim 32, 93, 94
jevahir-i khamsa 57
Jewish: and Christian traditions, mindfulness-based practices in 17–25; mystical tradition 17; prayer practices 19 see also prayers
jihad 66
al-Jilani, 'Abd al-Qadir 32, 41
Judaic spiritual practice 18; see also practices
Judaism 9, 18, 114
al-Junayd, Abu al-Qasim 34, 41
Jung, C. 3, 54, 112; analytic psychology 7; "coniunctio" 89
Jurayri 33

Kabat-Zinn, J. 4, 13
Kamada, S. 6
Kaplick, P. M. 75
al-Karam, C. Y. 73
Karimpour, G. 6
karma yoga 26
Keating, T. 25; *The Cloud of Unknowing* 24
kelimat-i qudsiyye 43
kenosis 20
Keshavarzi, H. 74, 77, 78, 90
khafi 44
khalwat 50, 51

Khalwati order 103; see also orders
Khanaqah-i Ni'mat Allahi: *Muraqabah* 7
Khan, F. 74, 77, 78
al-Khattab, U. ibn 95
khawatir 93
khawf 77
khirgah 43
Kitab al-adab 78
Kitab al-tawasin 36
Knabb, J. J. 24; *Christian Meditation in Clinical Practice: A Four-Step Model and Workbook for Therapists and Clients* 23
Koenig, H. 3, 4
Kugle, S. 1, 31, 48, 102, 103
Kulal, E. 43

la ilaha illa Allah 43–46, 99–100, 103
Larson, D. B. 4
lataif 46
latifah rabbaniyyah ruhaniyyah 59
Lectio Divina 22
Lee, J.: *The Influence of Swami Satyananda's Meditation on John Main's Christian Meditation* 23
levels, of *muraqabah* 42
Lew, A. 18
Linehan, M. 13
Lippard, P. V.: Society of Friends (Quakers) 19
Living from the Heart: Heart Rhythm Meditation (Bair) 50
Lobel, D. 26
Lodi, F. 75–76
loving-kindness, reflect on 138–139
low-level *muraqabah* 42
Loyola's Exercises 21; see also exercises

Maaseh Merkabah 17
mahabba 7
Main, J. 23
al-Makki, A. T. 32, 41; *Ḵut al-Ḵulub* 6
malaki 94
Mandel (Sufi master) 104
Margolin, A. 25
ma'rifah 33, 84, 92
Masalih al-Abdan wa al-Anfus 93
Maslow, A. 54
Mawlana Nur al-Din 'Abd al-Rahman 37

Index

Mawlana Shaykh Nazim 50
mawt 45
Mazhar Jan-ı Janan 45
MBCT *see* Mindfulness-Based Cognitive Therapy (MBCT)
MBSR *see* Mindfulness-Based Stress Reduction (MBSR)
McCarthy-Jones, S. 25
McCreery, J. L. 101
meditation: Christian meditation and mindfulness 23; *The Healing Power of Sufi Meditation* 50; Hindu mantra meditation 23; Ignatian method of 23; *Living from the Heart: Heart Rhythm Meditation* 50; meditation-based therapy, in Islamic psychotherapy 84; as stress-reduction techniques 13; techniques 15 *see also* techniques; Zen meditation 18
medium-level *muraqabah* 42
MER *see* Muslim Experiential Religiousness (MER)
merkabah 17–18
Mevlevi dance 52
Mevlevi order 105–106; *see also* orders
MiCBT *see* mindfulness-integrated CBT
Mijares, S. J. 112
Miles-Yepez, N. 86, 95
mind-focused mindfulness technique 73
mindfulness: Christian meditation and 23; in Christian tradition 22, 24; and contemplative practices **17**; in contemporary western psychotherapy 13–17; in English 12; Islam and 5, 25–29; meditation, secular and Buddhist forms of 23; meditation techniques 15; mindfulness-based Islamic psychotherapy 26; and mindfulness-based practices, in Jewish and Christian traditions 17–25; mindfulness-based psychotherapeutic modalities 8, 15; mindfulness-based spiritual practices, from Prophetic tradition 30; mindfulness-based therapies 11, 23; and modalities 9; in Pali language 12; practices *see* mindfulness practices; secular mindfulness 77; techniques 82, 87 *see also* techniques; working definition of **14**
Mindfulness-Based Cognitive Therapy (MBCT) 13, 16
Mindfulness-Based Stress Reduction (MBSR) 13, 14
mindfulness-integrated CBT (MiCBT) 13, 14
mindfulness practices 1, 4, 12; in Christian tradition 19; in Islamic psychotherapy 8; principles for 84; and Sufism 6; *see also* practices
Mirahmadi, N.: *The Healing Power of Sufi Meditation* 50
mi'raj 38
Mirdal, G. M. 49, 84, 90
misbahah 104
Miu, T.-A. 19
modalities 77; common psychotherapeutic modalities 82; evidence-based treatment modalities 1; mindfulness and 9; mindfulness-based psychotherapeutic modalities 8, 15; third-wave psychotherapy modality 15
Morris, J. W. 62
Mu'akabat al-nafs 'ala takṣiriha 7
mu'aqaba 39
Muḥasabat al-nafs ba'd al-'amal 7
mu'ataba 39
Muhammadan Rasulullah 46
Muhammad ibn Ishaq Sadr al-Din al-Qunawi 87–88
muhaqqiq 38
muharata 39
muhasaba 39
muhasabah 10, 87, 95–96
Mujaddidi system 45
mujahada 39
multiplicity 55
munjiyyat 61
murabaṭa, six degrees of 6–7
murabit 39
muraqabah 1–2, 5–11, 25–27, 39, 122–124; *ahadiyyah* 44; *ahadiyyet* 46; *akrabiyyat* 46; *aqrabiyya* 45; classical techniques in 85; context of 28 *see also* context; definitions of 85; *dhati* 45; *dhat-i*

baht 45, 46; *haqiqat-i-ka'ba* 45; *haqiqat-i-Qur'an* 45; high-level 42; and human nature *see* human nature; in Islamic psychotherapy techniques *see muraqabah*, in Islamic psychotherapy techniques; *kamalat-i-nubuwwa* 44; *kamalat-i-risala* 44; levels of 86; low-level 42; *ma 'budiyat-i-sirfa* 45; *mahabba* 44; *ma'iya* 44; *ma'iyya* 45; *maiyyat* 45, 46; medium-level 42; *muhabbat* 46; 99 Names of Allah in 105–110; physical movements in 110–113; practice of 26, 44; *qurba* 45; role of 82; as spiritual practice *see muraqabah*, as spiritual practice; techniques 96 *see also* techniques; theological foundation of 26; types of 44–45

muraqabah, as spiritual practice 30–34; Naqshibandi order 42–46; Ni'matullahi order 47–50; power of 34; space, music, and dance 50–52; Sufi orders and 41–42; and Sufism 31–32; Sufi tradition 35–41

muraqabah, in Islamic psychotherapy techniques 87; *muhasabah* 95–96; *mushahadah* 87–88; stages of human condition 96–98; *tadabbur* 91–95; *tafakkur* 91–95; *tasawwur* 88–91

Murata, S. 56, 63, 64, 70, 107–109; *The Tao of Islam* 106
murid 43
Murta'ish 34
mushahada 7, 10, 87–88
musharata 6
Muslim Experiential Religiousness (MER) 77
Muslims: clinicians 9; context 29 *see also* context; mental health professionals 1; with *muraqabah* 30; Sufi *see* Sufi/Sufism
Muslim Woman, Domestic Violence and Psychotherapy (Isgandarova) 28
mystical Islamic tradition 51; *see also* tradition/traditional
mystical path 18

Nachman, R. 18
nafas 63, 70, 71, 125

nafs 2, 32, 51, 56, 64–71, 74, 130–132; *al-ammara* 67–69, 71, 75; *al-lawammah* 60, 69; *al-marid'a* 60; *al-mutma'inna* 60, 70, 71, 75; *ittiham al-nafs* 95
nafsani 94
Najm ad-Din Abu Hafs 'Umar ibn Muhammad an-Nasafi 58, 64
Najm al-in Kubra 94
Naqshbandi: orders 41–46, 78, 90, 101, 105 *see also* orders; principles of 43
Nasimi, I. 5
Nasr, S. H. 26, 33, 52, 93
nazar 44
New Age "Eastern" religious trends 18
"new age" Jewish spirituality 18; *see also* spiritual/spirituality
Ni'matullahi order 47–50; *see also* orders
99 Names of Allah 105–110
niyyah (intention) 80
non-Muslim context 117; *see also* context
Nūrbakhsh, J. 6, 101
Nur ad-Din 'Abd ar-Rahman Jami 37
Nur ad-Din Ni'matullah Wali 47
Nurbakhsh, J. 7, 32, 44, 59, 98
nur Muhammad 36

Oman, D. 76
Omar, S. H. S., 39
omega 45
Om Mani Padme Hum (Sanskrit Mantras) 8
orders: Azeemia 47, 49; Chishti 45, 51; Khalwati 103; Mevlevi 105–106; Naqshbandi 41–46, 78, 90, 101, 105; Ni'matullahi 47–50; Qadiri Sufi 32, 41, 47; Rifa'i 41; Sufi/Sufism 40–72, 90, 105
Osmanli, I. 5

Pali language, mindfulness in 12
Pandolfo, S. 67
Pargament, K. I. 3, 25, 117
Parsa, M. 43
People of the Bench 31
Persico, T. 18
physical benefits, of Sufi whirling 111
physical movements, in *muraqabah* 110–113

Pickell, T. R.: Apophatic (negative) prayer 20 *see also* prayers; *The Cloud of Unknowing* 20
Piraino, F. 83
plerosis 20
PMIR *see* Psychological Measure of Islamic Religiousness (PMIR)
postmodern Western culture 18
practices: ancient Eastern practices 15; associated Buddhist practice 12; Christian-derived meditative practices 24; contemporary Islamic psychotherapeutic practices 18, 31, 57, 74, 85; in contemporary Western psychotherapy 25; Eastern Orthodox practices 22; healing practices 27; inward-directed spiritual practices 18; Judaic spiritual 18; mindfulness in 19, 22; mindfulness practices *see* mindfulness practices; of *muraqabah* 26, 44; *muraqabah*, as spiritual practice *see muraqabah*, as spiritual practice; prayer 19 *see also* prayers; of traditional *muraqabah* 39–41; worship practices 20
prayers: Apophatic (negative) prayer 20, 24; "centering prayer" 24–25; contemplative prayer 25; Jewish prayer practices 19; practices 19; Qur´an and 8
Pritchett, J. 4
Prophetic tradition 30, 67, 75, 78, 80, 81, 105, 108; *see also* tradition/traditional
Prophet Muhammad 1, 9–10, 30, 35–36, 38, 46, 80, 89
psyche 3; psychic equilibrium 54; psychic polarity 55; psychic reality 89
psychoeducation 16, 71, 75, 77, 83
Psychological Measure of Islamic Religiousness (PMIR) 77
psychology 4; Christian approach with 23; classical Sufi psychology 11; conflicts 44; Islamic psychology 66; Jungian analytic psychology 7; Sufi psychology 32, 54–56, 59, 62, 66, 69–71; *see also* psychotherapy
psycho-physiological energies 51

psychotherapy 4; classical Islamic spirituality and 6; contemporary Islamic psychotherapy 57, 85; contemporary Western psychotherapy 25; context 13 *see also* context; dance movements in 112; Islamic practice of 6; Islamic psychotherapy 8–10, 32, 54, 58, 61, 63, 78; Islamic spiritual care and 8; mindfulness-based Islamic psychotherapy 26; spiritually integrated psychotherapy 25; Sufi psychotherapy 82; traditional Chinese medicine psychotherapy 16; *see also* psychology; therapies
PsycINFO 6
PubMed 6
puleeta 104

Qadi ´Iyad b. Musa 36
Qadiri Sufi ´Abd-Allah Yefa´i 47
Qadiri Sufi order 32, 41, 47; *see also* orders
Qalandar Baba Auliya 47
qalb 2, 45, 56, 59–62
qudrat 62–63
quietism 47
Qur´an 1, 2, 9, 10, 28, 35, 38, 55, 56, 61, 80, 102, 106, 107, 109; ´aql 57–59; depiction of God 26; and hadith *see* hadith; *nafs see nafs*; and prayers *see* prayers; and Prophetic tradition 106; *qalb* 2, 45, 56, 59–62; Qur´anic verse 46; *riyah* 62–64; *ruh* 62–64; Sufi *see* Sufi/Sufism; *see also* Islam; *muraqabah*
qurb 7
al-Qushayri 32; *Tartib al-Suluk* 101

rabitah 39
Rahman, F. 56, 73; *Guide for Students* 73
rahmani 94
raja´ 7
rajaa 77
raqeeb 2
Rassool, G. H. 74
al-Razi, A. B. M. i. Z. 56, 73, 92
religious authority 4
Ricoeur, P. 22
al-Rifa´i, Ahmad 41

Rifa'i order 41; see also orders
"right vision" 18
riyah 62–64
Rogerian therapy 89; see also therapies
Rothman, A. 2, 57, 58, 74–75, 80, 95
ruh 2, 56, 62–64, 70
ruhani 77
The Rule of St. Benedict (6th century) 22
al-Rumi, M. Jalal-ad-Din 36, 63, 70, 78, 88, 107; concept of mindfulness 84; Mathnawi 109
Ruschoff, I. 75
Rye, M. S. 25

sabr 39
Sacred Law 73
sadr 61, 62
safar 40–41
Sahl [al-Tustari] 34
sahw 41
Salamah, U. 61
salawat 75
salik 2, 43
samsar 15
Saniotis, A. 66, 71, 81, 101, 104
Sarraj, A.: Kitab ul Luma 7
sati 12
Schimmel, A.: Al-insan al-kamil fi ma'rifat al awakhir w-al-awa'il 37
seclusion 30, 47
secular: and Buddhist forms, of mindfulness meditation 23; mindfulness 77
"self-actualized" personality 54
self-compassion 14
self-evaluation process 2
self-soothing system 15
Seyidbayli, H. 5
seyr ilallah 46
al-Shadhili, Abu al-Ḥasan 41
al-Shafi 'i, Imam 32
Shahada 100
Shah-e Naqshiband 42
Shah, I. 8, 13, 31, 51–52; The Study of Sufism in the West 45
Shahjahanabadi, S. K. 103
Shah Ni'matullah 47
shaikh 90
Shaikh, J. -H 83
shakhsiyyah 77

Shari'ah 33, 41
shauq 7
shaykhs 32
shaytani 94
Shia tradition 104; see also tradition/traditional
Shihab al-Din 'Umar Suhrawardi 44
Sirhindi, A. 103
sirr 44
Skinner, E. 13
Skorupski, J. 101
sophos 31
soul-related interventions 77
"the Soviet men" 5
spiritual practice, muraqabah as 30–34; Naqshibandi order 42–46; Ni'matullahi order 47–50; power of 34; space, music, and dance 50–52; Sufi orders and 41–42; and Sufism 31–32; Sufi tradition 35–41; see also practices
spiritual/spirituality: classical Islamic spirituality 6; Eastern Orthodox spirituality 22; exercises 8, 21, 48, 103 see also exercises; integrated psychotherapy 25; Islam spirituality 10, 28, 31–32, 109; "new age" Jewish spirituality 18; purification 124–125; self-schema 25; spirituality-based tools 6; surveillance 2
Stoller, P. 103
stress-reduction techniques, Buddhist meditation as 13
Subandi, M. A. 28, 74
subhanallah 75, 103
suffa 31
al-Sufi, A. H. 31
Sufi/Sufism 40, 44, 54, 116; and common psychotherapeutic modalities 82; context 99 see also context; disciples 9; focus of 32; literature 96; meditative tradition 49; methodology 39; mindfulness practices and 6; muraqabah and 31–32; mystics 36; orders see orders; practices see practices; practitioners 92; psychology see psychology; psychotherapy see psychotherapy; spiritual insights and practices of 7; Syrian Sufi 31;

teachings 68; terminology 90; tradition *see* tradition/traditional; writers 117; writings 56
Sufi whirling dervishes (SWDs) 111
al-Suhrawardi, Abu al-Najib 41, 92
al-Suhrawardi, Shihab al-Din 41
sukr 41
suluk 43
Sunan Abi Dawud 79
Sunnah 35, 38
superego 3
Susanty, R. 82
Swami Satyananda 23
SWDs *see* Sufi whirling dervishes (SWDs)

Tabrizi, S. 36
tadabbur 91–95
tafakkur 2, 10, 87, 91–95
tafraqah 98
tahannuth 30
tahara 79
tahlil 99
tahqiq 38
tajalli 107
talqin 44
taqwa 55, 75
ṭarīka 99
tariqah 33, 44
tasawwuf 31
tasawwur 10, 87–91
tasbih 100, 104, 105
tasfiyat al-qulub 31
'taskhir-i-jinn' 101
tassawuf 90
tawajjuh 43
tawakkul 77, 78
tawassut 37
tawbikh al-nafs wa-mu'atabatuha 7
tawhid 45, 47
ta'wil 89
tawwakul 75
tayammum 79, 81
tazkiyat al-nafs 27
techniques: Buddhist meditation, as stress-reduction techniques 13; Christian mindfulness techniques, unique psychospiritual benefits of 24; classical techniques, in *muraqabah* 85; Islamic psychotherapy *see muraqabah*, in Islamic psychotherapy techniques; meditation 15; mindfulness 82, 87; *muraqabah* 96; western psychotherapeutic techniques 75
theosis process 22
therapies: Acceptance and Commitment Therapy 13, 15, 16, 24; Buddhism and mindfulness-based therapy 23; Christian-based therapy 25; cognitive-behavioural therapy 94; cognitive therapy 88; Compassion Focused Therapy 14, 16; contemporary western psychotherapy 13–29; context of 91; Dance Movement Psychotherapy 112–113; Dhikr-Based Cognitive Therapy 74–75; dialectical behaviour therapy 13; heart-based therapy 73; Islamic psychotherapy *see* Islamic psychotherapy; psychotherapy *see* psychotherapy; Rogerian therapy 89
Theravada Buddhism 12
third-wave psychotherapy modality 15; *see also* modalities
"threat mind" 14
TIIP *see* Traditional Islamically Integrated Psychotherapy (TIIP)
al-Tirmidhi, Muhammad b. 'Ali 34
traditional Chinese medicine psychotherapy (TCMP) 16
Traditional Islamically Integrated Psychotherapy (TIIP) 73–74, 77
tradition/traditional: hadith 56; Islam 1, 8, 26, 33, 35, 75, 80; Jewish mystical tradition 17; mindfulness, in Christian tradition 22, 24; mystical Islamic tradition 51; Prophetic tradition 30, 67, 75, 78, 80, 81, 105, 108; Shia tradition 104; Sufism *see* Sufi/Sufism; traditional *muraqabah* 3, 39–41, 87
Trimingham, J. S. 99
al-Tustari, Sahl 36

ulu'l 'azrn 44
unity 55
uns 7

wahdat 45
wahdat-e wujud 108
wara' 7
wasawes al-sadr 93
wasawis 94
Western clinical work 15
western psychotherapeutic techniques 75; *see also* techniques
Wilhoit, J. C. 24
wird 99
Wolf, R. K. 51, 111
Worthington, E. L. Jr. 25

wudu 79, 81
wujud 38
wuquf qalbi 100

Yapko, M. D. 83
yaqin 7
Yasawiyah 41
ya sayidi madad al-haqa 50
Young, S. 12, **17**

Zen meditation 18; *see also* meditation
Zhu, Z. 16

For Product Safety Concerns and Information please contact our EU
representative GPSR@taylorandfrancis.com
Taylor & Francis Verlag GmbH, Kaufingerstraße 24, 80331 München, Germany

www.ingramcontent.com/pod-product-compliance
Lightning Source LLC
Chambersburg PA
CBHW071411300426
44114CB00016B/2260